Breakthrough Language Series

BUSINESS FRENCH

Brian Hill
with Didier Riccard, Mohammed Saad
and Steve Burrough

D0981120

General editor Brian Hill
Professor of Modern Languages, Brighton Polytechnic

Acknowledgements

Many people have contributed to the development of *Breakthrough Business French*. I am indebted to members of the French business community who gave their time to be interviewed and to participate in the various dialogues. Steve Burrough and Didier Riccard organized many of the recordings in Normandy, and the technical operations were directed by Gerald Ramshaw. Mohammed Saad was invaluable in advising on the business scene in France and on the appropriateness of business terminology, and Sue Jones helped in the compilation of the material. Colleagues at Macmillan, particularly Jane Wightwick and John Winckler, were constantly on hand with support and advice. The scrappy handwritten drafts could never have been understood without the expert help of Zamy Alibhai, who transformed the original material into professionally presented and comprehensible texts.

To all of the above I am extremely grateful. Without their invaluable help the course would never have seen the light of day.

The authors and publishers wish to thank the following for permission to use copyright material: Banque de France, France Telecom, Hertz France S.A., P&O Ferries Ltd, and SNCF for advertising material, and The New York Times Syndication Sales for a table from the 29 May 1987 edition of *L'Express*.

Every effort has been made to trace all the copyright holders, but if any have been inadvertently overlooked the publishers will be pleased to make the necessary arrangement at the first opportunity.

Actors: Yves Aubert, Philippe Monnet, Carolle Rousseau
Audio producer: Gerald Ramshaw, MAX II

First published 1992 by
THE MACMILLAN PRESS LTD
Houndmills, Basingstoke, Hampshire RG21 2XS
and London
Companies and representatives throughout the world

ISBN 0-333-54397-1
ISBN 0-333-54399-8 (3 cassette pack)
ISBN 0-333-54398-X (book and cassette pack)

A catalogue record for this book is available from the British Library

Printed in Great Britain by
Scotprint Ltd, Musselburgh

10 9 8 7 6 5 4 3 2 1
01 00 99 98 97 96 95 94 93 92

Contents

How to use this course

HOW TO USE THIS COURSE

Breakthrough Business French is the ideal course for business people who have little or no previous knowledge of French. Here are some of its main features:

- The key recordings have been made on location in French companies. The starting point for each unit is conversations and interviews with French people employed in a range of jobs.
- The language and the situations are, therefore, authentic – you are taken from boardrooms to the factory floor, from commercial exhibitions to banks financing small businesses.
- Business people have lives outside their jobs, and care is taken to provide training in the language which will help you to survive in hotels, restaurants and on the streets of France as well as in companies.
- The main emphasis throughout is on listening, speaking and reading – the skills you will find most useful in contacts with the French business world.
- Before producing the course, we talked to hundreds of people about *how* they learn languages. The result is that great care has been taken with the *Breakthrough Business* series to ensure that you get enough opportunities to practise the language. We have included in each unit a variety of activities that get you involved in using the French that has been introduced to you in the authentic dialogues.
- This is not a grammar course. You first understand and then you use the language; only then are the main grammar features introduced to provide some cement and to explain how the language works.
- Included in each unit is up-to-date information to ensure you are familiar with key features of the French business scene.

General hints

- Have confidence in us. Real language is complex and there are certain things in each unit which are not explained in detail and which you may find difficult to understand, particularly on the first hearing. We will build up your knowledge slowly, emphasizing only what you really need to remember at each stage and making a distinction between language you need to use and language where you only need to understand the gist.
- Try to practise regularly, but in short periods. 20–30 minutes a day is usually better than 3–4 hours once a week.
- To develop your speaking skills, do say the words and phrases out loud. This articulation of the language is important in building up a degree of confidence and fluency.
- If you don't understand something, don't panic. Leave it for a while. Learning a language is a bit like doing a jigsaw; it all eventually falls into place.
- Don't be afraid to write in the book and add your own notes.
- Go back over the units you have already studied. You'll often be surprised at how much you understand and it helps remind you of the vocabulary.
- If you are not attending language classes, try to pair up with somebody else and learn with them.
- If this is the first time you have used a recording to help you learn a language, practise using the pause and repeat-play controls on your cassette or CD player.
- Learning French may take more time than you thought. Just be patient and, above all, don't get angry with yourself.

How the course is organized and how to make the most of each unit

There are twelve units, each one focusing on a particular aspect of Business French. Each unit is divided in the same way. In the first section, you get a numberof authentic recordings with transcripts of what is said together with notes and vocabulary. Each recording is followed by three or four exercises, some practising comprehension, some practising speaking. When the new location recordings have been introduced, explained and practised, all the main words and phrases are brought together in a list called *Key words and phrases*. Then come short sections which focus on grammar, reading, background information and some final 'open-ended' speaking practice.

The book contains step-by-step instructions for working through the course: when to use the book or recording on its own, when to use them together. As the course progresses you may well evolve your own pattern of study and that's fine. As a starting point, here's how we suggest you approach each unit.

Dialogues

First, listen to each of the key dialogues without stopping the recording, just to get a feel for the task ahead. Then go over the dialogue bit by bit in conjunction with the explanatory notes and vocabulary. You should get into the habit of playing the recordings repeatedly to give yourself time to think, listen to sentences a number of times, and repeat them after the speaker. When you feel confident you have at least understood what the dialogue is about and you have become familiar with the most important phrases, move on and do the associated exercises.

Practise what you have learned

These exercises have been carefully chosen to practise key vocabulary and structures. During the course you will come across many different types of exercises. Our presenter, Yves, will guide you through what to do and there are clear instructions in the book.

Key words and phrases

By the time you get to this section you should be reasonably familiar with most of the words and phrases listed. Use the list to test yourself, covering up and checking what you know, first the English and then the French column. This should ensure that you can remember the most important items.

Read and understand and *Did you know?*

In these sections you will be able to read the kind of written material – signs, faxes, publicity brochures, etc. – that you are likely to come across in France; and you are given some up-to-date information on the organization of business and commerce.

Your turn to speak

This final activity is open-ended. It is an opportunity for you to adapt the language of the unit to your own particular circumstances, so there are normally no 'correct' answers. When you've had a go at this guided speaking activity, you will hear a model version on the recording. This will show you what someone else said and give you a few extra ideas.

Answers

The answers to all the exercises (except where the answers are given on the recording) can be found at the end of each unit.

Vocabulary

At the back of the book is a French–English and English–French vocabulary. This does not replace a dictionary, of course, but you should be able to use it as an alphabetical reference for most of the words you need.

All of us involved in producing *Breakthrough Business French* hope you will enjoy the course and find it useful.

Bon courage!

Symbols and abbreviations

For cassette players
If your cassette recorder has a counter, set it to zero at the start of each unit and then note the number in the headphone symbol at the start of each dialogue. This will help you to find the right place on the tape when you want to wind back.

For CD players
Your player will locate each unit as a track number. Note the number from your display in the headphone symbol at the start of each dialogue. This will help you find the right place on your disc when you want to repeat play.

◆   This indicates the most important words and phrases.

m.	masculine	sing.	singular
f.	feminine	pl.	plural
lit.	literally		

1 HELLO

You will learn

- to introduce yourself
- to answer simple questions about yourself
- to say where you work
- to understand simple questions about your company
- how best to address people in business

  and you will be given some information on France and the French language

Study guide

To help you keep a check on your progress, you could mark off the various tasks as you complete them.

Dialogue 1 + Practise what you have learned
Dialogue 2 + Practise what you have learned
Dialogue 3 + Practise what you have learned
Dialogue 4 + Practise what you have learned
Ensure you know the **Key words and phrases**
Study the **Grammar** section
Do the exercises in **Read and understand**
Did you know? The French-speaking world
Your turn to speak

Before you start, do make sure you've read the introduction, which explains the format of the course and how to make the most of it.

Dialogues

1   *A meeting at the Chamber of Commerce*

Steve	Ah bonjour Claude, comment vas-tu?
Claude	Bonjour Steve.
Steve	Ça va?
Claude	Ça va bien.
Steve	Bonjour Didier.
Claude	Ça va Jean-Pierre?
Jean-Pierre	Très bien merci et toi?
Steve	Bonjour monsieur ... Steve Burrough.
Pascal	Pascal Morel.
Steve	Enchanté.

♦ **très bien**   very good / very well
♦ **merci**   thank you

> ♦ **Bonjour** is the most common way of saying 'Hello'. Lit. 'Good day'.
>
> ♦ **Comment vas-tu?** How are you? Lit. 'How goes you?' To somebody you don't know too well you would say **Comment allez-vous?**
>
> ♦ **Ça va?** How are you? Lit. 'It goes?' Remember in English we can say *How's it going?* or even *How goes it?*
>
> ♦ **Très bien merci et toi?** Very well thanks and you? You can either reply to this with a smile, or you could simply answer with **Ça va** (OK) as a statement.
>
> **Enchanté** is linked with *enchanted* in English but in French it's an everyday way of saying 'Pleased to meet you'.

Practise what you have learned

After each dialogue there are a few practice activities to reinforce what you have learned. There are usually one or two comprehension activities then one to get you speaking. Where appropriate, you will find the answers at the end of each unit.

1 Listen on your recording to four people answering the question **Ça va?** See if you can spot (i) who is very well indeed, (ii) who is okay and (iii) who is actually not too happy. (Answers on p. 22.)

		i	ii	iii
(a)	François	✓		
(b)	Marie-Claude			✓
(c)	M. Gauthier		✓	
(d)	Jeanne	✓		

2 Before you tackle the first speaking activity make sure you have read the section on how to make the most of each unit on p.5. On the recording you will be asked to take part in a little exchange of greetings, so start playing the recording now.

Dialogues

2 *A first encounter in the managing director's office*

M. Leroy	Bonjour monsieur Grandchamp.
M. Grandchamp	Ah bonjour monsieur Leroy.
M. Leroy	Vous avez fait bon voyage?
M. Grandchamp	Excellent, très, très bien.
M. Leroy	Nous sommes très heureux de vous accueillir dans notre entreprise aujourd'hui.
M. Grandchamp	Et je suis ravi de faire votre connaissance.
M. Leroy	A quel hôtel êtes-vous descendu?
M. Grandchamp	A la Présidence.
M. Leroy	La Présidence, bon hôtel?
M. Grandchamp	Excellent, pas de problème.

excellent excellent
aujourd'hui today
pas de problème OK, no problem

> **Vous avez fait bon voyage?** Have you had a good journey? Lit. 'You have made good journey?' See grammar p. 17 for why 'you' is **vous** here, but **tu** in dialogue 1. As in English, one way of forming a question is to make a statement with your intonation rising at the end.
>
> **Nous sommes très heureux...** We are very happy...
>
> **de vous accueillir**. The verb **accueillir**, 'to welcome', is difficult but useful. You may also see **accueil**, which means 'welcome' or 'reception'.
>
> **dans notre entreprise** in our firm. **Entreprise** is the general word for a firm or business.
>
> **Et je suis ravi de faire votre connaissance**. This polite but often heard rejoinder means 'And I am delighted to make your acquaintance'.
>
> **A quel hôtel êtes-vous descendu?** At which hotel are you staying? **Descendu** comes from the verb **descendre**, 'to descend / go down', and here it is used idiomatically.

Practise what you have learned

3 Link together one phrase from the left-hand column with one from the right to make four statements or questions that make sense.
(Answers on p.22.)

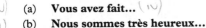

(a) **Vous avez fait...**   (i) **... de faire votre connaissance.**

(b) **Nous sommes très heureux...**   (ii) **... êtes-vous descendu?**

(c) **Je suis ravi...**   (iii) **... de vous accueillir.**

(d) **A quel hôtel...**   (iv) **... bon voyage?**

4 Listen now to the conversation on the recording. Below you will find twelve words or phrases only some of which appear in the conversation. Put a mark next to the *eight* words/phrases that you hear. You probably won't understand every word of the conversation, just listen out for those you recognise. (Answers on p. 22.)

- (a) **bonjour**
- (b) **aujourd'hui**
- (c) **de Londres**
- (d) **nous sommes très heureux**
- (e) **c'est très intéressant**
- (f) **merci beaucoup**
- (g) **je suis ravi**
- (h) **André est parisien**
- (i) **une entreprise américaine**
- (j) **pas pour le moment**
- (k) **bon voyage**
- (l) **pas de problème**

5 On the recording you'll be invited to take part in a conversation using the main words and phrases from the dialogue. It starts by your being asked **Quand êtes-vous arrivé?**, 'When did you arrive?'

Dialogues

3 *An English businessman arrives at the company reception*

M. Sawyer	Bonjour madame.
Receptionist	Bonjour monsieur. Vous désirez?
M. Sawyer	Euh je veux voir monsieur Lefebvre s'il vous plaît.
Receptionist	Oui bon, je vais vous faire remplir une petite fiche. Votre nom s'il vous plaît?
M. Sawyer	Sawyer.
Receptionist	Vous pouvez l'épeler?
M. Sawyer	S – A – W – Y – E – R.
Receptionist	Le prénom?
M. Sawyer	Andrew, A – N – D – R – E – W.
Receptionist	Le nom de votre société?
M. Sawyer	Ladipo.
Receptionist	Le but de votre visite?
M. Sawyer	J'ai rendez-vous avec monsieur Lefebvre.
Receptionist	Bon, je vous prie de vous asseoir. Ja vais lui transmettre votre fiche et il viendra vous chercher.
M. Sawyer	Merci madame.

bon good
petit(e) small/little
le nom de votre société the name of your company

le but the purpose
la visite the visit

Vous désirez? From **désirer** 'to desire/want'. Another example of a statement being turned into a question by using rising intonation. The direct translation, 'You want?', sounds a bit impolite in English but in French **Vous désirez?** is a perfectly good way of starting a conversation.

Je veux voir... I want to see... **Je veux** can be used with a lot of verbs: **Je veux descendre** 'I want to get down/off'; **Je veux faire** 'I want to do'; etc.

s'il vous plaît. We had **merci** 'thank you' earlier on. **S'il vous plaît** 'please' (lit. 'if it to you pleases') is its companion.

Je vais... From the verb **aller** 'to go'. **Je vais** I go / I am going' is used frequently to express intentions: **Je vais voir** 'I am going to see'; **Je vais visiter** 'I am going to visit'.

faire remplir une fiche. The phrase **remplir une fiche** means 'to fill in a slip/form'. **Faire** normally means 'to do' or 'to make' but when it is linked to a verb, as here in **faire remplir**, it conveys the sense of 'getting you to something'. So, if **écrire** means 'to write', 'I'm going to get you to write a letter' would be **Je vais vous faire écrire une lettre**.

Votre nom, s'il vous plaît? Your name, please? A phrase you will hear a lot. You'll also hear **Comment vous appelez-vous?** Lit. 'How do you call yourself?', to which the standard reply is **Je m'appelle...** 'I call myself...'.

Vous pouvez l'épeler? The phrase **vous pouvez** 'you can' is important. 'Can you...?' would more usually be translated as **Pouvez-vous...?** but here rising intonation is used to turn a statement into a question. **Epeler** is 'to spell (out)'.

J'ai rendez-vous avec... I have a meeting with...

Je vous prie de vous asseoir. A polite way of asking Andrew Sawyer to sit down / take a seat. **Je vous prie d'épeler votre nom** would be a polite way of saying 'Would you please spell your name'. The receptionist could also have said **Asseyez-vous, s'il vous plaît.**

Je vais lui transmettre votre fiche I'm going to give him (**lui** = to him) your slip. **Transmettre** literally means 'to transmit'.

et il viendra vous chercher and he will come and get (fetch) you. The whole of the last sentence may sound a bit long and complicated. Remember at this stage you only need understand it.

Practise what you have learned

6 Check your understanding of the dialogue. Without reading the transcript or notes, listen to the conversation with Andrew Sawyer again and indicate whether the following statements are true (**vrai**) or false (**faux**). Even though the verb forms are slightly different, e.g. 'he' instead of 'I', etc., you should recognize the meaning. (Answers on p. 22.)

		vrai	faux
(a)	**Andrew veut voir monsieur Lebrun.**		
(b)	**La secrétaire lui demande de remplir une fiche.**		
(c)	**Son prénom est André.**		
(d)	**Son nom est Ladipo.**		
(e)	**Il a rendez-vous avec M. Lefebvre.**		
(f)	**La secrétaire le prie de s'asseoir.**		
(g)	**M. Lefebvre vient le chercher.**		

7 On the recording you will hear Philippe giving you the pronunciation of the French alphabet. Pay particular attention to: **e, g, h, i, j, w,** and **y.** Most of the other letters are pronounced in a way which can be recognized reasonably easily. When you have grasped the pronunciation, you will be asked to write out five words which are spelled out to you. (Answers on p. 22.)

(a) _bonjour_ (d) _roude_

(b) _londres_ (e) _banque_

(c) _Wilson_

8 Write down your name, address and the name of your company, saying each letter aloud as you do it.

Votre nom: _Robert Grimwood_

Votre adresse: _57, Carver Hill Rd._
High Wycombe Bucks

Le nom de votre société: _Lorex Pharmaceuticals_

Dialogues

 4 *A secretary talks to a subcontractor waiting in reception*

Secretary	Qu'est-ce que vous faîtes dans la vie monsieur?
M. Lenoble	Je suis maître artisan du bâtiment.
Secretary	C'est-à-dire que vous avez une entreprise?
M. Lenoble	Oui c'est celà. Une petite entreprise avec quatre compagnons.
Secretary	Qu'est-ce que vous faîtes?
M. Lenoble	Oui on fait des installations électriques, beaucoup de rénovations des systèmes d'alarme et des antennes de télévision.
Secretary	Plomberie et sanitaire?
M. Lenoble	Pas du tout.
Secretary	Pas du tout?
M. Lenoble	Non.
Secretary	Vous avez combien d'ouvriers?
M. Lenoble	J'ai trois compagnons et une secrétaire.

   c'est-à-dire that is to say
   les rénovations (f.) renovations
♦ **petit(e)** small/little
   des systèmes (m.) **d'alarme** alarm systems
   les compagnons (m.) colleagues
   des antennes (f.) **de télévision** TV aerials
   les installations (f.) **électriques** electrical installations
   la plomberie the plumbing
♦ **beaucoup de** many / lots of
   sanitaire sanitary (installation)
   pas du tout not at all
♦ **combien de...?** how many...?

♦ **Qu'est-ce que vous faîtes dans la vie?** The secretary is asking about his profession. It is a useful phrase for finding out what somebody does. It's made up of **qu'est-ce que?** 'what?', **vous faîtes** from **faire** 'to do' and **dans la vie**, lit. 'in the life'.

♦ **Je suis maître artisan du bâtiment.** It is notoriously difficult to find exact equivalents for job titles. He is a **maître artisan** (lit. a master worker), which means a 'specialist' in his field. **Bâtiment** means 'building'.

Vous avez une entreprise? You have (your own) firm?

Oui, on fait... On is the royal 'one' in English but it is used much more widely in French, often replacing **nous** 'we' or **je** 'I'. So **on va au cinéma** would be translated as 'we're going to the cinema'.

Vous avez combien d'ouvriers...? You have how many workers...?
♦ **Combien de** 'how many' is a key phrase: **Combien de kilomètres?** 'How many kilometres?'; **Combien de secrétaires?** 'How many secretaries?'; etc.

♦ **j'ai** I have. From **avoir** 'to have', an important verb. See grammar, p. 17.

Practise what you have learned

9 The questions and answers have got mixed up in this transcript. See if you can sort them out. (Answers on p. 22.)

(a) **Qu'est-ce que vous faîtes dans la vie?**

(b) **Vous avez une entreprise?**

(c) **Qu'est-ce que vous installez?**

(d) **Vous avez combien d'ouvriers?**

(i) **J'ai trois compagnons et une secrétaire.**

(ii) **Des systèmes d'alarme.**

(iii) **Je suis maître artisan.**

(iv) **Oui, une petite entreprise.**

10 Listen a couple of times to the conversation on the recording where two business people meet each other for the first time at the **Chambre de Commerce.** Then answer the multiple-choice questions below. **Travailler** means 'to work'. (Answers on p. 22.)

(a) **Il est de Dieppe?**

(i) **Oui, de Dieppe.**
(ii) **Non, il est de Perpignan.**
(iii) **Non, il est de Paris.**

(b) **Qu'est-ce qu'il fait à Dieppe?**

(i) **Il est invité par la Chambre de Commerce.**
(ii) **Il veut rendre visite à son oncle.**
(iii) **Il a rendez-vous avec le maire.**

(c) **Qu'est ce qu'il fait dans la vie?**

(i) **Il est directeur d'une entreprise.**
(ii) **Il est maître artisan.**
(iii) **Il travaille pour une banque.**

(d) **Il va visiter quelle sorte d'entreprise?**

(i) **Une banque.**
(ii) **Une entreprise spécialisée dans la plomberie.**
(iii) **Une entreprise qui installe les systèmes électriques.**

(e) **Il est à quel hôtel?**

(i) **La Résidence.**
(ii) **La Présidence.**
(iii) **Le Président.**

11 In the speaking activity, you'll be asked to play the part of a visitor to Dieppe. Yves will prompt you with what to say.

Key words and phrases

Here are the most important words and phrases which you have met in this unit. You should make sure you know them as they will keep cropping up. Practise saying them aloud.

oui	yes
non	no
bonjour	good morning / good afternoon / hello
Comment vas-tu?	How are you?
Ça va?	How are you?
très bien	very good / very well
merci	thank you
s'il vous plaît	please
un bon voyage	a good journey/trip
heureux	happy
accueillir	to welcome
l'accueil (m.)	the reception/welcome
une entreprise	a firm
une société	a company
désirer	to want/desire
Je veux voir...	I want to see...
Il veut voir...	He wants to see...
Je vais voir...	I am going to see...
Je suis de...	I am from...
travailler	to work
faire	to do/make
le nom	the last name
le prénom	the first name
Comment vous appelez-vous?	What's your name?
Je m'appelle...	I am called...
J'ai rendez-vous avec...	I've a meeting with...
Qu'est-ce que...?	What...?
maître + profession	specialist/qualified
une secrétaire	a secretary
le collègue	the colleague (male)
la collègue	the colleague (female)
combien de...?	how many...?
j'ai	I have
vous avez	you have
petit(e)	small/little
beaucoup de...	many / lots of
demander	to ask
visiter	to visit (e.g. a monument)
rendre visite	to visit someone

Grammar

The word grammar can strike terror into many hearts and it is not the aim of this course to go into great detail about grammar points. We will present the basics and show how the language works so that you have firm ground to build on. *But* don't be afraid to make mistakes! You can still be understood and you can understand others without knowing all the ins and outs.

Gender and plurals

French nouns are divided into two categories: they are either masculine or feminine. Sometimes it is common sense whether something is masculine or feminine – **la mère** (the mother) is feminine, **le père** (the father) is masculine – but mostly it's not that easy. There is no logic as to why **le nom** should be masculine or **la société** feminine. One helpful feature is that in many cases nouns that end in -**e** are feminine (but there are lots of exceptions).

Making nouns plural is, however, much easier. In the majority of cases you just add -**s**. So 'mothers' are **mères**, 'fathers' are **pères**, 'names' are **noms** and 'societies' are **sociétés**.

How to say 'the'

With a masculine noun, the word for 'the' is **le**, as in **le but** 'the aim / purpose'. With a feminine noun, the word for 'the' is **la**, as in **la fiche** 'the slip / form'. In the plural the word for 'the' with both masculine and feminine nouns is **les**, as in **les buts** or **les fiches**.

In front of a vowel (**a, e, i, o, u**) or **h** (which counts as a vowel in French) both **le** and **la** are shortened to **l'**, as in **l'hôtel** (m.) or **l'entreprise** (f.).

How to say 'a'

With a masculine noun the word for 'a' is **un**, as in **un artisan** 'a craftsman'. With a feminine noun the word for 'a' is **une**, as in **une banque** 'a bank'.

Adjectives

In French, adjectives (descriptive words such as 'big', 'little', 'blue', etc.) have to *agree* with the noun they are linked to. So you get **un petit hôtel**, or **un nom américain** but **une petite entreprise** or **une société américaine**. In other words, you usually add an -**e** to the adjective when the word described is feminine

The verb 'to be'

As in most languages, the verb 'to be', **être**, is irregular. It is important so try to learn it by heart.

je suis	I am	**nous sommes**	we are
tu es	you are	**vous êtes**	you are
il est	he is	**ils sont**	they are (m.)
elle est	she is	**elles sont**	they are (f.)

Note that there are two words for 'you' – **tu** and **vous**. The French have maintained the distinction we used to have between *thou* and *you*. In everyday business situations the **vous** form is much more common. **Vous** is used in formal or polite speech or, indeed, to translate *you* in the plural. **Tu** is used when you are talking to one person you know well, to a friend, or to a child. So you get **Comment vas-tu?** 'How are you?' (friend) but **Comment allez-vous?** 'How are you?' (polite address to one person or addressing more that one person whether they are friends or not).

12 Try this exercise to practise the verb 'to be'. (Answers on p. 22.)

Translate the following phrases into French:

(a) I am from Chicago.
(b) How are you? (friend)
(c) He is American.
(d) She is a good (**bonne**) secretary.

(e) We are in (**dans**) the hotel.
(f) How are you? (polite)
(g) They (the two men) are in the bank.
(h) They (the two women) are from Brighton.

Read and understand

13 Here are a few French business cards. Have a look at them and answer the questions below. (Answers on p. 22.)

(a) Who works in a language centre *Steve Burrough*

(b) Which four people have post office box (**boîte postale**) numbers?

(c) The French do use the word **fax**, but fax machines are also called what?

(d) One of the cards belongs to a businesswoman. Which?

(e) What is Jacques Choteau's job?

(f) If you send a telex to Didier Reininger, for whose attention do you have to mark it?

(g) Who works in a nuclear power plant, and what is his job?

JEAN-CLAUDE MOYEN
ADJOINT AU DIRECTEUR

CENTRE RÉGIONAL DE FORMATION
ET D'ASSISTANCE NUCLÉAIRE
ATELIER-RELAIS PALUEL · 76450 CANY-BARVILLE
TÉL. 35 97 80 11 · FAX : 35 97 12 31

Jacques CHOTEAU
Attaché Commercial

FRANCE TELECOM AGENCE COMMERCIALE DIEPPE
VAL DRUEL · BP Y · 76884 DIEPPE CEDEX · TEL. 35 04 71 30

OMB **TOSHIBA**
Le Monde du Bureau PHOTOCOPIEURS
TÉLÉCOPIEURS

 Guillaume DA SILVA

Jacques TILLIETTE ORGANISATION S.A.
15, rue Victor Hugo 76200 DIEPPE
Tél. 35 84 87 00 · Télécopieur : 35 40 14 60

Steve BURROUGH
Centre d'Etude des Langues

Chambre de Commerce et d'Industrie de DIEPPE
INSTITUT CONSULAIRE · E.N.A.C.E. B.P. 62 · 76202 DIEPPE Cédex
Tél. : 35 82 24 99 · Télex : 180770 Chamcom. · Télécopie : 35 82 11 39

EDF
GDF *Agence de Dieppe*
Service Commercial

Patrice SCELLES

Route du Vallon · Le Val Druel · B.P. 104 · 76203 Dieppe Cédex · Tél : 35.84.10.20

Michel GIUDICELLI
Chef des Ventes Constructeurs
Division Industrie

Pall Hydraulique s.a.
3, rue des Gaudines
Boîte Postale n° 253
78104 Saint-Germain-en-Laye Cedex
Tél. : (1) 30.61.39.07 · Télex : 697 497
Télécopieur : (1) 30.61.38.98

FORUM TEXTILES

Etoffes d'intérieur · Tissus professionnels
Tissus Nonfeu "b. delacourt"

Didier REININGER
RESPONSABLE COMMERCIAL

5, Bd René Cassin
Quartier Beaulieu
86000 POITIERS · FRANCE

Tél. 49.44.25.44
Télex 790 586 F
attn forum textiles

---

14 When you check in at a hotel you are often asked to fill in this form – **une fiche de voyageur**. Have a go at filling it in now with your own real or imagined details. Note the French for the following key words. (Answers on p. 22.)

(a) establishment _établissement_

(b) first name _Prénom_

(c) to write _Ecrire_

(d) place _lieu_

(e) arrival _entrée_

(f) departure _sortie_

FICHE
D'ÉTRANGER

Nom et adresse de l'établissement:
....
....

Chambre nº ....

Ecrire en majuscules *(In block letters)*

NOM ...... *Rob* Grimwood ....
(Name / Name)

Prénom ...... Robert ....
(First name / Vorname)

Date de naissance ...... 5/3/1965 ....
(Date of birth / Geburtsdatum)

Lieu de naissance ...... Barnet ....
(Place of birth / Geburtsort)

Domicile habituel ...... High Wycombe ....
(Permanent address / Anschrift)

Profession ...... Chef Constable ....
(Occupation / Beruf)

Nationalité ...... Anglais ....
(Nationality / Staatsangehörigkeit)

Date d'entrée en France ...... 21 Septembre 1993 ....
(Date of arrival in France / Eingangsdatum)

Date probable de sortie ...... 22 Septembre 1993 ....
(Probable date of exit / Ausgangsdatum)

Signature ...... Moi. ....

Nombre d'enfants de moins de 15 ans accompagnant le voyageur .... Nil.
(Accompanying children under 15 / Kinder unter 15 Jahren)

15 Here's another form, this time for participants in Business Language Training. Read it through and see if you can find an equivalent in French for the terms listed below. (Answers on p. 22.)

INSCRIVEZ VOUS MAINTENANT   **A retourner au Centre de Formation**
                                       BP 62 76200 DIEPPE CEDEX

Nom: _____

Prénom: _____

Adresse privée: _____

_____

EMPLOYEUR: _____

Téléphone professionnel: _____   Domicile: _____

Langue souhaitée: _____

Horaires souhaités: _____

Fréquence souhaitée: _____

(a) home address ___Address Privée___

(b) language ___Langue___

(c) training centre ___Centre de Formation___

(d) frequency ___Fréquence___

(e) employer ___employeur___

(f) surname ___Nom___

(g) timetable ___souhaitée___

(h) business phone ___Téléphone Professionnel___

Did you know?

The French-speaking world

France is twice the size of Great Britain but has a slightly smaller population and, though 65 per cent of its people live in towns, it is still in the main a rural country. For administrative reasons it is divided into twenty-two **régions** (see map) and also into ninety-five **départements** (the nearest equivalent to the English county), classified in alphabetical order and numbered 1 to 95 (e.g. Ain 01, Paris 75, etc.). These numbers are also used on French car number-plates and indicate where the car is registered.

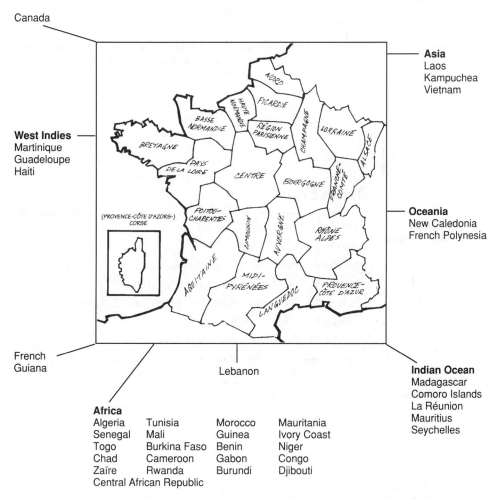

Canada

Asia
Laos
Kampuchea
Vietnam

West Indies
Martinique
Guadeloupe
Haiti

Oceania
New Caledonia
French Polynesia

French
Guiana

Lebanon

Indian Ocean
Madagascar
Comoro Islands
La Réunion
Mauritius
Seychelles

Africa

Algeria	Tunisia	Morocco	Mauritania
Senegal	Mali	Guinea	Ivory Coast
Togo	Burkina Faso	Benin	Niger
Chad	Cameroon	Gabon	Congo
Zaïre	Rwanda	Burundi	Djibouti
Central African Republic			

French is spoken in all five continents. It is one of the official languages of Belgium, Switzerland, Luxembourg and Canada and is either the official or main language in twenty-one African countries (former colonies). French is also widely spoken in the West Indies (Martinique, Guadeloupe and Haiti), in the Indian Ocean (Madagascar, the Comoro Islands, La Réunion, Mauritius and the Seychelles), in Oceania (New Caledonia and French Polynesia), in Asia (Laos, Kampuchea and Vietnam) and in South America (French Guiana), and in the Middle East (Lebanon). With English, French is used as an official language in most international organizations.

Your turn to speak

At the end of each unit there is an open-ended speaking activity – this means there is no correct or incorrect version, it's just an opportunity for you to adapt some of the words and phrases you have learned to your own personal circimstances. When you have had a go at the activity, listen to the 'model' answer on the recording, which gives you some of the structures and vocabulary you might have used.

16

(a) Think how you would introduce yourself to the company receptionist, then speak it out loud. You might want to say 'I'm Peter Turner from Brighton. I have an appointment with M. Lefebvre today. My company is Beechams and I have a problem.' (Don't expect too much of yourself this early on.)

(b) Work out five polite questions you might ask somebody you have just met. Say the questions out loud and then listen to some of the possibilities we have recorded for you.

Answers

Practise what you have learned

Exercise 1   (a) i (b) iii (c) ii (d) i

Exercise 3   (a) iv (b) iii (c) i (d) ii

Exercise 4   (a), (b), (d), (f), (g), (i), (k), (l)

Exercise 6   vrai: (b), (e), (f), (g); faux: (a), (c), (d)

Exercise 7   (a) Bonjour (b) Londres (c) Wilson (d) Route (e) Banque

Exercise 9   (a) iii (b) iv (c) ii (d) i

Exercise 10 (a) iii (b) ii (c) iii (d) iii (e) ii

Grammar

Exercise 12 (a) Je suis de Chicago (b) Comment vas-tu?
(c) Il est américain (d) Elle est une bonne secrétaire
(e) Nous sommes dans l'hôtel (f) Comment allez-vous?
(g) Ils sont dans la banque (h) Elles sont de Brighton

Read and understand

Exercise 13 (a) Steve Burrough (b) Giudicelli, Choteau, Scelles,
Burrough (c) télécopieur (d) Guilaine da Silva, OMB
(e) commercial attaché/assistant (f) attn. forum textiles
(g) Jean-Claude Moyen, assistant to the director

Exercise 14 (a) établissement (b) prénom (c) écrire (d) lieu
(e) entrée (f) sortie

Exercise 15 (a) adresse privée (b) langue (c) centre de formation
(d) fréquence (e) employeur (f) nom (g) horaire
(h) téléphone professionnel

HOW DO YOU GET TO...?

You will learn

- how to ask for directions in a town
- to discuss the layout of a company
- to introduce yourself at the reception desk
- some useful numbers

  and you will be given information on the transportation systems for passengers and freight in France

Study guide

To help you keep a check on your progress, you could mark off the various tasks as you complete them.

Dialogue 1 + Practise what you have learned
Dialogue 2 + Practise what you have learned
Dialogue 3 + Practise what you have learned
Dialogue 4 + Practise what you have learned
Ensure you know the **Key words and phrases**
Study the **Grammar** section
Do the exercises in **Read and understand**
Did you know? Transportation in France
Your turn to speak

Dialogues

Remember to set your display at zero before you start work on the recording.

1 *Steve and Didier want to get to the station*

Steve	Nous sommes perdus en fait, est-ce que vous pourriez nous renseigner pour aller à la gare?
Café owner	Vous descendez la rue ici à droite et vous allez jusqu'au carrefour, vous tournez à gauche et vous allez tout droit, c'est environ à 500 mètres d'ici.
Steve	A 500 mètres?
Café owner	Oui à 500 mètres, c'est tout droit vous ne pouvez pas vous tromper.
Steve	Bon, je vous remercie

- **en fait** a filler phrase; it means 'in fact'
- **descendre** to go down / descend
  environ about/approximately
  d'ici from here

- **Nous sommes perdus** We are lost. From **perdre** 'to lose'.

- **Est-ce que ...?** Another common way of forming a question: **Est-ce que vous avez fait bon voyage? Est-ce que vous avez beaucoup d'ouvriers?**

  vous pourriez nous renseigner ...? Could you (lit. you would be able to) inform us? **Renseigner** is 'to inform'; here it means 'to direct'.

- **Pour aller à la gare?** To go/get to the station – a crucial phrase. Similarly, **Pour aller à l'aéroport? Pour aller à Paris?**

- **à droite** to the right

- **Vous allez jusqu'au carrefour** You go as far as / up to the crossroads (**le carrefour**)

- **Vous tournez à gauche** You turn left

  Vous allez tout droit You go straight ahead. *Note:* don't confuse **à droite** 'to the right' with **tout droit** 'straight ahead'.

- **à... de...** An idiomatic expression for saying how far away something is, e.g. **Paris est à 200 kilomètres de Dieppe** or **L'aéroport est à 15 kilomètres du centre ville.**

  Vous ne pouvez pas vous tromper You can't go wrong. Famous last words. Notice the negative here, **ne ... pas...** It is used to turn a positive statement into a negative one. **Je peux aller à l'aéroport** I can go to the airport. **Je ne peux pas aller à l'aéroport** I can't go to the airport.

Practise what you have learned

1 Listen carefully to the recording where Steve is asking a lady passer-by the way to **la Route du Havre** 'the Le Havre road'. See if you can spot five key words or phrases that have already appeared in dialogue 1, and list them below. (*Note:* Steve says **Pouvez-vous nous indiquer…?** 'Can you show us…?' It isn't quite the same as **Pourriez-vous…?** 'Would you be able to…?', so you can't include it.) (Answers on p. 38.)

(a) _____   (d) _____

(b) _____   (e) _____

(c) _____

2 Some speaking practice. It always gives you a sense of achievement to direct somebody around a town. You'll be asked to give a few simple directions so make sure you know phrases such as **à droite, à gauche, tout droit, jusqu'au carrefour** and **à 2 kilomètres d'ici.**

Dialogues

2 *Didier asks the way to a bank, **la Société Générale***

Didier	Pardon madame, pourriez-vous m'indiquer la Société Générale, c'est une banque qui se situe dans la grande rue.
Passer-by	Eh bien, monsieur, vous allez prendre, ... vous allez contourner l'église, vous allez prendre la première à gauche et vous allez suivre la place. Ensuite vous allez prendre la première à droite et vous trouverez devant la Société Générale.
Didier	Donc je répète je pars de chez vous.
Passer-by	Oui, vous contournez l'église.
Didier	Je contourne l'église.
Passer-by	Oui.
Didier	Je tourne la première à gauche.
Passer-by	Oui.
Didier	Et ensuite la première sur la droite.
Passer-by	C'est ça.
Didier	C'est bien celà?
Passer-by	C'est ça.
Didier	Je vous remercie madame.

la grande rue   the main (lit. big) street
ensuite   then
◆ **devant**   in front of
répéter   to repeat
sur   on
c'est ça/celà   that's it

◆ **Pardon madame** Excuse me (madam). This is a very usual way of starting a conversation in French. It is normal to add **monsieur, madame** or **mademoiselle**.

Pourriez-vous m'indiquer...? Could you (would you be able to) direct me to...?

◆ **une banque que se situe** a bank which is situated. **Se situe** means 'situates itself', which might sound a bit strange but it's one way of conveying the idea of 'lies', 'is to be found', etc. **Est situé** is a more usual way of saying 'is situated'.

◆ **vous allez prendre.** Lit. 'you are going to take'. **Prendre** means 'to take'.

Vous allez contourner l'église. Lit. 'You are going to go round the church'.

la première à gauche the first on the left

Vous allez suivre la place. Lit. 'you are going to follow (go across) the square'. **Suivre** means 'to follow'.

◆ **Vous vous trouverez...** You will find yourself... **Trouver** means 'to find'.

◆ **Je pars de chez vous** I leave from your place. **Je pars** 'I leave', from **partir**. **Chez** is a useful word which means 'at somebody's place or home'.
◆ So **chez moi** would be 'at my home'. **De** here means 'from'.

◆ **Je vous remercie** is a polite way of saying thank you. Normally, **merci** is enough, though again it is usual to add **monsieur, madame** or **mademoiselle**.

Practise what you have learned

3 Look at the map below. On the recording you will hear directions to **la gare** (the station), **l'hôtel de ville** (the town hall), **le grand café**, **le syndicat d'initiative** (the tourist office), **la cathédrale** and **le musée du tourisme**, but, craftily, not in that order. Your task is to listen to each set of directions, to follow them on the map and then to note down where you are, **où vous êtes**. Write the place-names and the key letters on the map. You start each time at **le pont** (the bridge). (Answers on p. 38.)

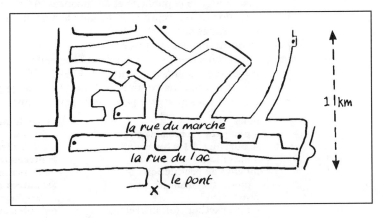

4 Use the notes and vocabulary to translate the following phrases into French. (For answers see exercise 5 below.)

(a) Excuse me (sir), would you be able to direct me to the church please?

_____

(b) Yes, you (are going to) take the first on the right.

_____

(c) The bank is (situated) in front of you.

_____

(d) You (are going to) go round the square.

_____

(e) Thank you (sir).

_____

5 When you have written down the answers to exercise 4, turn on the recording. You'll be asked to say out loud what you have written and then Brigitte will give you the correct version (it should be the same as yours).

_____

Dialogues

3 *The receptionist explains the layout of the company to a visitor*

Receptionist	Alors, au rez de chaussée vous avez le secteur production où travaillent à peu près soixante personnes. Juste à côté c'est le bureau du chef de production, M. Holtenbach. Puis, au premier étage il y a les services administratifs – les départements du personnel, du marketing, de la publicité et des finances. Au deuxième étage il y a la direction de l'entreprise, c'est-à-dire le bureau du directeur général et les autres chefs.
Visitor	Peut-on manger sur place?
Receptionist	Oui, bien sûr. Aussi au deuxième étage, il y a notre petite cantine où les repas sont servis entre 11.30 et 14.00.
Visitor	Merci ... Euh, ma voiture est devant la porte, je peux la laisser là?
Receptionist	Ah non, vous pouvez la garer sur le parking, juste derrière le bâtiment.

alors so
à peu près approximately
▸ **le bureau** (pl. **les bureaux**) the office(s)
du chef de production of the production manager
puis then
du marketing (of) marketing
de la publicité (of) publicity

et des finances (f.) and of finance
c'est-à-dire that is to say
le directeur général the managing director
les autres chefs (m.) the other managers
oui, bien sûr yes, certainly
aussi also

▸ **au rez de chaussée** on the ground floor (US first floor)

▸ **vous avez le secteur production** you have the production department/section

▸ **où travaillent soixante personnes** Lit. 'where are working sixty people'. **Travailler** 'to work' is an important verb.

juste à côté just here (lit. just at the side)

▸ **au premier étage** on the first floor (US second floor)

▸ **au deuxième étage** on the second floor (US third floor)

les départements du personnel. In French you have to say the equivalent of 'the departments of the personnel, of the marketing', etc.; **du** 'of the' (m.); **de la** 'of the' (f.).

▸ **il y a les services administratifs** there are the administrative services. **Il y a** is *crucial* – it means 'there is' or 'there are'. For example: **Il y a une banque juste à côté** or **Il y a beaucoup de bons hôtels à Dieppe**.

il y a la direction de l'enterprise. Lit. 'there is the management of the company'. **La direction** means 'the management'.

Peut-on manger sur place? Can you eat in the building? **Peut-on** means literally 'Can one?' The royal 'one' is often used to replace 'you' when you are talking about people in general.

▸ **Manger** 'to eat' is an important verb; **sur place** is an idiom meaning 'here / in the building'.

notre petite cantine our little canteen. **Petit(e)** 'little' is the opposite of **grand(e)** 'big'.

Les repas sont servis entre... Meals are served between...

▸ **Ma voiture est devant la porte** My car is in front of the door

Je peux la laisser là? Can I leave it there?

Vous pouvez la garer... You can park it... **Garer** is a slightly idiomatic verb very often used for 'to park'.

sur le parking in the car park (lit. on the parking)

juste derrière le bâtiment just behind the building

Practise what you have learned

6 Here are three little diagrams showing what three floors of the company might look like. Using information from the dialogue, label as many of the departments, offices, etc. as you can. (Answers on p. 38.)

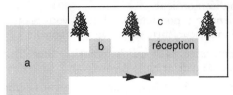

au rez de chaussée

au premier étage   au deuxième étage

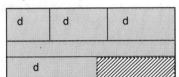
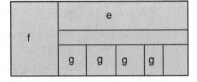

7 On the recording you will hear a number of visitors asking how to get to various offices and departments. Listen carefully, pausing after each exchange to mark on the grid where they are. (Answers on p. 38.)

	rez de chaussée	premier étage	deuxième étage
(a) **la réception**	✓		
(b) **le bureau du chef de production**		✓ 202.	
(c) **le département du personnel**			✓
(d) **le bureau du chef des finances**		✓	
(e) **la section marketing**	✓		
(f) **la direction de l'entreprise**			✓

8 Your turn to speak. You'll be prompted on the recording to ask for a number of different offices and departments. **L'ascenseur** (f.) means 'the lift/elevator'; **se trouver** 'to be located'.

Dialogues

4 *Steve Burrough introduces himself at the company reception*

Steve	Bonjour madame.
Receptionist	Bonjour monsieur.
Steve	Je viens voir monsieur Gédéon s'il vous plaît.
Receptionist	Oui monsieur, juste un instant, je l'appelle.
	Oui monsieur Gédéon, j'ai monsieur Steve Burrough qui vous demande dans le hall s'il vous plaît.
	Merci monsieur. Monsieur Gédéon vous demande de bien vouloir patienter quelques instants s'il vous plaît.
Steve	Merci bien.
Receptionist	Alcatel Business Systems bonjour. Oui madame un instant s'il vous plaît.
Receptionist	Il vient vous accueillir dans quelques instants.
Steve	Très bien.

After the meeting Steve gets directions to the city centre

Steve	Je dois repartir. Pouvez-vous m'expliquer comment aller en ville?
Receptionist	Oui.
Steve	J'ai peur de me perdre. *I am afraid to get lost.*
Receptionist	Oui bien sûr monsieur. A la sortie de l'usine vous aurez à tourner à droite.
Steve	Oui.
Receptionist	Puis vous prendrez la première à gauche et ensuite la grande avenue vous dirige directement vers Dieppe.
Steve	Très bien.
Receptionist	Vous traversez un village qui s'appelle Arques la Bataille et Dieppe sera indiquée.
Steve	Bon je vous remercie, au revoir.
Receptionist	Y a pas de quoi monsieur, au revoir.
Steve	Au revoir.

> **s'il vous plaît** please
> **juste un instant** just a moment
> **dans le hall** lit. in the hall (reception)
> **quelques instants** a few moments
> **oui, bien sûr** yes, certainly
> **la première à gauche** the first on the left
> **la grande avenue** the big avenue
> **qui s'appelle** which is called

Je viens voir... I am coming to see... **Viens** is an irregular present tense from **venir** 'to come'. Note that it is possible to use the simple present tense in French where in English we might say *I have come to see...*

Je l'appelle I (will) call him. Remember in Unit 1 we had **Je m'appelle...**, lit. 'I call myself...', i.e. 'My name is...'

J'ai monsieur... I have Mr... See grammar, p. 33, for the full form of 'to have'

qui vous demande who is asking for you. There have already been a number of examples illustrating that the direct object pronoun (me, him, her, you, us, them, etc.) goes in front of the verb. Here is another, with **vous demande**. (See grammar, p. 33.)

---

de bien vouloir patienter. The verb **patienter** is polite, and means 'to wait / have patience'. **Bien vouloir** is part of an idiom which has the sense of 'if you wouldn't mind'.

- **Il vient vous accueillir** He is coming to receive/welcome/get you.

Je dois repartir I have to go/leave (again). **Je dois** comes from the verb **devoir** 'to must' or 'to have to'.

- **Pouvez-vous m'expliquer...** Can you explain to me...
...comment aller en ville? ...how to get into town? Two useful phrases here for asking directions. Steve could have just used the simpler question from dialogue 1: **Pour aller en ville, s'il vous plaît?**

J'ai peur de me perdre I'm afraid of losing my way (lit. of myself losing)

- **à la sortie de l'usine** at the exit from the factory. The opposite of **sortie** is **entrée**.

Vous aurez à tourner à droite You will have to turn right. **Aurez** comes from **avoir** 'to have', and it is an irregular future form.

vous dirige directement vers Dieppe takes you directly to Dieppe. Lit. '(la grande avenue) you directs directly towards Dieppe'.

- **vous traversez un village** you go through (lit. you cross) a village.
Dieppe sera indiquée Dieppe will be indicated. **Sera** is another way of saying 'will be'.

Y a pas de quoi. Short for **il n'y a pas de quoi**, an idiom that means 'don't mention it / no problem'. You can also just say **Pas de quoi**.

Practise what you have learned

9 Pairing: in the two lists below are six pairs of statements or questions which went together in the dialogue. The only problem is that they have been mixed up. Draw lines to link the pairs and to make sense of what was actually said in the dialogue. (Answers on p. 38.)

(a)	**Je viens voir M. Gédéon s'il vous plaît**	(i)	**Bien sûr, monsieur, vous prendrez la première à gauche**
(b)	**M. Gédéon vous demande de bien vouloir patienter**	(ii)	**dans quelques instants**
(c)	**Pouvez-vous m'expliquer comment aller en ville**	(iii)	**Au revoir**
(d)	**Il vient vous accueillir**	(iv)	**Oui, monsieur, juste un instant, je l'appelle**
(e)	**Vous traversez un village et Dieppe sera indiquée**	(v)	**Bon, je vous remercie**
(f)	**(Il n') y a pas de quoi**	(vi)	**quelques instants**

10 First listen to Philippe pronouncing the numbers from 1 to 10 and learn them. You'll find them written down on p. 33. Then note down the numbers that are used in the recorded conversation in the order in which you hear them. Just look out for the numbers, don't worry if you don't understand the rest. (Answers on the recording.)

(a) _____   (d) _____

(b) _____   (e) _____

(c) _____   (f) _____

11 Your turn to speak. You're at the company reception and you are going to introduce yourself and say who you have come to see. When you are ready, start the recording.

Key words and phrases

Here are the most important words and phrases from Unit 2. Make sure you have learned them before going on. Practise saying them aloud.

Nous sommes perdu(e)s	We are lost (from **perdre** 'to lose')
Je suis perdu(e)	I am lost (add the -e if you are female)
Est-ce que vous avez...?	Have you...?
Pour aller à...?	To get to...?
à droite	to the right
à gauche	to the left
tout droit	straight on/ahead
le carrefour	the crossroads
à (10 kilomètres) de...	10 kilometres from...
Je ne parle pas français	I do not speak French
Pardon monsieur/madame	Excuse me (sir/madam)
la banque	the bank
prendre	to take
l'église (f.)	the church
la rue	the road
la place	the square
trouver	to find
devant	in front of
partir	to leave/depart
chez vous	at (your) home
chez moi	at (my) home
je vous remercie	I thank you
le rez de chaussée	the ground floor
au premier étage	on the first floor (US second floor)
au deuxième étage	on the second floor (US third floor)
le bureau	the office
le secteur production	the production department
le département du personnel	the personnel department
les services (m.) administratifs	the admin. department
l'entreprise (f.)	the firm
manger	to eat
la voiture	the car
la porte	the door
le bâtiment	the building
le chef (de production)	the head (of production)
le directeur du marketing	the director of marketing (male)
la directrice du marketing	the director of marketing (female)
l'accueil (m.)	the reception
Pouvez-vous...?	Can you...?
la sortie (de l'usine)	the exit (of the factory)
traverser	to cross / go through
il y a	there is / there are

Grammar

avoir *(to have)*

As in most languages, the verb 'to have' is irregular. This is how it goes in French:

j'ai	I have	**nous avons**	we have
tu as	you have	**vous avez**	you have
il a	he / it has	**ils ont**	they have (m.)
elle a	she / it has	**elles ont**	they have (f.)

By the way, if you want to say 'it', use either **il** or **elle**; **il** is when it relates to a masculine noun, **elle** when it relates to a feminine noun.

il y a

This is a really useful phrase. It means both 'there is' and 'there are'.
For example:
Il y a une grande église sur la place There is a big church on the square
Il y a beaucoup de voitures sur le parking There are a lot of cars in the car park

It can equally be used in a question:
Y a-t'il...? Is there...? / Are there...?

The **t** is added just to make it sound better:
Y a-t'il une cantine ici? Is there a canteen here?
Y a-t'il beaucoup d'ouvriers? Are there a lot of workers?

Numbers

Here are the numbers from 1 to 10. They are pronounced for you in exercise 10.

un	**deux**	**trois**	**quatre**	**cinq**
six	**sept**	**huit**	**neuf**	**dix**

If you want to get over the idea of 'second', 'third' and so on, you just add **-ième**: **deuxième, troisième, huitième**, etc. 'First' is **premier** or, with a feminine noun, **première**.

Negatives

The usual way of forming the negative is to put **ne** before the verb and **pas** afterwards. For example:
Je suis perdu I am lost → **Je ne suis pas perdu** I am not lost

In front of a vowel the **ne** becomes **n'**:
Le bureau est au premier étage The office is on the first floor →
Le bureau n'est pas au premier étage The office is not on the first floor.

In speech the **ne** is often omitted.

12 Here's a short exercise to practise the use of **avoir** 'to have'. Translate the following sentences into French. (Answers on p. 38.)

(a) I have a car.

_____

(b) We have two cars.

_____

(c) Do you have a personnel department?

_____

(d) They (m.) have a big office.

_____

(e) They (f.) do not have two cars.

_____

Read and understand

13 Here is part of a map showing where some of the main buildings in Dieppe are located. Have a look at it and note down which number is associated with the places listed below. (Answers on p. 38.)

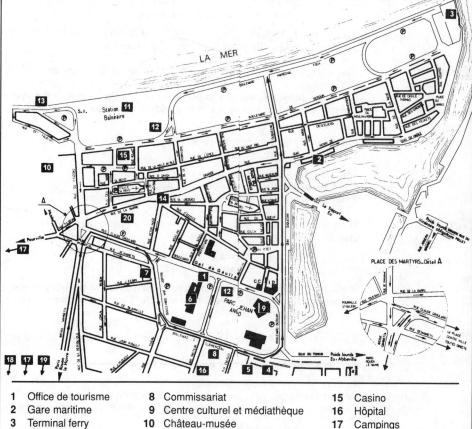

1	Office de tourisme	8	Commissariat	15	Casino
2	Gare maritime	9	Centre culturel et médiathèque	16	Hôpital
3	Terminal ferry	10	Château-musée	17	Campings
4	Gare SNCF	11	Piscine découverte	18	Auberge de Jeunesse
5	Gare routière	12	Jardin d'enfants	19	Mammouth
6	Hôtel de ville	13	MJC plage	20	Shopi
7	Bureau de poste	14	Café des Tribunaux		

(a) hospital

(b) tourist office

(c) train station

(d) castle museum

(e) post office

(f) town hall (beware!)

(g) open-air pool

(h) youth hostel

14 The French are rightly very proud of their high-speed trains – **trains à grande vitesse (TGV)**. SNCF's rail network (**un réseau**) spans the country. Here is an extract from one of their publicity brochures. See if you can understand the gist and answer the questions below. (Answers on p. 38.)

Le TGV (Train à Grande Vitesse) est le train le plus rapide du monde en service commercial. Depuis 1981, sa silhouette orange, effilée, traverse chaque jour le quart Sud-Est de la France atteignant une vitesse de 270 km/h.

NAISSANCE D'UN RESEAU
Les trains à grande vitesse s'apprêtent à conquérir l'EUROPE et la SNCF construit le premier réseau de train à grande vitesse du monde: TGV SUD-EST (1981), ATLANTIQUE (1989-1990), LYON-VALENCE (1992-1994), soit 1230 km de lignes nouvelles avec **le projet** du **TGV NORD** (1993) et **L'INTERCONNEXION** des TGV en ILE-DE-FRANCE (1994-1995).

UN PROJET ORIGINAL
- La continuité de transport est assurée:
  - PARIS-LONDRES sans changement, grâce au tunnel sous la Manche,
  - liaisons directes PROVINCE-PROVINCE, c'est la fin du centralisme ferroviaire parisien.
- A ROISSY le train et l'avion deviennent complémentaires,
- Le projet est au cœur du réseau européen à grande vitesse et en est un des premiers maillons,
- Le train et la grande vitesse seront au rendez-vous du grand marché européen.

(a) What is the claim made for the TGV?

_____

(b) When did it go into service?

_____

(c) What speed does it go at?

_____

(d) How big will the network be when it is finished?

_____

(e) Why don't you have to change between Paris and London?

_____

(f) Where do the trains link with airlines?

_____

_____

Duty-free allowances

And you will probably want to take advantage of the duty-free offers. Here's a table from the French Customs and Excise (**la Douane Française**) telling travellers what they can legally bring into France. You'll need a few of the words below to help you understand it.

Denrées et articles divers	Voyageurs en provenance	
	Pays membres de la CEE	Autres pays
1. TABACS		
Cigarettes (unités).............	300	200
ou		
Cigarillos (unités)..............	150	100
ou		
Cigares (unités)...............	75	50
ou		
Tabacs à fumer (grammes).......	400	250
2. BOISSONS ALCOOLISÉES		
Vins tranquilles	5 l	2 l
et		
soit Boissons titrant plus de 22°	1,5 l	1 l
soit Boissons titrant 22° ou moins	3 l	2 l
3. PARFUMS..................	75 g	50 g
4. EAUX DE TOILETTE	3/8 l	1/4 l
5. CAFÉ	1 000 g	500 g
ou Extraits et essences de café...	400 g	200 g
6. THÉ	200 g	100 g
ou Extraits et essences de thé ...	80 g	40 g
7. MÉDICAMENTS	Quantités correspondant aux besoins des voyageurs	
8. AUTRES MARCHANDISES		
Par voyageur âgé de 15 ans et plus	2 800 FF	300 FF
Par voyageur âgé de moins de 15 ans	700 FF	150 FF

pays membres de la CEE EC countries
autres pays other countries
boissons drinks
vins tranquilles still wines
plus de more than
moins less
médicaments medicines
autres marchandises other goods

Did you know?

Transportation in France

Transportation is at the heart of the economic system of a country. In France the transportation sector employs 6 per cent of the working population and represents around 6 per cent of the GDP. In each branch of this sector, France has succeeded in becoming a world leader, with the development of the TGV (**train à grande vitesse**), the Airbus and the underground network (**le métro**).

The road network, with more than 1.5 million km of roads, is also undergoing considerable improvements. Within the EC, France has the second-largest motorway network after Germany. The main types of road in France are:

Category A   **Autoroutes** (motorways), 7,000km. As they are constructed and run by private institutions, a toll (**le péage**) is payable. However, no toll is charged 50km around Paris.

Category B   **Les routes nationales** (corresponding to the 'A' roads in Great Britain), 28,000km.

Category C   **Les routes communales** (roads connecting villages), 420,000km.

Like the motorway system, the rail network is basically built up like a spider's web, with Paris as the nerve centre. With 36,000km of track, French railways operate the most extensive rail network in Western Europe. French railways, run by the state-owned SNCF (**Société des Chemins de Fer**), with a workforce of 200,000 and a turnover of FF 48 billion, is by far the largest transporter in France. Each day two million travellers and 500,000 tonnes of goods are transported by train. The main lines are served by high-speed trains (TGVs and Corail), which are punctual and comfortable. In addition, French Motorail enables users to save journey time by taking their cars on the train. With the completion of the Channel tunnel, and the high-speed link between Paris, Brussels, Cologne, Amsterdam and London, the use of trains is increasing and competing with other means of transportation.

Transportation between major French cities is also well covered by a domestic air network which brings most of the large cities to within no more than a 90-minute flight from Paris. These domestic flights are basically operated by Air Inter (330 flights daily). Air France and UTA operate international flights from cities such as Paris, Lyon, Marseille, Bordeaux, Nice, Strasbourg and Toulouse.

Your turn to speak

15 As in Unit 1 this is an open-ended speaking activity. This means there is no 'correct' answer, but it's an opportunity for you to adapt the vocabulary you've learned to your own situation.

Try to work out how you would explain to a French speaker how to get from your company offices to a place in the centre of town. Think through your answer first and then speak it aloud. On the recording you'll find a 'model' answer giving you some ideas of what you might have said.

Answers

WHAT DO YOU DO?

You will learn

- to ask people about their job
- to answer basic questions about yourself
- something about working and living in France
- more on numbers
- about business customs

and you will be given some information on the French economy

Study guide

To help you keep a check on your progress, you could mark off the various tasks as you complete them.

Dialogue 1 + Practise what you have learned
Dialogue 2 + Practise what you have learned
Dialogue 3 + Practise what you have learned
Dialogue 4 + Practise what you have learned
Section 5 + Practise what you have learned
Ensure you know the **Key words and phrases**
Study the **Grammar** section
Do the exercises in **Read and understand**
Did you know? The French economy
Your turn to speak

Dialogues

1 *The receptionist talks to a visitor at the company reception*

Receptionist	Monsieur Liçois vous demande de patienter quelques minutes.
Visitor	Oui d'accord.
Receptionist	Vous habitez la région?
Visitor	Oui pas très loin d'ici, Offranville.
Receptionist	Et vous êtes native de la région?
Visitor	Oh non vous n'entendez pas mon accent? Non, je suis du Midi.
Receptionist	Vous avez des enfants?
Visitor	Oui j'ai deux filles.
Receptionist	Elles ont quel âge?
Visitor	Euh 17 et 19 ans à peu près.

A few moments later

Receptionist	Donc vous habitez Offranville?
Visitor	Oui oui oui oui.
Receptionist	Vous connaissez monsieur Christian à Offranville?
Visitor	Monsieur Christian oui oui oui oui. Ah il est très gentil. Il habite près de chez nous, euh une petite rue à côté de chez nous.
Receptionist	Oui c'est ça.
Visitor	Vous le connaissez bien?
Receptionist	Oui très bien c'est un bon ami.
Visitor	Ah que le monde est petit!

♦ **patienter** to wait
native native
♦ **des enfants** children
à peu près about/approximately

donc so
très gentil very nice
♦ **une rue** road
bien well

♦ **quelques minutes** a few minutes. Similarly **quelques kilomètres** 'a few kilometres', **quelques visites** 'a few visits', etc.

♦ **d'accord** is an important phrase for expressing agreement. It means 'OK / alright / I agree'.

♦ **Vous habitez la région?** You live in the area? From **habiter** 'to live (inhabit)'.

♦ **pas très loin de** not very far from. Note the use of **pas** for saying 'not'.

♦ **Vous n'entendez pas mon accent?** You can't hear my accent? **Entendre** means 'to hear'.

♦ **Je suis du Midi** I'm from the South of France. **Le Midi** is the usual way of saying 'the South'; **midi** without a capital letter means 'midday'. So **le Midi** has the idea of the land of the midday sun. **Du** comes from **de + le** and means 'from the'. See p. 67.

♦ **J'ai deux filles** I have two daughters. 'A son' would be **un fils**.

Elles ont quel âge? How old are they? Lit. 'They have what age?' In French you say: 'I have 25 years', etc.: **J'ai 25 ans** 'I am 25 years old'.

♦ **Vous connaissez...?** Do you know...? From the verb **connaître** 'to know a person or place': **Je connais John Peel** 'I know John Peel'.

♦ **Il habite près de chez nous** He lives near to us (our house)

♦ **un bon ami** a good friend. A female good friend would be **une bonne amie**.

Que le monde est petit! How small the world is! Without **que** this would be simply 'the world is small'. **Que** in this idiom means 'How...!' **Que le bâtiment est grand!** 'How big the building is!'

Practise what you have learned

1 Using the transcript and the notes, write down the French equivalent of the following sentences. (Answers on p. 56.)

(a) Mme Lebrun asks you to wait a few minutes.

(b) He lives not far from Nice.

(c) I have two sons.

(d) They are 15 and 17 years old.

(e) Do you know a good friend, Pierre Selas?

(f) How beautiful (**belle**) the region is!

2 Listen to the conversation on the recording and then say whether the statements below are true (**vrai**) or false (**faux**). (Answers on p. 56.)

		vrai	faux
(a)	The visitor is asked to wait 20 minutes.		
(b)	She comes from the South of France.		
(c)	Her children live in Lille.		
(d)	Her son is 16 years old.		
(e)	She knows M. Bernard.		
(f)	M. Bernard lives in Nice.		

3 In the speaking activity you'll be asked to play the part of a visitor waiting in the company reception. Remember an appointment is **un rendez-vous**.

Dialogues

2 *A tailor talks about his job*

Visitor Bonsoir monsieur.
Tailor Bonsoir monsieur.
Visitor Qu'est-ce qu'il fait beau!
Tailor Ce fut un temps formidable aujourd'hui.
Visitor Ah oui vous êtes d'ici?
Tailor Oui je suis d'ici.
Visitor Qu'est-ce que vous faîtes?
Tailor Je suis tailleur.
Visitor Tailleur?
Tailor Tailleur, dans la fabrication de vêtements pour hommes et dames.
Visitor Industrielle?
Tailor Non absolument artisanale.
Visitor Vous avez beaucoup d'employés?
Tailor Je n'ai pas d'employés seulement mon épouse m'aide dans l'entreprise.
Visitor Vous êtes deux?
Tailor Nous sommes deux. Le matin je suis seul. L'après-midi, mon épouse me rejoint et nous travaillons ensemble.
Visitor Ah ça existe encore?
Tailor Ça existe encore pour une année seulement. Je prends ma retraite.
Visitor Ah très bien.
Tailor En novembre, le premier novembre.
Visitor Alors si vous prenez votre retraite l'année prochaine qu'est-ce que vous ferez?
Tailor Eh bien je jardinerai.
Visitor C'est tout?
Tailor Non j'aime les activités sportives, j'irai me baigner comme je le fais actuellement chaque jour.
Visitor Très bien.

d'ici from here
le tailleur tailor
pour hommes et dammes for men and women
l'artisan (m.) crafstmen
pour dames for women
beaucoup d'employés lots of employees
seul alone

exister to exist
encore still
le premier novembre first of November
eh bien... well...
C'est tout? Is that all?
chaque jour each day

◆ **Bonsoir** Good evening. **Le soir** means 'evening'.

Qu'est-ce qu'il fait beau! What beautiful weather! **Il fait beau** means 'It's beautiful weather'. By adding **qu'est-ce que** you get an exclamation like **Que le monde est petit!**

Ce fut un temps formidable aujourd'hui. Lit. 'It was a weather fabulous today'. **Un temps formidable** means 'wonderful weather'.

◆ **la fabrication de vêtements** the production of clothes. **La fabrication** is the important general word for 'production', linked to **fabriquer** 'to produce'.

artisanale. He is not producing on an industrial scale; he is a self-employed craftsman.

Mon épouse m'aide My wife helps me. **Epouse** (cf. *spouse*) is slightly formal.

◆ **le matin... l'après-midi...** in the morning... in the afternoon...

me rejoint joins me. From **rejoindre** 'to join'. **Nous travaillons ensemble** We work together

une année seulement one year only; **l'année prochaine** next year

◆ **Je prends ma retraite** I'm going to retire (lit. I take my retirement)

Qu'est-ce que vous ferez? What will you do? In French, one way of conveying the future
◆ is by changing the form of the verb. **Vous ferez** 'you will do' comes from **faire** 'to do'.

Je jardinerai I will do some gardening. **Le jardin** 'garden'; **jardiner** 'to do the gardening'.

J'aime les activités sportives I like sporting activities

J'irai me baigner I'll go swimming. **J'irai** is an irregular future from **aller** 'to go'.

◆ **actuellement** at the present time / now (*not* actually)

Practise what you have learned

4 Using the information you've just got from the dialogue, answer the
following questions with **oui** (yes) or **non** (no). (Answers on p. 56.)

(a) **Il fait un temps formidable.** _____

(b) **Le tailleur fabrique des vêtements pour enfants.** _____

(c) **Il est artisan.** _____

(d) **Il a beaucoup d'employés.** _____

(e) **Sa femme l'aide dans l'entreprise.** _____

(f) **Il prend sa retraite en octobre.** _____

(g) **Il va se baigner chaque jour.** _____

5 In the box there are a number of jumbled up answers to the questions
below. Try and complete the dialogue and then switch on the recording and
see if you got it right. **Rester** means 'to stay' and **une maison** is 'a house'.

> **Moi, personnellement, je prends ma
> retraite à la fin de l'année, en décembre.**
>
> Pas beaucoup, environ 50.
>
> Je suis representant d'une compagnie d'assurance.
>
> Non, ma femme m'aide.
>
> **Oui parce que j'aime les activités sportives.
> J'aime le tennis et j'aime me baigner.**
>
> Ah non, nous avons une petite maison dans le Midi.

Qu'est-ce que vous faîtes?

_____

Il y a beaucoup d'employés dans votre compagnie?

_____

Et vous travaillez seul?

_____

Qu'est-ce que vous allez faire l'année prochaine?

_____

Et vous allez rester ici chez vous?

_____

Mm, que c'est beau le Midi! Et vous y irez souvent?

_____

6 And now for the speaking exercise. You'll be practising the main words and
phrases from the dialogue as you use the prompts to answer the questions
about your company and yourself.

Dialogues

3 *A financier who works at the Stock Exchange and the commercial director of a machine tool firm meet at the Chamber of Commerce*

Steve   Vous êtes nouveau à Dieppe?

Financier   Je viens d'arriver à Dieppe mais je ne suis pas nouveau car j'ai mes origines à Dieppe, bien sûr, et ... mais je suis Parisien.

Steve   Ah?

Financier   Pour le travail.

Steve   Ah vous êtes Parisien?

Financier   Tout à fait.

Steve   Et vous faîtes quoi exactement comme activité?

Financier   Je travaille principalement à la Bourse. Mais dans deux secteurs d'activité de la finance.

Steve   Ah intéressant.

Financier   Bien oui.

Steve   Et vous venez nous voir pour affaire?

Financier   Euh c'est-à-dire que j'ai pas mal de famille qui réside à Dieppe et j'ai eu l'occasion de rencontrer quelqu'un de la Chambre de Commerce qui m'a invité, donc c'est la raison pour laquelle je suis ici. Mais ce n'est pas mon but premier. Et vous, vous êtes Dieppois?

Steve   Oui, je suis Dieppois. J'habite cette région depuis une quarantaine d'années.

Financier   Ça vous plaît? Quelle activité faîtes vous?

Steve   Je suis spécialisé dans la vente de machine-outils sur le territoire français et je suis directeur commercial de la société Framo. Notre activité principale sont des machines par usinage ... par enlèvement de copeaux. Activité bien différente de la vôtre mais qui se rejoignent très proches avec la finance.

Financier   Bon tout à fait. De toute façon c'est très intéressant d'avoir des informations sur les entreprises puisque c'est la base de l'investissement.

---

car   because/for/since
mes origines   my origins
Parisien   from Paris
tout à fait   quite/exactly
principalement   principally
♦ **secteurs** (m.)   sectors/areas
intéressant   interesting
c'est-à-dire   that is to say
résider   to reside/live
donc   so
Dieppois   from Dieppe
depuis   since
spécialiser   to specialize
le territoire   territory
♦ **des informations**   information

- **Vous êtes nouveau à Dieppe?** You are new in Dieppe? If the newcomer were a woman you would ask **Vous êtes nouvelle à Dieppe?**

- **Je viens d'arriver** I have just arrived (lit. I come from arriving). This is the way of saying you have just done something. **Je viens de visiter** means 'I have just visited'; **Il vient de parler** 'He has just spoken'.

  pour le travail for (the) work. In French you often have the definite article (the) when it is not needed in English.

  Vous faîtes quoi comme activité? What do you do? (lit. You do what as activity?). So this is another typical way of asking **Qu'est-ce que vous faîtes?**

- **Je travaille à la Bourse** I work at the Stock Exchange. **La bourse** also means 'purse'.

- **Vous venez nous voir pour affaire?** You are coming to see us on business?

  J'ai pas mal de famille. The expression **pas mal** is a way of saying 'quite a lot', e.g. **J'ai pas mal d'employés.** Here **famille** (family) is used to mean 'relations'.

- **J'ai eu l'occasion de rencontrer...** I (have) had the opportunity of meeting... **J'ai l'occasion de...** means 'I have the opportunity of...' **Rencontrer** is the regular verb for 'to meet'.

- **quelqu'un** someone (m.). If he were meeting a female, he would say **quelqu'une.**

  qui m'a invité who has invited me

  la raison pour laquelle the reason for which

  mon but premier my main aim/purpose

- **J'habite cette région depuis une quarantaine d'années** I've lived in this area for about forty years. **Quarante** would be forty exactly, **quarantaine** means 'about forty'. Similarly, 'fifty' is **cinquante** and **une cinquantaine** means 'about fifty'.

- **Ça vous plaît?** A neat little phrase for 'Do you like it?' He could have answered: **Oui, ça me plaît beaucoup** 'Yes, I like it a lot'.

- **la vente de machines-outils** the sale of machine tools. **La vente** is linked to **vendre** 'to sell'. **Les outils** is the general word for 'tools'.

- **Je suis directeur commercial** I'm the commercial director. When you're saying what you do you often miss out 'the' or 'a'. 'I'm a doctor' would be **Je suis médecin.**

  des machines par usinage par enlèvement de copeaux. He got into a bit of a mess here. **Usinage** means 'machinery' and **l'enlèvement de copeaux** 'the removal of shavings'. Don't worry you won't be tested on this!

  différente de la vôtre different from yours

  se rejoignent from **rejoindre** 'to join/link'

- **très proches avec la finance** very closely with finance

  tout à fait, de tout façon quite, anyway (two filler phrases)

  puisque c'est la base de l'investissement since it is the basis of investment. **Investissement** is linked to **investir** 'to invest'.

Now turn over to p.46 and do the exercises based on this dialogue.

Practise what you have learned

7 An exercise in spotting synonyms. On the left are some phrases which have more or less the same meaning as certain words and phrases used in dialogue 3. Draw lines to match up the two columns. (Answers on p. 56.)

(a) **Je viens originalement de Dieppe.**   (i) **Je suis Parisien.**
(b) **Qu'est-ce que vous faîtes?**   (ii) **Je suis spécialisé dans la vente.**
(c) **Je suis employé à la Bourse.**   (iii) **J'ai mes origines à Dieppe.**
(d) **J'ai la possibilité d'un**   (iv) **Qui se rejoignent avec la finance.**
     rendez-vous avec quelqu'un.
(e) **Je viens de Paris.**   (v) **Vous faîtes quoi comme activité?**
(f) **depuis environ quarante années**   (vi) **Je travaille à la Bourse.**
(g) **Je travaille principalement**   (vii) **J'ai l'occasion de rencontrer**
     dans la vente.   **quelqu'un.**
(h) **Il y a beaucoup en commun**   (viii) **depuis une quarantaine d'années**
     avec la finance.

8 Below is a transcript of a short exchange between two business colleagues, but there are a number of gaps still to be filled in. First read the transcript through to get a feel for what it's about and then switch on the recording. All the gaps can be filled with words that occurred in dialogue 3. (Answers on p. 56.)

– Bonjour madame.
– Bonjour, vous êtes nouveau ici?
– Oui, je viens d'____(a)____ . Et vous, vous travaillez à Dieppe depuis longtemps?
– Oui, en effet, je travaille pour la même entreprise depuis une vingtaine d'____(b)____ . Vous ____(c)____ quoi exactement comme ____(d)____ ?
– Je viens travailler dans le bureau de ____(e)____ . Jusqu'au présent j'étais à Paris, à la ____(f)____ .
– Ah intéressant. Oh excusez-moi. Je m'appelle François Tissaud et je suis le ____(g)____ . Nos deux secteurs se rejoignent parce que la finance est ____(h)____ de l'investissement. Alors, bienvenue à notre ____(i)____ . J'éspère que vous serez heureux chez nous. Au revoir.
– Au revoir, merci.

9 In the speaking exercise you'll play the role of somebody just arriving at the Chamber of Commerce. Switch on when you're ready.

Dialogues

4 *An immigration official explains about permission to enter France*

Traveller Monsieur l'inspecteur pourriez-vous me dire quelles sont les formalités d'entrée en France s'il vous plaît?

Official Bien sûr, tout dépend de l'origine du voyageur. S'il s'agit d'un voyageur en provenance d'un pays de la Communauté Européenne, il lui suffit d'être en possession d'une carte nationale d'identité ou d'un passeport en cours de validité et revêtu d'un visa également en cours de validité à l'exception de quelques pays particuliers comme les Etats-Unis d'Amérique, le Canada, l'Australie et le Japon; ainsi évidemment que les Principautés comme le Vatican, Monaco, etc.

le voyageur traveller
la Communauté Européenne (CE) European Community (EC)
en possession de in possession of
revêtu d'un visa bearing a visa
également equally/similarly
les Etats-Unis (d'Amérique) USA
ainsi so/similarly
évidemment evidently/obviously
les Principautés Principalities

> ▸ **Pourriez-vous me dire...?** Could you (lit. would you be able to) tell me...? A useful phrase for starting a conversation.
>
> **Quelles sont...?** What are...? **Quelles** is spelled like this because it refers to **formalités**, which is feminine and in the plural. You use **quel(s)** when it refers to a masculine, e.g. **Quel est votre âge? Quels sont vos documents?** And **quelle** when it refers to a feminine singular noun.
>
> ▸ **tout dépend de...** everything depends on...
>
> ▸ **s'il s'agit de...** if it is a question of... **Il s'agit de combien de temps vous avez** means 'It's a question of how much time you have'. **Si**, shortened here to **s'**, means 'if'.
>
> **en provenance de**. A phrase often used in transportation. **Le train en provenance de Marseilles** means 'the train arriving from Marseille'.
>
> **il lui suffit d'être...** it is enough (sufficient) for him/her to be...
>
> **une carte nationale d'identité** national identity card. French citizens (and many others) have to carry this at all times.
>
> **en cours de validité** valid (officialese)
>
> **à l'exception de** with the exception of
>
> **quelques pays particuliers** some specific countries

Now turn to p.49 and do the exercises 10 and 11 which are based on this dialogue.

5 *Numbers over 10*

Here, first of all, are the numbers 11 to 20:

onze	**douze**	**treize**	**quatorze**	**quinze**
seize	**dix-sept**	**dix-huit**	**dix-neuf**	**vingt**

And here's how to say the numbers from 30 to 100:

trente (30)	**soixante** (60)	**quatre-vingt-dix** (90)
quarante (40)	**soixante-dix** (70)	**cent** (100)
cinquante (50)	**quatre-vingt** (80)	

Up to 70, making up the intermediate numbers is fairly easy as the same pattern is used as in English:

vingt-deux (22)	**cinquante-neuf** (59)
trente-cinq (35)	**soixante-quatre** (64)
quarante-huit (48)	

It's in the 70s, 80s and 90s that things get difficult. In French, 71 is the equivalent of 'sixty eleven', **soixante et onze**; 72 is **soixante-douze**; 73 is **soixante-treize**; 77 is **soixante-dix-sept**; and 79 is **soixante-dix-neuf**.

For the 80s you just add the numbers 1 to 10. So 82 is **quatre-vingt-deux**; 84 is **quatre-vingt-quatre**; 85 is **quatre-vingt-cinq** and 88 is **quatre-vingt-huit**.

But for the 90s you go back to the 'eighty eleven', 'eighty twelve', 'eighty seventeen' format:

quatre-vingt-onze (91)	**quatre-vingt-dix-sept** (97)
quatre-vingt-douze (92)	**quatre-vingt-dix-neuf** (99)
quatre-vingt-quatorze (94)	

For numbers in the 100s and 1000s you just have to put everything together; at least the same pattern is followed as in English (100 = **cent**; 1000 = **mille**):

526	**cinq cent vingt-six**
748	**sept cent quarante-huit**
973	**neuf cent soixante-treize**
992	**neuf cent quatre-vingt-douze**
1233	**mille deux cent trente-trois**
4657	**quatre mille six cent cinquante-sept**
6774	**six mille sept cent soixante-quatorze**
8894	**huit mille huit cent quatre-vingt-quatorze**

Now do exercises 12 and 13 (opposite).

Practise what you have learned

10 Using the notes and vocabulary from dialogue 4, translate the following sentences and questions into French. (Answers on p. 56.)

(a) Would you be able to work in France?

Pourriez-vous travailler en France

(b) Everything depends on the documents.

(c) It's a question of the investment.

il s'agit d'investissement

(d) It's enough to have a national identity card.

(e) The train is arriving from Monaco.

Le train en provenance de Monaco.

(f) It's enough to have a valid passport.

(g) With the exception of the European Community.

à l'exception de la commu Euro

11 Now for a speaking exercise in which you will be telling a French colleague what documents are necessary for a business trip to the States. The UK is **le Royaume Uni**.

12 Before you start this exercise, read the section on numbers over 10 (opposite).

You're going to hear some numbers spoken on the recording. See if you can fill them in correctly. (Answers on p. 56.)

(a) **Vous avez la chambre _____ monsieur.**

(b) **Elle habite rue du Havre numéro _____**

(c) **Nous avons _____ employés dans notre entreprise.**

(d) **Ma mère a _____ ans.**

(e) **Notre numéro de téléphone au bureau est le _____**

(f) **J'ai commencé à travailler pour Chambourcy en _____**

(g) **La Renault coûte _____ francs.**

(h) **Le numéro de notre Fax est _____**

13 Now it's your turn to get your tongue around some of the numbers. Follow the prompts.

Key words and phrases

patienter	to wait
quelques (minutes)	some / a few (minutes)
d'accord	OK/alright
habiter	to live (in)
loin	far
entendre	to hear
le Midi	South of France
midi	noon
les enfants (m.)	children
une fille	daughter
un fils	son
connaître	to know (a person or place)
chez nous	at our house
un bon ami / une bonne ami	good friend (m.) / good friend (f.)
une rue	road
bonsoir	good evening
la fabrication	production
un homme	man
une dame/femme	woman
un employé	employee
aider	to help
le matin	morning
l'après-midi	afternoon
travailler	to work
la retraite	retirement
faire	to do/make
aimer	to like/love
actuellement	at present
chaque jour	each day
nouveau (nouvelle)	new
je viens (d'arriver)	I have just (arrived)
la Bourse	Stock Exchange
le secteur	area
pour affaire	on business
l'occasion (f.)	opportunity
quelqu'un(e)	someone
une quarantaine	about forty
Ça vous plaît	Do you like it?
la vente	sale
le directeur commercial	commercial director (m.)
la directrice commerciale	commercial director (f.)
la finance	finance
l'investissement (m.)	investment
des informations (f.)	information
dire	to say/tell
tout dépend de	everything depends on
il s'agit de	it's a question of

And don't forget numbers, perhaps the most important of all.

Grammar

The present tense of verbs

In French there are three 'types' of verb. There are verbs which in their infinitive (full) form end in -**er** (e.g. **travailler, arriver, habiter**); verbs which end in -**re** (e.g. **vendre, prendre, dépendre**) and verbs which end in -**ir** (e.g. **finir, partir, investir**).

In English, verbs change slightly depending on their subject: *I sell, he sells,* etc. In French, unfortunately, verbs change rather more. At this stage you need not learn all the endings, but it is as well to be aware of them.

The largest group of verbs is the -**er** type and the good news is that most of them are regular. The -**er** ending is left off and the following endings are added:

	-er	-er
I	je travaille	j'arrive
you	tu travailles	tu arrives
he	il travaille	il arrive
she	elle travaille	elle arrive
we	nous travaillons	nous arrivons
you	vous travaillez	vous arrivez
they (m.)	ils travaillent	ils arrivent
they (f.)	elles travaillent	elles arrivent

The comparable endings for the -**re** group and for the -**ir** group are:

	-re	-ir
I	je vends	je finis
you	tu vends	tu finis
he	il vend	il finit
she	elle vend	elle finit
we	nous vendons	nous finissons
you	vous vendez	finissez
they (m.)	ils vendent	ils finissent
they (f.)	elles vendent	elles finissent

Note the -**iss** in some forms of -**ir** verbs.

Incidentally when you're speaking you don't pronounce the -**ent**. Obviously there are quite a lot of verbs that are not regular, but even if there are changes in the stem, the endings remain the same. For instance, with **prendre** 'to take' you say **nous prenons** or **vous prenez**. The **d** has got lost but the **nous** and **vous** endings are still -**ons** and -**ez**.

Things are made a little easier for learners because there is no present continuous (progressive) tense in French. *I am arriving* or *they are working*, etc., is simply translated as **j'arrive** (I arrive) or **ils travaillent** (they work).

14 See if you can fill in the correct form of the verb in the following sentences or phrases. (Answers on p. 56.)

(a) **Nous** _____ **à Londres.** (habiter)

(b) **Ils** _____ **les machines-outils.** (vendre)

(c) **Je** _____ **ma retraite en novembre.** (prendre)

(d) _____ **vous pour une grande entreprise?** (travailler)

(e) **Elles** _____ **à 5 heures.** (arriver)

(f) **Il** _____ **ses employés.** (aider)

A note on countries

Here are some of the countries you might come across. Most of them are easily recognizable.

l'Allemagne (f.) (Germany)	**l'Italie** (f.) (Italy)
l'Angleterre (f.) (England)	**le Japon**
le Brésil (Brazil)	**le Mexique** (Mexico)
les Etats-Unis (m.) (USA)	**le Pérou**
la France	**le Royaume-Uni** (UK)
la Grèce (Greece)	**la Russie** (Russia)

If you want to say 'I come from...' or 'he comes from...', etc., you have to know whether a country is masculine or feminine. For *feminine* countries you say **Je viens de la France** or **Il vient de l'Angleterre**. For *masculine* countries you say **Je viens du Canada** or **Il vient du Mexique**. 'He comes from the USA' is **Il vient des Etats-Unis**.

If you want to say 'in' or 'to' + a country, again you have to know whether it is masculine or feminine. For *feminine* countries you use **en**, e.g. **Il exporte en France** or **Nous travaillons en Allemagne**. For *masculine* countries you use **au**, e.g. **Il exporte au Canada** or **Nous travaillons au Royaume-Uni**. 'In the USA' is **aux Etats-Unis**.

Read and understand

15 Here are the results of a recent opinion poll asking whether the public believes that the service they get from various professions and trades is improving (**s'améliorer**) or getting worse (**se dégrader**). There's also a column for those who thought the quality of service had stayed the same and one for respondents with no opinion. Some of the professions have been translated into English and some haven't. Try to fill in the gaps by spotting the links with similar English words. (Answers on p. 56.)

Pour chacune des professions et activités suivantes, la qualité du service ou de la prestation a-t-elle eu tendance à s'améliorer ou à se dégrader au cours des dernières années ?

		S'améliorer	Se dégrader	Est restée la même*	Sans opinion
(a)	Les pharmaciens	59 %	12 %	24 %	5 %
(b)	Les médecins	59	20	17	4
(c)	Les coiffeurs	56	12	20	12
	Les grandes surfaces	56	18	19	7
(d)	Les banques	52	27	14	7
(e)	Les agents de voyages	49	8	6	37
(f)	Les restaurateurs	47	17	14	22
	Les petits commerçants et artisans en général	42	37	16	5
(g)	Les pompistes	41	25	19	15
(h)	Les hôteliers	40	14	15	31
	Les assureurs	37	37	15	11
(i)	Les garagistes	34	39	14	13
(j)	Les cafetiers	30	19	18	33
	Les enseignants	30	43	14	13
(k)	Les taxis	26	15	13	46
	Les agents immobiliers	25	26	10	39
	Les notaires	23	15	15	47
	Les pompes funèbres	17	15	9	59

(a) _Chemists_

(b) _doctors_

(c) _Hairdressers_

supermarket staff

(d) _banks_

(e) _Travel Agents_

(f) _Restaurateurs_

small businesses and trades

(g) _petrol pump attendants_

(h) _hoteliers_

insurance agents

(i) _garage_

(j) _____

teachers

(k) _____

(real-) estate agents

notaries/solicitors/lawyers

undertakers

16 Here is a selection of **offres d'emploi** (job ads). Obviously you are not expected to understand everything at the moment, but see if you can match the mini-profiles below to the most appropriate job vacancy. (Answers on p. 56.)

(a)
SOCIÉTÉ DE SERVICES AMERICAINE
recherche
ASSISTANT (E) DIRECTEUR FINANCIER
- Niveau DECS
- Anglais courant indispensable
- Connaissance de la micro-informatique
- Expérience cabinet souhaitée.

Merci d'adresser lettre manuscrite, photo et CV détaillé mentionnant votre rémunération actuelle à :
Mme D. BENHAIM - RUSSELL REYNOLDS Associates
7, place Vendôme - 75001 Paris

(b) **FUTURS VENDEURS SENIORS**
Fort de son concept novateur et exclusif

EASYCOM
RECRUTE
2 VENDEURS JUNIORS
Après une formation rémunérée à la vente **pure** et **dure**, sur le terrain, pendant une période de 6 mois, vous rejoindrez notre équipe "SENIORS" (240 à 350 KF + frais)

NOUS DEMANDONS :
- Esprit battant et gagneur.
- Organisation et rigueur.
- Positionnement et conviction.
- Excellente présentation.
- Mobilité totale.

Pour entretien, envoyer C.V. + photo + lettre à **EASYCOM,** service commercial, chemin de Marceron, 33160 SAINT-AUBIN-DE-MÉDOC.

(c) Employés administratifs

algeco

BRIE CTE ROBERT 77

recherche

SPECIALISTE RECOUVREMENTS CLIENTS

Sous l'autorité du Responsable Administratif, il anime une petite cellule de 3 personnes spécialisées dans la relance des créances commerciales
— en-cours environ 1000 dossiers & 25 MF
— Il est nécessaire d'avoir une expérience de la fonction.

Pour postuler, écrire s/ref.TC1196E à :

ALLIANCE H. & E.
10, rue Jean Perrin
93330 Neuilly s/Marne

(e) **GROUPE DE PRESSE**
En pleine expansion
Recherche
ASSISTANTE DE PUBLICITE
22 ANS MINI
Bac, excellente présentation pour contacts Ciaux haut niveau. Formation assurée.
Poss. évolution
Mini. 8000F.
Env. C.V + photo + prétentions à :
RPPP 17, rue Letellier, 75015 Paris,
ss réf.: L1/1705.

(d) Secrétaires

SECRETAIRE
EXPERIMENTEE
parfaitement bilingue
ALLEMAND FRANÇAIS
Connaissances anglais, négoce international.
Quartier Saint-Lazare.

Tél. de 9 h à 12 h 30
au 46.07.91.17

Candidate 1   23 years old, good appearance, wants to work in advertising
Candidate 2   bi-lingual in French and German with some English, experienced secretary
Candidate 3   specialist in recovering and collecting debts from clients, happy to lead a small team of 3 people
Candidate 4   qualified in finance, speaks good English, used to working with computers, prefers a foreign company
Candidate 5   no experience but would like to work in sales, well organized, mobile, of good appearance

Did you know?

The French economy

France's population is 55.5m, and 80% of this population live in cities. The major cities are Paris (9m for Greater Paris), Lyon (1.3m), Marseille (1.2m) Lille and Bordeaux. The total working population is around 24m.

France is today the fourth-largest economic power in the West, and second in the European Community. It is the main agricultural power in the EC. Although agriculture still plays an important role in the French economy (food and drink), only 7% of the working population are engaged in this sector, as opposed to 30% in 1945.

The 1980s were marked by profound industrial change in France. The older manufacturing industries declined, bringing economic difficulties to many regions, especially in the North and East of the country. But on the whole, French industry has been successfully developed and the main industrial strengths are in vehicle production, transportation, engineering, aerospace, telecommunications, defence, energy and software. The most significant achievements of French industry include:

- world leadership in the production of nuclear power, with 70% of energy generated by nuclear power

- leadership of Europe in aeronautics, satellites and space research (Airbus, Ariane)

- one of the world's fastest trains (TGV)

- one of the world's most advanced telecommunications systems (conversion to an 8-digit numbering system, Minitel)

- successful innovation in car design

In general, there has been a tendency to specialize in high-technology sectors (electronics, automation systems, telecommunications, computers and data processing) to the detriment of medium and low technology. Luxury goods (clothing, perfumes, wine and food) is also one of the sectors which continues to show significant growth.

Companies in France are classified according to the number of employees:

- below 500: **petites et moyennes entreprises** (small and medium-sized enterprises)

- above 500: **grandes entreprises** (large companies)

There is in the French economy a long tradition of public enterprise and of state intervention. Indeed France has one of the largest nationalized sectors in Western Europe, ranging from banking (Crédit Lyonnais, Banque Nationale de Paris), insurance, aerospace (Aérospatial), transportation (SNCF and Air France), electricity and gas (Electricité de France, Gaz de France) to cars (Renault).

Your turn to speak

 17 See if you can work out a few simple sentences to describe your job, where you work and where you live. Imagine you are talking to someone you have just met. When you've thought out what you might say, speak it aloud and then listen to the recording to see how Philippe tackled the exercise.

Answers

Exercise 1 (a) Mme Lebrun vous demande de patienter quelques minutes (b) Il habite pas loin de Nice (c) J'ai deux fils (d) Ils ont 15 et 17 ans (e) Connaissez-vous un bon ami, Pierre Selas? (f) Que la région est belle!

Exercise 2 (a) faux (b) vrai (c) vrai (d) faux (e) vrai (f) faux

Exercise 4 (a) oui (b) non (c) oui (d) non (e) oui (f) non (g) oui

Exercise 7 (a) iii (b) v (c) vi (d) vii (e) i (f) viii (g) ii (h) iv

Exercise 8 (a) arriver (b) années (c) faîtes (d) activité (e) finance (f) Bourse (g) directeur commercial (h) la base (i) entreprise

Exercise 10 (a) Pourriez-vous travailler en France? (b) Tout dépend des documents (c) Il s'agit de l'investissement (d) Il suffit d'avoir une carte nationale d'identité (e) Le train est en provenance de Monaco (f) Il suffit d'avoir un passeport en cours de validité (g) A l'exception de la Communauté Européenne

Grammar

Exercise 12 (a) quarante-trois (b) soixante-sept (c) deux cent (d) quatre-vingt-douze (e) 89 74 36 29 (f) 1986 (g) 80700 (h) 71 48 26 98

Read and understand

Exercise 14 (a) habitons (b) vendent (c) prends (d) travaillez (e) arrivent (f) aide

Exercise 15 (a) pharmacists (b) doctors (c) hairdressers (d) staff in banks (e) travel agents (f) restaurateurs (g) petrol-pump attendants (h) hoteliers (i) garage staff (j) café owners (k) taxi drivers

Exercise 16 (a) 4 (b) 5 (c) 3 (d) 2 (e) 1

4 AT THE HOTEL

You will learn

- how to book a room and check in
- to understand documents and hotel formalities
- how to enquire about the hotel's business services
- how to find out about what to do in a town

and you will be given some information about France's political and administrative structures

Study guide

To help you keep a check on your progress, you could mark off the various tasks as you complete them.

Dialogue 1 + Practise what you have learned
Dialogue 2 + Practise what you have learned
Dialogue 3 + Practise what you have learned
Dialogue 4 + Practise what you have learned
Ensure you know the **Key words and phrases**
Study the **Grammar** section
Do the exercises in **Read and understand**
Did you know? France's political and administrative structures
Your turn to speak

Dialogues

1 *A businessman checks into a hotel where he has a reservation*

John Smith	Bonjour mademoiselle, Vous devez avoir une réservation pour moi, je crois?
Receptionist	Oui, bonjour, monsieur. C'est à quel nom, s'il vous plaît?
John Smith	Euh, Smith, John Smith.
Receptionist	Oui. Alors un petit instant ... c'était une chambre à un grand lit, je crois?
John Smith	Oui.
Receptionist	Une nuit?
John Smith	Euh, peut-être deux, hein.
Receptionist	Peut-être deux. D'accord donc je la réserve maintenant et puis vous me direz demain si vous restez ou si vous partez.
John Smith	D'accord. Et le prix?
Receptionist	Alors le prix pour une personne, c'est 355 francs la chambre.
John Smith	D'accord merci.
Receptionist	Et on ajoutera le petit déjeuner qui sera de 35 francs.
John Smith	D'accord.
Receptionist	Voilà. Je vous donne votre clef. C'est au deuxième étage.
John Smith	Merci.
Receptionist	L'ascenseur se trouve juste là.

♦	**une réservation** reservation		**puis** then
	pour moi for me	♦	**le prix** price
	peut-être perhaps		**pour une personne** for one person
	maintenant now		**w.c.** toilet

> ♦ **Vous devez avoir...** You should/ought to have... From **devoir**, which you have already met: **je dois** means 'I must'.
>
> ♦ **je crois** I think
>
> **C'est à quel nom?** It is in what name?
>
> ♦ **C'était une chambre à un grand lit** It was a room with a double (lit. big) bed. The **un** is often 'swallowed' – so you hear **une chambre à grand lit**.
>
> ♦ **Une nuit?** One night?
>
> ♦ **Vous me direz demain** You will tell me tomorrow. **Direz** is a future form of **dire** 'to say' or 'to tell'.
>
> ♦ **si vous restez ou si vous partez** if you are staying or if you are leaving – **rester** 'to stay', **partir** 'to leave'.
>
> ♦ **On ajoutera le petit déjeuner** Breakfast will be added. **Ajouter** means 'to add'. In French **on** (one) is often used to replace the passive.
>
> **qui sera 35 francs** which will be 35 francs – **sera** is an irregular future form of **être** 'to be'.
>
> ♦ **Je vous donne votre clef** I'll give you your key
>
> ♦ **L'ascenseur se trouve juste là** The lift (elevator) is just over there. **Se trouver** (lit. finds itself) is often used to get over the idea of 'is located' or 'is situated'.
>
> ♦ **Avec douche, salle de bains et w.c.** with shower, bathroom and toilet

Practise what you have learned

1 Look back at the dialogue and find the phrases which are roughly equivalent to the following ones. (Answers on p. 72.)

(a) **Avez-vous une réservation pour moi?**

_____

(b) **Quel est votre nom?**

_____

(c) **Une seconde s'il vous plaît.**

_____

(d) **Je réserve votre chambre immédiatement.**

_____

(e) **C'est combien?**

_____

(f) **Ça va, merci.**

_____

(g) **Voici votre clef.**

_____

(h) **L'ascenseur est à côté.**

_____

2 Listen to a similar exchange at another hotel reception and then answer the questions below. **Ne... aucun(e)** means 'no'. **Il n'a aucune clef** means 'He has no key / He doesn't have a key'. (Answers on p. 72.)

(a) **Est-ce qu'il reste des chambres à l'hôtel?** _____Oui_____

(b) **Le voyageur prend la chambre pour combien de nuits?** _____3_____

(c) **Est-ce qu'il a un problème?** _____Non_____

(d) **Quel est son prénom?** _____John_____

(e) **C'est combien pour une personne?** _____355_____

(f) **Et pour deux?** _____390_____

3 And now imagine you are checking into a hotel. Yves will prompt you on the recording.

Dialogues

2 *The receptionist fills in the arrival form*

Receptionist Alors, je vais vous demander votre nom, s'il vous plaît, et puis je (vais) vous demander de remplir cette petite fiche voyageur ...
Guest Oui.
Receptionist Où vous indiquerez votre nom, prénom, adresse complète et votre numéro de passeport, s'il vous plaît.
Guest C'est pour quoi?
Receptionist C'est une fiche voyageur qui doit être destinée à la police. Euh, c'est une fiche de police en fait.
Guest Pour la police?
Receptionist Pour tous les étrangers qui viennent en France.
Guest Ah bon; c'est obligatoire?
Receptionist Un petit peu, oui.
Guest Bien, d'accord.

alors so
♦ **votre nom** your surname
♦ **votre prénom** your first name
votre adresse complète your full address

♦ **je vais vous demander** I am going to ask you

♦ **de remplir cette fiche voyageur** to fill in this travellers' form. **Remplir** is 'to fill in'; **une fiche** is 'card', 'slip' or 'form'; and **une fiche voyageur** (traveller) is what you have to fill in when staying in hotels in France.

où vous indiquerez where you will indicate (write in)

C'est pour quoi? It's for what? **Pourquoi** (one word) means 'why', e.g. **Pourquoi êtes-vous en France?** Why are you in France?

qui doit être destiné(e) which is supposed to be destined/meant for. **Elle doit être une bonne secrétaire** means 'She is supposed to be a good secretary'.

♦ **pour tous les étrangers** for all foreigners. **Etranger** has links with the English word *stranger* but it has come to mean 'foreigner'.

♦ **qui viennent en France** who come to France. **Viennent** comes from **venir** 'to come': **je viens** 'I come', **tu viens, il/elle vient, nous venons, vous venez, ils/elles viennent**.

♦ **C'est obligatoire?** It's compulsory?

Practise what you have learned

4 Here are some clues to words used in the dialogue. See if you can find those words. (Answers on p. 72.)

(a) **La réceptioniste vous demande votre** _____nom_____

(b) **Vous devez la remplir à la réception d'un hôtel.** _la fiche voyageur_

(c) **Vos amis vous appellent par votre ...** _prénom._

(d) **Chaque passeport a un ... particulier.** _numero_

(e) **Les fiches voyageurs sont destinées à la ...** _police._

(f) **Vous devez absolument le faire. Alors, c'est ...** _obligatoire_

5 You are going to fill in a **fiche voyageur**. Switch on the recording and pause after each question to fill in your own details below. Obviously there are no standard answers.

(i)	Rob Greenwood
(ii)	Home Address
(iii)	16/11/93
(iv)	
(v)	occupation Chef comptable de Luvey
(vi)	passeport
(vii)	nuits

6 Now, using the information from the **fiche** you have completed, reply to the questions on the recording. Remember **épeler** means 'to spell out'.

Dialogues

3 *Arranging seminar facilities in a hotel*

Receptionist Avez-vous besoin de matériel audio-visuel dans cette salle?
Businessman Ah si c'est possible oui.
Receptionist Voulez-vous, euh, un rétroprojecteur?
Businessman Un rétroprojecteur ce serait une bonne chose. Avec un écran.
Receptionist Vous voulez un appareil à diapositives?
Businessman Un appareil à diapositives, je pense qu'on en aura besoin également oui.
Receptionist Sinon nous avons également un magnétoscope VHS avec les moniteurs TV.
Businessman Non ça ce ne sera pas nécessaire.
Receptionist Ce ne sera pas nécessaire? Euh des paperboards, ça se met d'office dans une installation de salle de conférence.
Businessman Bien sûr, bien sûr.
Receptionist La salle fait environ 50 m².

si if
c'est possible it is possible
un écran screen
également equally (also)
sinon if not
♦ **un magnétoscope VHS** VHS video
♦ **un moniteur TV** TV set
nécessaire necessary
salle de conférence conference/seminar room
parfait perfect
♦ **un tarif reduit** discounted price
♦ **un télécopieur** fax machine
♦ **une télécopie** fax
♦ **un télex** telex

♦ **Avez-vous besoin de...?** Lit. 'Have you need of...?' An important phrase.
Avez-vous besoin de quelque chose? 'Do you need something/anything?'.

matériel audio-visuel audio-visual material

dans cette salle in this room

Voulez-vous un rétroprojecteur? Do you want an overhead projector?

Ce serait une bonne chose It would be a good thing. In dialogue 1 we had **sera** 'it will be'. **Serait** also comes from **être** and means 'it would be'.

un appareil à diapositives slide projector

♦ **Je pense qu'on en aura besoin** I think that we (one) will have need of it. **Je pense**, like **je crois**, means 'I think'. **En** is a difficult word which crops up in different contexts. Here it means 'of it'.

ça se met d'office is an idiomatic phrase meaning 'as a matter of course', i.e. flip charts are standard in a conference room.

La salle fait environ 50m² The room is (lit. makes) about 50 square metres. **Faire** means basically 'to do' or 'to make' but it is often used idiomatically. The receptionist could have said **La salle est de 50m²**.

Practise what you have learned

7 Below is a list of ten facilities you might need in a conference room. Seven of them are mentioned in the conversation with the conference organizer. When you've read through the list, listen to the recording and mark off those you hear. (Answers on p. 72.)

(a) **un rétroprojecteur** _____

(b) **un appareil à diapositives** _____

(c) **un téléphone** _____

(d) **un télécopieur** _____

(e) **une caméra** _____

(f) **un magnétoscope** _____

(g) **un moniteur TV** _____

(h) **un paperboard** _____

(i) **une cafetière** (coffee maker) _____

(j) **un télex** _____

8 And now imagine you are arranging the facilities for a conference with the hotel's business service. Follow the prompts on the recording.

Dialogues

4   *The conference receptionist gives a few ideas for what to do in three hours in the evening*

Receptionist   En trois heures, vous pouvez faire de la thalassothérapie, vous pouvez faire du tennis, vous pouvez faire une partie de squash, le golf, c'est un petit peu plus juste mais ça peut ...

Organizer   C'est envisageable.

Receptionist   C'est envisageable, vous pouvez faire du plus culturel avec visite du château et la collection d'ivoire qui est absolument splendide.

Organizer   Oui.

Receptionist   Vous pouvez visiter les jardins, vous serez à la très bonne époque avec les rhododendrons qui sont superbes et après le dîner, bon, bien vous pouvez faire un petit tour au casino avec ... aller dans une boîte de nuit.

en trois heures   in three hours
de la thalassothérapie   sea-water therapy (very popular in spas and resorts)
envisageable   possible
du plus culturel   (something) more cultural
la collection d'ivoire   ivory collection
absolument splendide   absolutely splendid
les rhododendrons (m.)   rhododendrons
superbe(s)   superb
après le dîner   after (the) dinner

Vous pouvez faire de... Lit. 'You can do...', but again the verb **faire** 'to do' is used rather idiomatically. There is a verb for 'to play' – **jouer** – but it is often replaced by **faire**, e.g. **faire du tennis**.

faire une partie de... to have a game of...

C'est un peu juste. A useful phrase used to get over the idea that time is short. You might ask if you have time to get to the bank and if it were near closing time you'd probably hear **C'est un peu juste** 'You haven't much time'.

avec visite de château with a visit of the castle. (See p. 67 for a note on **de, du, de la** and **des**.)

▶ **Vous pouvez visiter les jardins** You can visit the gardens

Vous serez à la très bonne époque Lit. 'You will be at the very good time'. **Epoque** is used more than *epoch* in English. It means 'a *period* (of time)'.

Vous pouvez faire un petit tour au casino You can go to the casino. **Faire un petit tour** is an idiomatic way of saying **visiter**.

(Vous pouvez) aller dans une boîte de nuit. Normally **une boîte** means 'a box' but **une boîte de nuit** is definitely 'a night club' and not a night box. Remember **aller** means 'to go'.

Practise what you have learned

9 Go back over the last two dialogues and make up two lists. One list of three words/phrases which convey the idea of want/like/need; the other of four words/phrases meaning good/great. (Answers on p. 72.)

(a) want/like/need

(b) good/great

_____ _____

_____ _____

_____ _____

_____

10 Match the following jumbled captions to the appropriate pictures. (Answers on p. 72.)

(a)

(b)

(c)

(d)

(e)

(f)

(g)

(h)

(i) **Vous pouvez faire du golf.**

(ii) **Connaissez-vous un bon restaurant?**

(iii) **J'aime le foot.**

(iv) **Attention! Vous risquez de perdre votre argent**

(v) **Faîtes de la thalossothérapie. C'est super!**

(vi) **Il y a beaucoup de boîtes de nuit à Paris.**

(vii) **Mon fils fait du basket.**

(viii) **Le musée est ouvert à 3 heures.**

11 A slightly different speaking exercise. Look at the phrases below and one by one try to work out what you would say in French. Say each sentence out loud and then check your answers on the recording. Go through them one by one. For 'Can I?' or 'Can we?' use **Peut-on?** (Can one?). Remember too 'I would like' is **je voudrais**.

(a) You can play tennis.

(b) You can play a game of squash

(c) Can we play golf here?

(d) I would like to visit the castle.

(e) Is there a casino here?

(f) I would like to go to a night club.

Key words and phrases

Vous devez avoir...	You must have...
une réservation	reservation
je crois / je pense	I think
le nom	name
le prénom	first name
une chambre à (un) grand lit	double-bedded room
une nuit	night
demain	tomorrow (remember **aujourd'hui** 'today')
rester	to stay/remain
partir	to depart/leave
le petit déjeuner	breakfast
donner	to give
la clef	key
un ascenseur	lift/elevator
se trouver	to be located/situated
la douche	shower
la salle de bain	bathroom
le prix	price
demander	to ask (for)
remplir une fiche	to fill in a form
un étranger / une étrangère	foreigner (m./f.)
venir	to come
obligatoire	compulsory
avoir besoin de	to have need of / to need
la salle	room (for conference, seminar, etc.)
un magnétoscope VHS	VHS video
un moniteur TV	TV set
tarif réduit	discount price
un télécopieur	fax machine
une télécopie	fax
un télex	telex
un paperboard	flip chart
faire du sport	to play sport
visiter	to visit (e.g. a museum)
aller	to go

Grammar

Prepositions

Prepositions are little words such as 'in', 'at', 'of', 'for' and 'with'. Here are some of the main prepositions you have met:

à	to/at
dans	in
avec	with
pour	for
sur	on/over
de	of/from
chez	at (the home of)
à côté de	beside

Although French prepositions do have specific meanings, they are, unfortunately, often used idiomatically. This idiomatic usage is sometimes linked to verbs so, for instance, 'to depend on' is **dépendre de**. For example: **Ça dépend de ma directrice** 'It depends on my (female) boss'. 'To play sport' is **faire du sport**. Sometimes the idiomatic usage is linked to a specific phrase, e.g. **A quel nom?** 'In what name?'; **beaucoup d'employés** 'many employees'; **à gauche** 'on the left'; **j'ai l'occasion de rencontrer** 'I have the opportunity to meet'; **je suis ravi de faire votre connaissance** 'I am delighted to make your acquaintance'; **pas de problème** 'no problem'.

In fact it is with **à** and **de** that most of these idiomatic uses occur. Don't worry if you can't get the usage right when you are speaking, just don't be thrown if you *hear or read* something a little unexpected. In most cases you can understand the gist in spite of **à** and **de**.

*A further note on **de***

You will have noticed that **de** is sometimes modified to **du, de la** or **des**. There are two main examples of this.

1 *To translate 'of the'*

de + **le** becomes **du**:
   La voiture du directeur The car of the director

de + **les** becomes **des**:
   Le prix des chambres The price of the rooms

2 *To translate 'some'.* A choice of **du, de la** or **des** depends on whether the noun is masculine, feminine or plural.

some coffee	**du café**
some beer	**de la bière**
some rooms	**des chambres**

*A further note on **à***

The same sort of thing happens with **à**.

à + **le** becomes **au**:
   au musée to/at the museum

à + **les** becomes **aux**:
   aux ascenseurs to/at the lifts/elevators

With **à** + **la** or **de** + **la** there is no change from what you would expect.

   Je vais à la banque I am going to the bank
   Nous venons de la ville We're coming from the town

You might find it helpful to read back through some of the earlier dialogues and to note the use of prepositions.

The months of the year and the days of the week

In Unit 2 the number system was introduced. Here are the days of the week.

lundi	Monday	**vendredi**	Friday
mardi	Tuesday	**samedi**	Saturday
mercredi	Wednesday	**dimanche**	Sunday
jeudi	Thursday		

And the months of the year:

janvier	January	**juillet**	July
février	February	**août**	August
mars	March	**septembre**	September
avril	April	**octobre**	October
mai	May	**novembre**	November
juin	June	**décembre**	December

Read and understand

12 You have been given the job of sorting out some translations on a bi-lingual report form that have been put in the wrong order. Insert the correct version in the central panel. (Answers on p. 72.)

FRENCH VERSION	YOUR VERSION	INCORRECT VERSION
Etes-vous satisfait de:	_____	Would you recommend TIMHOTEL?
Votre chambre n°	_____	Your breakfast
Calme de la chambre	_____	Quality of welcome
Confort du lit	_____	Quality of food
Image TV	_____	General cleanliness
Réglage du chauffage	_____	Friendly staff
Qualité du linge	_____	Bathroom in good order
Etat des sanitaires	_____	Comfortable bed
Propreté générale	_____	Good value for money
Votre petit-déjeuner →	_____	← Your stay
Qualité du service	_____	Quality of linen
Qualité des produits	_____	Sufficient quantity
Quantité suffisante	_____	Heating control
Votre séjour	_____	Your room no.
Qualité de l'accueil	_____	Quietness of the room
Efficacité du personnel	_____	Quality of service
Amabilité du personnel	_____	Efficient staff
Bon rapport qualité/prix	_____	TV correctly tuned
Recommanderiez-vous TIMHOTEL?	_____	Are you satisfied with:

A few key words you might not recognize:

réglage du chauffage	heating control
le linge	linen
la propreté	cleanliness
efficacité	efficiency

13 Read through the publicity issued by the Hotel Présidence in Dieppe and the Meridien in Montreal, then ✓ the facilities table below. (Answers on p. 72.)

MATIÈRE GRISE + CONFORT + DÉTENTE = EFFICACITÉ

— 5 salles de conférences de 10 à 200 personnes pourvues d'éclairage naturel

— équipement audio-visuel

— traduction simultanée

— 89 chambres équipées
  • salle de bains
  • téléphone à prise directe

• réveil automatique
• bar
• T.V. (la plupart en couleur)
— 1 restaurant panoramique face à la mer
• un choix important de poissons selon l'arrivage

— un golf de 18 trous
— tennis
— thalassothérapie
— équitation
— yachting
— casino

HOTEL « LA PRESIDENCE » Bd de Verdun 76201 DIEPPE Cedex.
Tél. : (35) 84.31.31. Telex 180865F

Accès
Centre ville.
Aéroport international de Montréal/Dorval : 19 km.
Aéroport international de Montréal/Mirabel : 40 km.
Gares Canadian National et Canadian Pacifique : 5 mn par taxi. Port : à proximité.
Parking souterrain. Location de voitures.

Hébergement
Catégorie luxe.
603 chambres.
Climatisation, insonorisation, téléphone, radio, télévision couleur.

Restauration
La Rôtisserie carte (160 couverts).
L'Universel spécialités locales (120 couverts).
Le Vieux Marché coffee-shop (275 couverts).
Le Caroussel snack (70 couverts).
L'Été des Indiens bar-restaurant (100 couverts).

HÔTEL MERIDIEN

Activité sportive
Piscine.

Santé
Sauna, service médical, club de santé.

Services divers
Télex, photocopie, secrétariat multilingue, coffres, change, banque.

* Congrès - Séminaires
9 salons. Accueil : jusqu'à 1 500 personnes.

Animation - Loisirs
Discothèque.
Spectacles de chansonniers.
4 bars.

Facilités de règlement
Les principales cartes de crédit.

	Présidence	Meridien
(a) conference/seminar rooms		
(b) close to international airport		
(c) language services		
(d) automatic wake-up		
(e) restaurant with sea-view		
(f) shows in the evening		
(g) accommodates more than 1000 guests		
(h) air- and sound-conditioned		
(i) provides A/V equipment		
(j) swimming pool		
(k) outdoor sports		

Did you know?

Political and administrative structures

Since 1870 France has had a republican form of government with a president, a prime minister and two houses of parliament. The current political system is derived from the 1958 constitution, which created the Fifth Republic and in which political power is shared between the president with his appointed government and parliament. It is a system based on the separation and balance of powers. The French president is elected by universal suffrage for a seven-year term. He appoints the prime minister, who in turn recommends ministers for the government, appointed by the president. The president defines the guidelines of policy and has the right to dissolve parliament and call new elections. He cannot block legislation passed by parliament but can bypass it by calling a referendum.

Legislative power is held by parliament, which has two houses: l'**Assemblée Nationale** (National Assembly) and the **Sénat** (Senate). Members of the National Assembly (**députés**) are elected by universal suffrage for five years. The members of the Senate (**sénateurs**), elected for nine years by an electoral college (around 130,000 local councillors), have certain limited powers to amend or reject legislation passed by the Assembly.

A constitutional court (**conseil constitutionnel**) is responsible for the enforcement of the constitution and ensures that all elections are fair and that laws passed by the parliament comply with the constitution. Its nine members are independent and appointed by the president, the president of the national Assembly and the president of the Senate (three members each) for a period of nine years.

There are three administrative levels in France: **régions, départements** and **communes**. Each region has its own elected assembly and executive and is in charge of adult education, culture, tourism and industrial development. Departments have an elected council and are responsible for welfare and social services. At the level of each department, a **préfet** appointed by the government is responsible for co-ordination, arbitration and security. The communes have their council and mayor and look after local affairs such as town planning, building and the environment. The revolutionary reforms introduced in 1982 transferred most of the executive power of the **préfet** to the local authorities. However, education, justice and the health service are firmly under the control of the state and thus under the administrative control of the **préfet**.

Your turn to speak

 14 Imagine you are making arrangements for a conference. Explain to the person responsible for business services what you will want. Remember **j'ai besoin de, je voudrais, il faut avoir, je dois avoir**, and try to bring them into your explanation. You might also ask about **un tarif réduit** by saying **Je voudrais savoir si vous avez un tarif réduit pour conférences**.

Answers

Practise what you have learned

Exercise 1 (a) Vous devez avoir une réservation pour moi? (b) C'est à quel nom? (c) Alors, un petit instant (d) Je la réserve maintenant (e) Et le prix? (f) D'accord, merci (g) Je vous donne votre clef (h) L'ascenseur se trouve juste là

Exercise 2 (a) oui (b) trois (c) non (d) John (e) 355 francs (f) 390 francs

Exercise 4 (a) nom (b) une fiche (c) prénom (d) numéro (e) police (f) obligatoire

Exercise 7 You hear the following facilities mentioned: (a), (c), (d), (f), (g), (h)

Exercise 9 Here are some of the phrases you might have noted: (a) avez-vous besoin de (3); voulez-vous (3); je pense qu'on en aura besoin (3); (b) ce serait une bonne chose (3); c'est parfait (3); absolument splendide (4); superbes (4)

Exercise 10 (a) vi (b) i (c) v (d) vii (e) viii (f) iii (g) ii (h) iv

Read and understand

Exercise 12 The order of the English translations should be: Are you satisfied with; your room no.; quietness of the room; comfortable bed; TV correctly tuned; right temperature; quality of linen; bathroom in good order; general cleanliness; your breakfast; quality of service; quality of food; sufficient quantity; your stay; quality of welcome; efficient staff; friendly staff; good value for money; would you recommend TIMHOTEL?

Exercise 13 Présidence: (a), (c), (d), (e), (i), (k); Meridien: (a), (b), (c), (f), (g), (h), (j)

You will learn

- to order drinks and snacks
- to arrange your hire car
- how to open an account in France
- how to get hold of cash when you need it

  and you will be given some information about French cuisine

Study guide

To help you keep a check on your progress, you could mark off the various tasks as you complete them.

Dialogue 1 + Practise what you have learned
Dialogue 2 + Practise what you have learned
Dialogue 3 + Practise what you have learned
Dialogue 4 + Practise what you have learned
Ensure you know the **Key words and phrases**
Study the **Grammar** section
Do the exercises in **Read and understand**
Did you know? French cuisine
Your turn to speak

Dialogues

1 *In a hurry and needing a snack*

Customer	Oui, s'il vous plaît, je voudrais manger là maintenant.
Café owner	Que désirez-vous?
Customer	Qu'est-ce que vous pouvez me proposer?
Café owner	Euh … quelque chose de vite fait?
Customer	Oui.
Café owner	Alors saucisses, pizzas, omelettes frites, croques-monsieur, sandwiches?
Customer	Omelettes frites.
Café owner	Que désirez-vous boire?
Customer	Un demi s'il vous plaît.
Café owner	Bien.

♦ **maintenant** now
♦ **une saucisse** sausage

♦ **Je voudrais manger là** I would like to eat here. **Je voudrais** 'I would like' is a useful way of getting what you want. **Là** 'here' is more often used to mean 'there'!

♦ **Qu'est-ce que vous pouvez me proposer?** Lit. 'What you can to me propose?' A good way of asking for a suggestion.

♦ **Quelque chose de vite fait?** Something quick? (lit. quickly done). **Une chose** is the word for 'a thing'; **quelque chose** 'something'.

♦ **frites** chips / French fries. If you ask for 'chips' in France you'll get crisps (potato chips).

♦ **un croque-monsieur** is a popular snack, available in most cafés. It's grilled cheese and ham on toast. A **croque-madame** is the same but with an egg.

♦ **Que désirez-vous boire?** What do you want to drink? **Boire** means 'to drink'. Notice the two ways of asking 'what'-questions in this dialogue. Both are equally possible. The café owner could just as well have said **Qu'est-ce que vous désirez boire?**

♦ **un demi** a half (-litre of beer). A standard way of ordering draft beer.

Practise what you have learned

1 On the recording is another example of ordering. Below is a transcript of what was said. See if you can fill in the gaps. (Answers on p. 88.)

- Je peux vous _____(a)_____ du café, _____(b)_____ ça intéresse quelqu'un?
- Oh, oui.
- Volontiers.
- _____(c)_____ , oui merci.
- _____(d)_____ noir. Pour tout le monde?
- Noir mais avec sucre _____(e)_____
- Alors, sucre également.
- Oui.
- Egalement.
- _____(f)_____ , trois sucres, et un café noir. Très bien _____(g)_____ vous chercher ça.
- Merci.

Note **Intéresser** is 'to interest' and **quelqu'un(e)** is 'someone'. **Volontiers** means literally 'willingly' but is often used when in English you might say *mmm, please* or *that would be nice*.

café noir is 'black coffee', as opposed to **café au lait** 'coffee with milk' or **café crème**. Beware, if you just ask for **un café s'il vous plaît** you will probably get the strong black variety. If you want white you must say **café au lait** or **café crème**.

le sucre is 'sugar', and **chercher** means 'to look for' but is often used idiomatically with the sense of 'to fetch'.

2 And now you're in a café ordering a snack. You'll be prompted what to say. Let's hope you'll like it!

Dialogues

2 *An English guest struggles to get a 'proper' breakfast in a hotel*

Guest	Pour le petit déjeuner.
Waitress	Oui, monsieur, qu'est-ce que vous désirez?
Guest	Qu'est-ce que vous avez?
Waitress	Du thé, du café, du chocolat? Vous désirez un jus d'orange? Il y a des toasts, du pain grillé.
Guest	Jus d'orange?
Waitress	Oui, du jus d'orange si vous le désirez.
Guest	Et café?
Waitress	... Jus de fruit, du café, café au lait?
Guest	Café au lait. Oui. Le café comment? Au lait? Lait chaud?
Waitress	Comme vous voulez monsieur. Lait chaud ou lait froid.
Guest	Un café avec du lait chaud.
Waitress	Oui.
Guest	Et puis il y a des saucisses?
Waitress	Eh, pas de saucisses, monsieur. Mais je peux vous faire des œufs sur le plat si vous désirez?
Guest	Ah oui, très bien.
Waitress	Avec des toasts?
Guest	Oui avec du pain, du toast, des toasts.
Waitress	Avec du beurre et de la confiture?
Guest	Très bien. Dans ma chambre?
Waitress	Si vous voulez, monsieur, et à l'heure que vous désirez.
Guest	A huit heures.
Waitress	Bon, très bien, monsieur, vous aurez votre petit déjeuner demain à huit heures.
Guest	Merci.

◆	**le petit déjeuner** breakfast	◆	**le chocolat** chocolate
◆	**désirer** to want (desire)	◆	**un jus d'orange** orange juice
◆	**le thé** tea	◆	**le pain** bread

---

du pain grillé long toasted rolls (usually)

Le café comment? Lit. 'The coffee how?' **Comment** is a useful question word: **Comment allez-vous?** How are you? (lit. How goes you?).

lait chaud. Lit. 'milk hot'. Adjectives often follow the noun. **Lait froid** means 'cold milk'.

◆ **Il y a des saucisses?** Are there any sausages?

Pas de saucisses is short for **Il n'y a pas de saucisses** 'There are no sausages'.

Je peux vous faire des œufs sur le plat I can do you fried eggs

◆ **avec des toasts**. You will often find **toasts** in the plural. This is usually mass-produced cold 'toast' bought like sliced bread in supermarkets.

avec du beurre et de la confiture with butter and jam. You rarely get 'real' orange marmalade in **le petit déjeuner français**. Here are two good examples of **du** and **de la** meaning 'some', as described in the grammar section of Unit 4.

◆ **à l'heure que vous désirez** at the time that you want. Unit 6 goes more fully into time.

à huit heures at 8 o'clock

vous aurez votre petit déjeuner demain à huit heures You'll have your breakfast tomorrow at 8 o'clock. **Aurez** 'will have' is an irregular future form of **avoir** 'to have'.

Practise what you have learned

3 Here's an extract from one of those breakfast menus that you hang on the door before going to bed (it's been slightly doctored). Help your colleague who doesn't speak such good French as you to translate it. (Answers on p. 88.)

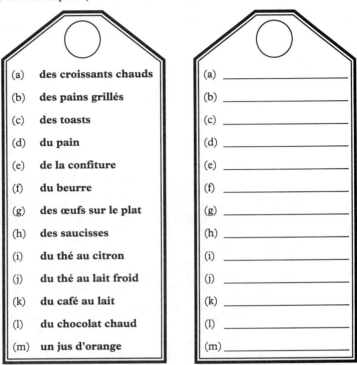

(a)	**des croissants chauds**
(b)	**des pains grillés**
(c)	**des toasts**
(d)	**du pain**
(e)	**de la confiture**
(f)	**du beurre**
(g)	**des œufs sur le plat**
(h)	**des saucisses**
(i)	**du thé au citron**
(j)	**du thé au lait froid**
(k)	**du café au lait**
(l)	**du chocolat chaud**
(m)	**un jus d'orange**

(a) _____
(b) _____
(c) _____
(d) _____
(e) _____
(f) _____
(g) _____
(h) _____
(i) _____
(j) _____
(k) _____
(l) _____
(m) _____

In fact most French people staying in a hotel take **un café complet**. This is **café au lait** served with croissants, rolls or bread, jam and butter.

4 You've just come down for breakfast in the hotel and you ask the waiter for various things. Switch on the recording when you're ready.

Dialogues

3 *Collecting a hire car*

M. Burrough Ma secrétaire m'a dit lorsque j'ai quitté Londres ce matin qu'il y avait une voiture reservée pour moi au nom de Burrough.

Clerk C'est exact monsieur j'ai bien votre réservation. Elle m'a demandé de vous réserver une catégorie C. C'est en l'occurrence une Renault 19. Ça vous convient?

M. Burrough Oui très bien, oui.

Clerk Bien, monsieur, c'est une voiture que vous allez garder trois jours et que vous allez rendre à l'aéroport de Roissy. Est-ce que c'est exact?

M. Burrough Roissy ou bien Bordeaux, je ne sais pas.

Clerk Ou bien Bordeaux, très bien, je note. Vous avez vos papiers, monsieur? J'aurai besoin de votre permis de conduire.

M. Burrough Oui les voilà.

Clerk Je vous remercie, bien, parfait. Vous prenez une assurance complète?

M. Burrough Oui.

Clerk Donc pour la voiture et les personnes transportées. Pour le paiement, monsieur, vous réglez avec une carte Avis ou une carte de crédit?

M. Burrough Vous ne pouvez pas facturer directement ma société?

Clerk Si, tout à fait. J'ai reçu un telex. Je ferai donc parvenir la facture à votre société en direct.

M. Burrough Parfait.

Clerk Je vais vous demander d'imposer vos initales ici et ici et de faire une signature ici. Merci, voilà, je vous donne vos documents, les documents de la voiture et votre contrat de location.

ce matin this morning	**les voilà** here they are
au nom de in the name of	**parfait** perfect
une catégorie category	**donc** so
en l'occurrence on this occasion	**une carte Avis** Avis card
◆ **garder** to keep	**ou** or
◆ **rendre** to return	**carte de crédit** credit card
noter to note	**tout à fait** quite/exactly
vos papiers your papers	**imposer vos initiales** to initial

◆ **ma secrétaire m'a dit** my secretary told me. **Dit** is from the verb **dire** 'to say/tell'.

lorsque j'ai quitté Londres ce matin when I left London this morning. **Quitter** 'to leave'.

◆ **il y avait** there was / there were. Remember **il y a** 'there is / there are'. This is the past tense.

J'ai bien votre réservation. By adding **bien**, the Avis lady is changing the statement 'I have your booking' to a confirmation, 'Yes, I do have your booking'. **Réserver** means 'to book'.

◆ **Elle m'a demandé de...** She asked me to... **Demander** is 'to ask'.

Ça vous convient? Is that alright? Lit. 'That to you is convenient?'

◆ **Je ne sais pas** I don't know. **Sais** comes from **savoir** 'to know a fact'.

◆ **J'aurai besoin de votre permis de conduire** I will need your driving licence

◆ **Vous prenez une assurance complète?** Are you taking comprehensive insurance?

◆ **Pour le paiement...vous réglez...?** **Le paiement** 'payment'; **régler** 'to settle an account'.

◆ **Vous ne pouvez pas facturer directement ma société?** Can't you bill my company direct? **Une facture** 'a bill'. **Si** means 'yes' when you are affirming or contradicting.

◆ **J'ai reçu un télex** I have received a telex. From **recevoir** 'to receive'.

Je ferai donc parvenir la facture à... I will have the bill sent to...

votre contrat de location your hire contract. **Location** is linked to **louer** 'to hire'.

Practise what you have learned

5 Referring back to the dialogue at the Avis car hire, answer the following questions in French, or fill in the gaps. (Answers on p. 88.)

(a) **Est-ce qu'il a quitté Londres aujourd'hui?** _____

(b) **Qui a reservé la voiture de location?** _____

(c) **Il va la garder combien de jours?** _____

(d) **Il va la rendre à** _____ **ou à** _____ **?**

(e) **Elle a besoin de ses** _____ **spécifiquement son** _____

(f) **Il prend quelle sorte d'assurance?** _____

(g) **On utilise une carte de crédit pour le** _____

(h) **Qui doit-elle facturer en direct?** _____

(i) **Elle lui donne les documents de la voiture et le** _____

(j) **On dit 'Bonne route' quand on part ou lorsqu'on arrive?** _____

6 On the recording you will hear a number of statements or questions. Pause after each one and write in the translation. (Answers on p. 88.)

(a) _____

(b) _____

(c) _____

(d) _____

(e) _____

(f) _____

(g) _____

(h) _____

7 And now it is your turn to pick up your hire car, **votre voiture de location**. As usual you'll be prompted what to say. Most of the vocabulary comes from the dialogue so make sure you know the main words before you start.

Dialogues

Opening an account at the bank

Bank clerk C'est tout à fait possible. Il vous suffit de me justifier de votre identité et de votre domicile qu'il soit en France ou qu'il soit dans votre pays d'origine.

Didier Bien. J'ai besoin d'un certificat de domicile?

Bank clerk Vous n'avez besoin que de me donner l'adresse si vous êtes résident en France. Si vous avez un domicile en France, vous avez vraisemblablement un permis de séjour ou tout simplement une adresse connue et reconnue.

Didier Oui c'est ça, c'est ma maison de campagne, c'est bon?

Bank clerk Tout à fait, c'est tout à fait possible.

Didier Bien, je vous remercie. Bien alors une autre question. Je suis détenteur d'un compte à la Barclays et je voudrais retirer de l'argent ici en France.

Bank clerk Bien ... Bien, monsieur, euh vous ... êtes-vous détenteur d'une carte bancaire?

Didier Oui.

Bank clerk Alors, là c'est très simple. Vous allez donc me confier votre carte, me demander le montant que vous désirez retirer et nous allons interroger notre centre de traitement des cartes bancaires parce que je vois que notamment vous êtes affilié au système Visa. Vous avez une autre possibilité si vous ne voulez pas passer par le système Visa, vous avez peut-être la carte Eurochèque et donc possibilité de me faire des chèques libellés en francs français à contre valeur de 1400 francs.

Didier Et c'est immédiat?

Bank clerk C'est immédiat. On vous donne la contre valeur immédiatement et sans limitation de montant.

Didier Très bien. Je vous remercie beaucoup.

le pays d'origine country of origin
un certificat certificate
vraisemblablement probably (also **probablement**)
simplement simply
ma maison de campagne my house in the country
le détenteur holder
♦ **parce que** because
notamment in particular
immédiat immediate

Il vous suffit de... It's enough/sufficient... Lit. 'It to you suffices...'

me justifier de votre identité to give me proof of your identity

et de votre domicile and of your home address

qu'il soit...ou qu'il soit... whether...or... A rather difficult idiom but one you might hear quite often.

♦ **ne ... que** only. Works like **ne ... pas**, e.g. **Je n'ai pas de voiture** 'I haven't a car'; **Je n'ai qu'une voiture** 'I have only one car'. **Vous n'avez besoin que de me donner...** 'You only need to give me...'

Si – this is **si** meaning 'if'

---

un permis de séjour a residential permit. **Un séjour** means 'a stay' and you often hear **Bon séjour** 'Have a nice stay'. It is linked to the English word *sojourn*.

une adresse connue et reconnue. Lit. 'an address known and recognized'. Here it just means 'a fixed address'.

◆ **un compte** account

Je voudrais retirer de l'argent I would like to withdraw some money

une carte bancaire cheque card

vous allez me confier. Lit 'you are going to let me have'.

◆ **le montant que vous désirez** the amount you want

◆ **nous allons interroger notre centre de traitement.** The literal meaning of **interroger** is 'to interrogate'; **un centre de traitement** is 'a data processing centre'.

◆ **Je vois que...** I see that... From **voir** 'to see'.

Vous êtes affilié au système Visa You're linked to the Visa network

une autre possibilité another possibility. **Autre** is a useful word: **une autre personne** 'another person'; **un autre compte** 'another account'.

des chèques libellés en francs français cheques made out in French francs

la contre valeur exchange value

sans limitation de montant without any limitation in the amount. **Sans** is a useful little word meaning 'without'; 'with' is **avec**.

This mention of the Eurocheque may be a little confusing. The system is that the bank guarantees any single cheque up to 1400FF. You may, however, write as many cheques as you like. So, to get 14,000FF you would write ten cheques each of 1400FF. The following additional words associated with banking might be useful.

◆ **la commission** commission
le crédit credit
◆ **en devises** in local currency

◆ **faire un virement** to make a transfer
◆ **les frais** charges
◆ **le taux d'intérêt** rate of interest

Practise what you have learned

8 Try a bit of text manipulation. Take the six words/phrases and try to make a simple sentence or question out of each one. For instance, with **la commission**, you might come up with **Je voudrais une commission** 'I would like a commission' or **Est-ce que vous demandez une commission?** Are you asking for a commission? There are obviously no right or wrong answers here.

(a) **la commission:** _____

(b) **le crédit:** _____

(c) **en devises:** _____

(d) **faire un virement:** _____

(e) **les frais:** _____

(f) **le taux d'intérêt:** _____

9 Listen to the dialogue on the recording, where a businessman is wanting to open an account. Then answer the questions below in English. (Answers on p. 88.)

(a) Why does he want to open an account?

(b) What does the bank official ask M. Tissand to do with his name?

(c) What document does she request?

(d) Which address does she require?

(e) How much will he put into the account initially?

(f) What does he want straight away?

(g) What sort of cheque will he be paying in?

(h) When can he start using a cheque book?

10 Now you're in a bank. You'll be asked to take part in a conversation with the bank clerk. Check that you have learned the main words in the dialogue, then switch on and have a go.

Key words and phrases

je voudrais manger	I would like to eat
maintenant	now
Qu'est-ce que...?	What...?
proposer	to suggest/propose
quelque chose	something
vite fait	quickly done
une saucisse	sausage
frites (f.)	chips / French fries
un croque monsieur	cheese and ham on toast
un croque madame	cheese and ham on toast with an egg
Que désirez-vous boire?	What do you want to drink?
un demi	a half of beer (i.e. half a litre)
le petit déjeuner	breakfast
le jus d'orange	orange juice
le thé	tea
le chocolat	chocolate
café au lait	coffee with milk
le sucre	sugar
café complet	'continental' breakfast
œufs sur le plat	fried eggs
le beurre	butter
la confiture	jam
le pain	bread
chercher	to look for / fetch
demain	tomorrow
dire	to tell/say
quand/lorsque	when
quitter	to leave
il y avait	there was / there were
au nom de	in the name of
demander	to ask
Ça vous convient?	Is that alright?
Je ne sais pas	I don't know
le permis de conduire	driving licence
l'assurance (f.)	insurance
régler	to settle (a bill)
payer / le paiement	to pay / payment
une carte de crédit	credit card
facturer / la facture	to bill / bill
à l'avance	in advance
la location de voitures	car hire
recevoir / j'ai reçu	to receive / I have received
garder	to keep
rendre	to return
ne...que...	only
un compte bancaire	bank account
le montant	amount
le centre de traitement	data processing centre
je vois que... (voir)	I see that... (to see)
la commission	commission
en devises	in local money
les frais (f.)	charges
faire un virement	to make a transfer (of money)
retirer de l'argent	to withdraw money
le taux d'intérêt	rate of interest
parce que	because
Le/La/Les voilà	Here it is / they are

Grammar

Adjectives

Most adjectives *follow* the noun in French: **un chocolat chaud** 'a hot chocolate', **un compte bancaire** 'a bank account', **l'argent étranger** 'foreign money'.

However, some do come before the noun, particularly some of the most common ones: **une grande chambre** 'a large bedroom', **une petite voiture** 'a little car', **une bonne idée** 'a good idea', **le premier étage** 'the first floor'. Here are a few of those adjectives that come before the noun:

grand	big	**petit**	small
bon(ne)	good	**mauvais**	bad
premier, deuxième, etc.	first, second, etc.	**joli**	pretty
beau (m.), **beaux** (m.pl.), **belle** (f.), **belles** (f.pl.)	beautiful		

You may have noticed that adjectives 'agree with' the noun to which they are referring. In practise this means that an -**e** is added with a feminine singular noun; -**s** with a masculine plural and -**es** with a feminine plural. For example, you would say **un grand pays** 'a large country', **une grande banque** 'a large bank', **les grands contrats** 'the large contracts', **les grandes entreprises** 'the large firms'.

Some adverbs

To get over the idea of -*ly*, as in *probably, firstly*, etc. you normally add -**ement** or -**ment** to the adjective. Hence 'probably' is **probablement/vraisemblablement**, 'possibly' **possiblement**, 'secondly' **deuxièmement**, 'exactly' **exactement**, 'equally' **également**, 'directly' **directement**, 'perfectly' **parfaitement**, 'simply' **simplement**, etc.

11 Select the correct form of the adjective and put it in the right place when you translate these phrases. (Answers on p. 88.)

(a) a little firm   _____

(b) a foreign company   _____

(c) a big credit   _____

(d) the important expenses   _____

(e) the good ideas   _____

(f) the first commission   _____

(g) a good interest rate   _____

Pronouns

Pronouns are those little words such as *me, you, it, them*, etc. that you use instead of a noun: *I see the man* → *I see him*, etc.

Here are the pronouns in French, most of which you will already have come across:

me	me	**il me voit**	he sees me
te	you	**il te connaît**	he knows you
le	him / it (m.)	**il le mange**	he eats it (m.)
la	her / it (f.)	**il la mange**	he eats it (f.)
nous	us	**il nous quitte**	he leaves us
vous	you	**il vous demande**	he asks you
les	them (m. + f.)	**il les garde**	he keeps them

And here is how to say 'to me', 'to you', 'to them', etc.:

me	to me	**il me donne de l'argent**
		he gives money to me
te	to you	**il te propose l'idée**
		he proposes the idea to you
lui	to him/her/it	**il lui demande une question**
		he asks (to) her/him a question
nous	to us	**il nous paie le montant**
		he pays the sum to us
vous	to you	**il vous dit l'heure**
		he tells (to) you the time
leur	to them (m. + f.)	**il leur rend la voiture**
		he returns the car to them

Notice that in French the pronouns always come before the verb!

Read and understand

12 Here are some advertisements for restaurants in Brittany. Have a look at them and answer the questions below. (Answers on p. 88.)

LES BONNES TABLES DE LA RÉGION

HÔTEL RESTAURANT ★★NN

LES GRANDES ROCHES
à Trégunc
Dans un cadre de verdure, calme et tranquillité,
Spécialités régionales
OUVERT TOUTE L'ANNÉE
Téléphone : (98) 97.62.97
ENGLISH SPOKEN
WIR SPRECHEN DEUTSCH

KERLAND
Mr et Mme CHATELAIN
AUBERGE GOURMANDE
Vue panoramique sur le Belon
Route de Moëlan
RIEC-SUR-BELON
Réservation :
Tél : (98) 06.42.98
jusqu'à 72 heures

RESTAURANT LA PIZZA
Spécialités italiennes
12, rue du Lin **CONCARNEAU**
Tél. 97.06.11
de 7 heures à minuit

CASA JOAN
Spécialités Catalanes
1, rue Duguay-Trouin
CONCARNEAU

RESTAURANT ESPAGNOL ET CATALAN
Ouvert toute l'année
Tél. 97.32.56

HÔTEL RESTAURANT LE MENHIR★★
Spécialités Régionales
TRÉGUNC Réservation 97.62.35

LA PAILLOTE
authentique restaurant vietnamien
rive gauche de CONCARNEAU
Douric-ar-Zin 100 m de l'hôpital
spécialités vietnamiennes et chinoises
Tél. (98) 97.34.02

Le Galion
Restaurateur
Henri Gaonac'h
15, rue Saint-Guénolé
Ville Close - Concarneau
Téléphone : (98) 97.30.16

RESTAURANT ★★★ La Gallandière
3, place de la Mairie
(entrée 1, rue Villebois-Mareuil 29110 CONCARNEAU)
Tél. (98) 97.18.34
Ouvert tous les jours sauf le jeudi

LA CRÊPE D'OR
HÔTEL-RESTAURANT
Spécialités de Fruits de Mer
NOCES - BANQUETS
SALLE POUR SÉMINAIRE
SOIRÉE ÉTAPE V.R.P.
3, rue du Lin - CONCARNEAU
Téléphone : (98) 97.08.61

RELAIS LA COQUILLE
Jean-François Le Maitre
SALLE PANORAMIQUE
1, rue du Moros - Port de Pêche
29110 CONCARNEAU
Téléphone : (98) 97.08.52

(a) What is Henri Gaonac'h's profession?

(b) Which is the best place for a business seminar?

(Continued on next page.)

(c)   Which three restaurants are definitely open throughout the year?

_____

(d)   What time does 'Kerland' close?

_____

(e)   Which restaurant is open 17 hours a day?

_____

(f)   Where would you go for Chinese-style food?

_____

(g)   Which two restaurants have particularly good views?

_____

(h)   If you fancy Spanish food, which restaurant would you go to?

_____

(i)   Which restaurant specializes in seafood?

_____

(j)   What is the big selling point of 'Les Grandes Roches'?

_____

13   Read through this extract from a special Hertz offer to business people (**Formule Affaires**). See if you can list three of the main advantages and also three of the conditions which are applied. (Answers on p. 88.)

CAT	MODELES	PRIX TTC PAR JOUR
A	Ford Fiesta 1.1 CLX	980
B	Ford Escort 1.6 CLX Peugeot 309 GL profil Renault 19 GTS	1 190
C	Ford Sierra 2.0 CLX Peugeot 405 GR Renault 21 GTS Lancia Dedra 1800 iE	1 410
D	Peugeot 605 SL Renault 25 GTS Lancia Thema 2.0 16S Volvo 740 GL	1 620
E	Mercedes 190 E BMW 520 i	1 900
L	Peugeot 605 SR 3.0 Volvo 760 GLE	1 930
G	Mercedes 190 E AC	2 050

Hertz

"FORMULE AFFAIRES"
Le tarif parfaitement adapté
aux exigences des hommes d'affaires.

Sur simple réservation 24 heures à l'avance (préciser *"TARIF AFFAIRES "*) bénéficiez d'un tarif journalier sans surprise, incluant les assurances, le kilométrage illimité et la possibilité de restituer sans supplément le véhicule dans n'importe quelle agence HERTZ en France.

- Tarif applicable au 14.01.91, modifiable sans préavis.
- Réservation 24 h à l'avance.
- Rachat de franchise et assurance personnes transportées incluses.
- Kilométrage illimité.
- TVA incluse.
- Durée de la location 24 h minimun.
- Tarif non remisable.
- Carburant en sus.

Pour toutes informations complémentaires,
consultez votre agence Hertz ou votre centre de réservation.

RESERVATIONS ET INFORMATIONS

PARIS	(1) 47 88 51 51	Telex : 610 335
LYON	78 49 75 75	Telex : 370 944
AUTRES	05 05 33 11	Telex : 610 335

Hertz loue des Ford et d'autres grandes marques

Advantages   *Conditions*

_____   _____

_____   _____

_____   _____

_____   _____

Did you know?

French cuisine

France has always enjoyed a high reputation for food prepared in traditional ways. This reputation is, to some extent, based on its agricultural industry, which is the largest food producer in Europe. Only the USA exports more agricultural products. French agriculture, characterized by the diversity of its products, accounts for 5.3% of GNP, more than twice the figure for the UK. France is the world's fifth biggest and the EC's biggest producer of cereals. As well as cereals and sugars, there is a large variety of dairy products and wines. The climate makes possible the cultivation of a wide range of fruit and vegetables. Livestock is another major sector: 38% of the total value of farm production.

France's world-famous dairy products include over 300 cheeses such as Camembert from Normandy, Brie from east of Paris, and Roquefort from the Massif Central. High quality butter from Normandy and the Charente is also much sought after. In France, wine is more than a farm product, it is an art form, with complex traditions, rules and methods.

The acknowledged quality of French **cuisine** relies heavily on the availability of a wide variety of 'fresh' ingredients. French cuisine is divided into **paysanne** (country cooking), with dishes such as the **pôt au feu** (boiled beef and vegetables), **bourgeoise**, with the famous **coq au vin**, and **haute cuisine**, which is very sophisticated and makes extensive use of expensive ingredients such as **foie gras** and truffles. Much use is made of cream, butter and cognac for the sauces. In addition, each region has its own style of cooking which often takes its character from the local ingredients (**bouillabaisse** in Marseille, **choucroute** in Alsace, **boeuf bourgignon** in Burgundy, etc).

In spite of the high reputation of French dishes, foreign ones have been introduced and adopted. **La cuisine chinoise, les spaghettis à la bolognaise, les pizzas, le couscous** and **les merguez** (hot spicy mutton sausages) have all grown in popularity in recent years. With an increasing emphasis on speed and convenience – the French now tend to work **à la journée continue,** with only a limited break for lunch – snackbars, self-service restaurants and fast-food takeaways are flourishing.

Another area where business is booming is in health foods. The traditional image of wine guzzling gourmands is far from the truth. Simple foods, organically grown, taken with plenty of exercise, would be much closer to the accurate picture of life for many, especially young French people.

Your turn to speak

14

(a) Imagine you are in a café. Compose a few sentences to order what you and your colleagues want to eat and drink. When you've spoken aloud your version, switch on and see what Philippe ordered.

(b) Think up some short sentences (or questions) using the following words or phrases and speak your version aloud. Remember there is no right or wrong.

Je voudrais...	**voulez**
Il me faut...	**Qu'est-ce que je peux...?** (What...?)
J'ai besoin de...	**Est-ce que vous pouvez...?** (Can you...?)
désirez	**le taux d'intérêt**

Answers

Practise what you have learned

Exercise 1 (a) proposer (b) si (c) s'il vous plaît (d) café (e) pour moi (f) deux sucres (g) je vais

Exercise 3 (a) hot croissants (b) toasted rolls (c) toast (d) bread (e) jam (f) butter (g) fried eggs (h) sausages (i) tea with lemon (j) tea with cold milk (k) white coffee (l) hot chocolate (m) an orange juice

Exercise 5 (a) oui, ce matin (b) sa secrétaire (c) trois (d) l'aéroport de Roissy ... Bordeaux (e) papiers ... permis de conduire (f) assurance complète (g) paiement (h) sa société (i) contrat de location (j) quand on part

Exercise 6 (a) There is a car reserved for me (b) It's a 'D' category. Is that alright? (c) Can I take it back to Roissy airport? (d) I'll need your driving licence (e) Are you going to take comprehensive insurance? (f) Do you want to pay by credit card? (g) Can you bill my company in England? (h) There you are. You have the car's documents and hire contract

Exercise 9 (a) He has quite a lot of clients in the area (b) to spell it (c) identity card (d) a fixed address (e) 30,000 francs (f) cheque book (g) in dollars (h) in a few days

Grammar

Exercise 11 (a) une petite entreprise (b) une société étrangère (c) un grand crédit (d) les frais importants (e) les bonnes idées (f) la première commission (g) un bon taux d'intérêt

Read and understand

Exercise 12 (a) restaurateur (b) La Crêpe d'Or (c) Les Grandes Roches, La Gallandière, Casa Joan (d) 10 p.m. (e) La Pizza (f) La Paillote (g) Kerland, Relais la Coquille (h) Casa Joan (i) La Crêpe d'Or (j) calm, tranquillity and surrounded by greenery (la verdure)

Exercise 13 *Advantages:* reasonable daily tarif, insurance included, unlimited kilometres, return to any Hertz agency in France, VAT and passenger insurance included. *Conditions:* tarif can be changed without notice, reservations 24 hrs in advance, minimum 24 hr hire period, no further discounts possible (a discount – **une remise**), fuel in addition

6 PLANNING

You will learn

- how to arrange a seminar
- to organize your diary
- times and days of the week
- about the working conditions of a new employee

  and you will be given some information about setting up a business in France

Study guide

To help you keep a check on your progress, you could mark off the various tasks as you complete them.

Dialogue 1 + Practise what you have learned
Dialogue 2 + Practise what you have learned
Dialogue 3 + Practise what you have learned
Dialogue 4 + Practise what you have learned
Ensure you know the **Key words and phrases**
Study the **Grammar** section
Do the exercises in **Read and understand**
Did you know? Setting up a business in France
Your turn to speak

Dialogues

1 *Arranging a two-day seminar at the Hôtel Présidence*

Businessman	Bien, alors comme je vous disais tout à l'heure, nous voudrions organiser un séminaire de deux jours: jeudi, vendredi, dans ... à peu près dans trois semaines et je voudrais voir vos conditions.
Receptionist	Vous voulez faire un séminaire résidentiel ou un...
Businessman	Tout à fait. Tout à fait, à cent pour cent.
Receptionist	Donc quel est le schéma ... type de votre programme envisagé?
Businessman	Et bien, nous arriverions le matin du premier jour pour rester dans vos murs en permanence jusqu'au lendemain soir.
Receptionist	Combien de personnes?
Businessman	Une vingtaine.
Receptionist	Vingt personnes?
Businessman	Hum.
Receptionist	Un jeudi et un vendredi?
Businessman	C'est ça.
Receptionist	Le vendredi, vous partez vers dix-huit heures?
Businessman	Nous partirons vers dix-huit heures.
Receptionist	Vous avez besoin de combien de salles de conférences?
Businessman	Oh! Ben pour vingt personnes je pense qu'une seule salle sera suffisante, hein?
Receptionist	Vous n'avez pas de sous commissions à faire?
Businessman	Non, non, non.
Receptionist	Vous prenez des chambres individuelles pour tout le monde?
Businessman	Oui tout à fait.
Receptionist	Oui, personne ne sera en chambre double?
Businessman	Écoutez, pour l'instant, je n'ai pas encore évalué ce genre de choses. Peut être ... Je ne pense pas que nous aurons de couples ou de ...
Receptionist	D'accord. Est-ce que vous prévoyez peut-être un dîner de gala en milieu?
Businessman	Le soir du jeudi alors?
Receptionist	Par exemple.
Businessman	Ça serait possible, ça serait envisageable.
Receptionist	Ça sera bien hein? Et pour l'arrivée, vous voulez peut-être un petit café d'accueil? Est-ce que vos participants viennent de loin?
Businessman	Ils vont venir de loin, euh de la région parisienne, quand même.
Receptionist	Oui donc ils vont se lever de bonne heure. On va peut-être prévoir un petit café d'accueil avec des petits croissants.
Businessman	Ah bien, ca serait très bien.
Receptionist	Et des petites brioches?
Businessman	Oui.

de deux jours of two days	**écoutez** listen
♦ **une semaine** week	♦ **peut-être** perhaps
♦ **voir** to see	**en milieu** in the middle
un séminaire residentiel residential seminar	♦ **par exemple** for example
	envisageable possible
donc so	**l'arrivée** (f.) arrival
une chambre individuelle single room	♦ **quand même** nevertheless
	une brioche a sort of bun

comme je vous disais tout à l'heure as I was telling you just now. **Tout à l'heure** can mean both 'a short time ago' or 'in a short time'. For instance, you often hear people say **à tout à l'heure**, which means 'see you again soon'.

Nous voudrions organiser... We would like to organize... Remember **je voudrais** 'I would like'. Here it is **nous voudrions** 'we would like'.

à cent pour cent one hundred per cent. Another way of saying 'for sure' or 'exactly'.

Quel est le schéma ... type? The receptionist first uses the word **schéma** 'outline' and then changes her question to ask what type of programme.

nous arriverions we would arrive. In French the concept of 'would do something' is conveyed by changing the ending on the verb. 'We are arriving' is simply **nous arrivons**.

pour rester. An important (and easy to use) construction. **Pour** + verb means 'in order to'. So 'in order to arrange' would be **pour arranger**; 'in order to drink' **pour boire**, etc.

dans vos murs en permanence. Lit. 'within your walls in permanence'. A rather convoluted way of saying the seminar will go on continuously, **en permanence**, for the two days.

◆ **jusqu'au lendemain soir** until the evening of the following day. 'Until the morning of the following day' would be **jusqu'au lendemain matin**.

Un jeudi et un vendredi? A Thursday and a Friday? See p. 68 for the days of the week.

Vous partez vers dix-huit heures? You're leaving about 6 p.m.? **Vers** is used for 'about' in relation to the time of day. So, **vers cinq heures** would be 'about 5 o'clock'.

◆ **nous partirons vers** we will leave about. As with 'would' above, there is no separate word for 'will' in the future. The ending on the verb conveys the idea. **Nous partons** is 'we are leaving' (we leave); **nous partirons** 'we will leave' (see p. 214 for more explanation).

Je pense qu'une seule salle sera suffisante I think that just one room will be sufficient. **Une seule personne** means 'just one person'; **un seul employé** 'just one employee'. **Seul(e)** means 'single' or 'alone'.

sous commissions. The meaning of **sous** is 'sub' or 'deputy'. The receptionist thinks he might need syndicate rooms. Note also **un sous-chef** 'deputy head'; **un sous-groupe** 'sub-group', etc.

◆ **toute le monde** everybody (lit. all the world)

◆ **personne ne...** nobody... So, **personne ne vient** means 'nobody is coming'; **personne ne mange** 'nobody is eating'.

◆ **Je n'ai pas encore évalué ce genre de choses** I haven't yet (**encore**) considered this type of thing

Je ne pense pas que nous aurons I don't think that we will have

Est-ce que vous prévoyez un dîner de gala? Lit. 'Do you foresee a special dinner?' A polite way of asking if he is planning a special dinner.

Ça serait ... ça sera... It would be ... it will be... Two examples of irregular forms of **être** 'to be'. **Je serais ravi de** 'I would be delighted to...'; **Je serai là** 'I will be there'.

un petit café d'accueil a little welcoming coffee

Est-ce que vos participants viennent de loin? Are your participants coming from far away? **Viennent** is from **venir** 'to come'; **de loin** 'from far away'.

◆ **Ils vont se lever de bonne heure** They are going to get up early. **De bonne heure** means 'early'; **se lever** is the verb for 'to get up'.

Turn over for the exercises based on this dialogue.

Practise what you have learned

1 Listen again to dialogue 1 and note who said what. (Answers on p. 108.)

	Receptionist	Businessman
(a) **tout à l'heure**		
(b) **tout à fait**		
(c) **Combien de personnes?**		
(d) **Nous partirons vers dix-huit heures.**		
(e) **Vous avez besoin de ... ?**		
(f) **Personne ne sera en chambre double?**		
(g) **peut-être**		
(h) **Ils vont se lever de bonne heure.**		

2 In this exercise we eavesdrop on a conversation where two people are planning a visit from the managing director. Listen to the recording and fill in the gaps in the discussion. (Answers on p. 108.)

Jean-Claude **Alors, il va arriver _____ (a)**

Marie **Est-ce que nous savons _____ (b)**

Jean-Claude **Pas exactement. Le matin de bonne heure, je suppose.**

Marie **Il faut _____ (c) _____ préparer un petit café d'accueil.**

Jean-Claude **Oui, pourquoi pas?**

Marie **_____ (d) directement de l'aéroport, je crois.**

Jean-Claude **Oui, c'est ce que _____ (e) m'a dit au téléphone.**

Marie **Alors, il va _____ (f) deux jours. Vous voulez que je réserve une chambre individuelle à l'hôtel Présidence?**

Jean-Claude **Bonne, idée. Alors, le premier soir nous pouvons organiser**

_____ (g)

Marie **Il veut visiter tous les départements pour éxpliquer la nouvelle**

structure à _____ (h)

Jean-Claude **Mm, ça _____ (i) difficile en deux jours mais c'est envisageable, je suppose.**

3 In the speaking exercise you will have a chance to organize a seminar. Switch on when you are ready and follow the prompts.

Dialogues

2 *The managing director and the head of personnel at Renault try to find a time to meet. There are lots of mms, ahs, and non-sequiturs, but some useful vocabulary as well. The transcript has been simplified a bit to omit some of the repetitions.*

Managing director Bon, dis donc Janick, il faudrait qu'on se voit cette semaine là pour avancer sur le recadrage du budget du service personnel ...

Janick Hou là là oui oui je suis tout à fait d'accord avec ça. Il faut absolument qu'on se voit, c'est une nécessité mais par contre je suis comme toi sans doute complètement débordé cette semaine, alors il faudrait peut-être ...

Managing director On va trouver un petit créneau d'une heure une heure et demie là.

Janick Alors sortons nos agendas.

Managing director Aujourd'hui, non ce n'est pas possible. Demain. Tu pourrais demain toi demain le mardi 20?

Janick Demain je ne peux pas. J'ai une conférence à l'extérieur.

Managing director Là zut zut zut bon alors moi 21 ... j'ai un informaticien qui vient le matin et j'ai une réunion ...

Janick Je pourrai en soirée.

Managing director En début d'après-midi avec Comolog. Ah oui mais bon moi j'ai un banquier après ... Je pourrais supprimer le ... annuler le banquier bien sûr mais non ça pose un problème. Jeudi jeudi 22, est-ce que tu peux jeudi?

Janick Le jeudi je reçois l'inspecteur du travail. Je ne sais jamais combien de temps il me consacrera.

Managing director Mais il vient le matin seulement non il ...

Janick Il vient le matin.

Managing director Il vient le matin et tu penses que ça peut durer toute la journée?

Janick Pas toute la journée en fin de matinée j'aurai peut-être un petit créneau d'une demie heure.

Managing director Moi ça m'arrangerait. Et en début d'après-midi ça m'arrangerait qu'on se planifie quelque chose en début d'après-midi.

Janick Ah oui mais souviens-toi qu'il y a un comité de direction.

Managing director Vendredi vendredi je suis en séminaire, donc je ne pourrai pas ou alors il faudrait que j'annule ce séminaire mais ça m' ...

Janick Le vendredi de toute façon je ne peux pas j'ai un ...

Managing director Tu ne peux pas.

Janick J'ai un entretien d'embauche je ne peux pas le remettre.

Managing director On peut essayer jeudi 22 alors après ton inspecteur du travail jeudi jeudi après midi.

Janick D'accord tout à fait.

Managing director Donc jeudi 22 à 14 heures.

Janick A 14 heures.

Managing director C'est parfait...

par contre on the other hand
comme toi like you
sans doute without doubt
▶ **trouver** to find
un créneau gap
à l'extérieur outside
un informaticien computer processor
l'informatique computing

▶ **un banquier** banker
consacrer to devote
(lit. to consecrate)
seulement only
planifier to plan
de toute façon in any case
parfait perfect

Turn over to the notes on this dialogue.

dis donc is a good way of starting a conversation. It means literally 'say then' but has the sense of 'so, let's see...'.

il faudrait it would be necessary. **Il faut** means 'it is necessary / one must / we must', etc.

se voit. Lit. 'see oneself'. **Se voir** is a verb often used for 'to meet': **Nous devons nous voir cet après-midi** means 'We must meet this afternoon'.

pour avancer sur le budget in order to make progress on the budget

♦ **Je suis complètement débordé** I'm completely swamped / overwhelmed / full up. **Débordé** is a good word for saying you're 'very busy'.

♦ **Sortons nos agendas** Let's get out our diaries. **Un agenda** 'appointments diary'. To say 'let's do something', you simply use the **nous** (**-ons**) form of the verb. 'Let's go' is **allons**; 'let's see' is **voyons**, etc.

♦ **aujourd'hui ... demain** today ... tomorrow. Remember **le lendemain** 'the following day'. Also important is **hier** 'yesterday' and **avant-hier** 'the day before yesterday'.

Je ne peux pas I cannot. From **pouvoir** 'to be able to'.

Je pourrai en soirée I will be able to in the evening. **Pourrai** is the future form of **pouvoir**.

en début d'après-midi at the start of the afternoon

♦ **Je pourrais supprimer/annuler ...** I could cancel ... **Supprimer** and **annuler** are two useful verbs.

♦ **Ça pose un problème** That poses a problem

♦ **Je reçois l'inspecteur du travail**. Lit. 'I'm receiving the work inspector', from **recevoir** 'to receive'.

♦ **Je ne sais jamais** I never know. **Ne ... jamais** is the way to translate 'never', e.g. **Je ne pars jamais avant 6 heures** I never leave before 6 o'clock.

♦ **Ça peut durer toute la journée?** That might last all day long?

En fin de matinée j'aurai ... At the end of the morning I will have ...

Ça m'arrangerait That would suit me. Similarly, **Ça m'arrange** 'That suits me' or **Ça vous arrange?** 'Does that suit you?'

Mais souviens-toi que ... But remember that ... The two colleagues are using the **tu/toi** familiar form to address each other. In a business context the formal **vous** form of address is more usual. So this would be: **Mais souvenez vous que ...**

♦ **Il y a un comité de direction** There is a management committee

J'ai un entretien d'embauche. Lit. 'I have a meeting of vacancy'. This is one way of saying he's interviewing somebody for a job.

♦ **Je ne peux pas le remettre** I cannot postpone it. **Remettre** 'to postpone'.

♦ **On peut essayer...** One can try...

Practise what you have learned

4 Using the information from dialogue 2, see if you can fill in the diaries of Janick and the managing director in English. There will be some gaps – these times have been crossed out. (Answers on p. 108.)

		Managing director	Janick
Tuesday 20th	a.m.	✕	
	p.m.	✕	
Wednesday 21st	a.m.		✕
	p.m.		✕
Thursday 22nd	a.m.	✕	
	p.m.		
Friday 23rd	a.m.		
	p.m.		✕

5 Listen to the conversation on the recording. The head of marketing is trying to find a time when she is free. (Answers on p. 108.)

(a) What sort of a meeting is she wanting to fix up? _____

(b) She chooses the week beginning the _____

(c) What's wrong with Monday morning? _____

(d) And at 3 o'clock she has what? _____

(e) What will she be discussing with the managing director all day Tuesday?

_____

(f) Where is she likely to be between 12.30 and 2.00 p.m on Wednesday?

_____

(g) Then she will be out of the the office from _____

to _____

(h) How do you know Mme Grenier is important? _____

(i) So when does she decide to meet M. Thibaud? _____

6 Now for a speaking exercise. On the recording you'll be invited to sort out your diary. For 'meeting' use **réunion**.

Dialogues

3 *At the **Institut Consulaire** an industrialist asks M. Pasquier, the vice president of the Franco-British Chamber of Commerce, if he can attend the meetings. While he is there, the phone rings and the secretary takes a message.*

Industrialist   Monsieur Pasquier je suis un industriel nouvellement installé dans la région dieppoise et j'ai entendu parler de l'existence d'une chambre de commerce franco-britannique dont vous êtes le vice président. Je serais intéressé de participer à une de vos réunions. Est-ce que vous pourriez m'expliquer comment il faut que je fasse?

M. Pasquier   Alors c'est très simple. Pour participer à une de nos réunions il suffit qu'on vous donne les dates de réunions et que vous veniez à ces dates. C'est une chambre qui fonctionne euh un petit peu sous la coupole de la Chambre de Commerce de Dieppe, sous la coupole de la Chambre de Commerce Franco-Britannique de Paris et nous travaillons beaucoup avec les conciles anglais qui sont l'équivalent de nos chefs de nos Chambres de Commerce. Donc la prochaine réunion c'est le mercredi 24 mars et nous vous y attendons à 11 heures et demie.

Industrialist   Et bien je vous remercie.

Secretary   Institut Consulaire de Dieppe, bonsoir.

Caller   Oui bonsoir Madame, pourrais-je parler à Monsieur Jean-Claude Moyant s'il vous plaît?

Secretary   Monsieur Jean-Claude Moyant est absent. C'était de la part de qui monsieur?

Caller   Alain Chehodet.

Secretary   Pouvez-vous m'épeler votre nom s'il vous plaît?

Caller   Oui, C – H – É – H – O – D – E – T.

Secretary   Et pourriez-vous me laisser également votre numéro de téléphone pour qu'il vous rappelle?

Caller   Oui et bien c'est le 42 24 11 33.

Secretary   Merci. Il n'y a pas de message à lui laisser?

Caller   Non mais qu'il me rappelle.

Secretary   Entendu monsieur.

Caller   Merci bien.

Secretary   Au revoir.

- ◗ **un industriel** industrialist
- **nouvellement** recently/newly
- ◗ **installer** to install / set up
- **dont** of which
- **simple** simple
- ◗ **participer à** to participate in
- ◗ **fonctionner** to function/operate
- ◗ **travailler** to work
- **l'équivalent** (m.) the equivalent
- **absent** absent / not here
- **épeler** to spell
- **également** equally/also
- **laisser** to leave

- **J'ai entendu parler de...** Lit. 'I have heard speak of...' The normal way to get over the idea of 'I have heard about...'

Je serais intéressé de participer à... I would be interested to participate in...

- **Est-ce que vous pourriez m'expliquer...?** Could you explain to me...?

comment il faut que je fasse is a very idiomatic phrase meaning 'how I should go about it' (lit. how it is necessary that I do).

- **Il suffit qu'on vous donne** It is sufficient that one gives you. Notice how the royal 'one' is again used where in English we would have something like 'you are given'. With certain phrases such as **il suffit que**, the form of the verb which follows is sometimes slightly changed. The rules are complicated so just make sure you understand the meaning and don't worry about the verb ending.

un petit peu sous la coupole de a little under the umbrella. **La coupole** literally means 'dome'.

les conciles anglais English councils

- **la prochaine réunion** the next meeting

- **nous vous y attendons.** The verb **attendre** is 'to expect' (also 'to wait for'). Breaking this phrase down you get 'we you there expect'. **Y** means 'there' and it is placed before the verb: **J'y vais** 'I'm going there'.

Pourrais-je parler à...? Could I (lit. would I be able to) speak to...?

De la part de qui? A phrase you hear over and over again at the reception. You are being invited to say who you are. Its literal meaning is 'On behalf of whom?'

Pourriez-vous me laisser...? Could you leave me...?

- **pour qu'il vous rappelle** in order that he calls you back. Here **rappeler** means 'to call back'. Remember **je m'appelle** 'I am called'.

Il n'y a pas de message? There is no message?

- **Entendu, monsieur** is a good way of saying 'OK' or 'alright' politely. It is often used to finish off conversations when you have agreed to do something for somebody. **Entendu** (heard) comes from **entendre** 'to hear'.

Turn over for the excercises based on this dialogue.

Practise what you have learned

7 Using dialogue 3, find the French equivalent of the following phrases. *Note* that they are not a straight translation from the dialogue. (Answers on p. 108.)

(a) I have heard of your firm.

(b) I would be interested to arrange a meeting.

(c) Could you explain to me how...?

(d) It is sufficient that you come Wednesday.

(e) We work a lot with American companies.

(f) Charles isn't here at the moment.

(g) Who shall I say it is?

(h) Would you be able to call back at the beginning of the afternoon?

(i) There is no message.

8 On the recording you will hear a phone call where someone is enquiring about the meetings of a Chamber of Commerce. Try to fill in below when the various events will happen. Use numbers, don't write everything out in words. (Answers on p. 108.) You will come across the following new words: **une séance** 'session/sitting'; **un(e) délégué(e)** 'delegate'; **le droit** 'the right'; **un(e) salarié(e)** 'a salaried employee'.

Programme de la Chambre de Commerce

(a) _____ Séance plénière de la Chambre de Commerce

(b) _____ Réunion des délégués consulaires

(c) _____ Réunion du bureau de l'Institut Franco-Britannique

(d) _____ Réunion du Directoire

(e) _____ Réunion de la Commission des Finances

(f) _____ Réunion de la Promotion de l'Industrie et du Commerce extérieur

(g) _____ Droits d'expression des salariés

(h) _____ Réunion des délégués du personnel

Dialogues

4 *The personnel director welcomes a new employee and outlines his conditions of employment*

Employee Bonjour monsieur.
Personnel director Bonjour, eh bien je suis très heureux de vous revoir à nouveau puisque...
Employee Merci.
Personnel director Votre candidature a eu une suite positive.
Employee Merci.
Personnel director Je vous accueille donc ici au nom de notre directeur général dans cette entreprise qui bientôt sera la vôtre. Alors à ce sujet je vous rappelle quels sont nos horaires. Vous êtes amené à travailler de 7 heures le matin à 16 heures 30 l'après-midi. Je vous rappelle que vous avez une coupure autorisée de 45 minutes pour vous permettre de prendre vos repas, repas que vous pouvez prendre à l'extérieur, bien qu'il n'y a pas grande chose dans la région. Bon vous pouvez aussi bénéficier de notre restaurant d'entreprise qui se trouve sur le site. Vous savez que le repos hebdomadaire a lieu le samedi et le vendredi. A ce sujet, j'ai oublié de vous préciser que les horaires sont modifiés le vendredi puisque par accord nous ne travaillons pas le vendredi après-midi; la journée se termine à 12 heures 30. En ce qui concerne les congés annuels la solution est très simple; le mois d'août est le congé annuel pour tout le monde puisque l'entreprise est fermée. Nous avions déjà évoqué les problèmes de transport, les transports sont pratiquement inexistants, les transports publics.
Employee Il n'y a pas de transports collectifs?
Personnel director Il n'y a pas de transports collectifs, ni du point de vue municipal ni du point de vue entreprise ce qui veut dire si vous vous déplacez par vos propres moyens...
Employee Ce qui est le cas...
Personnel director Vous avez à votre disposition juste devant mon bureau soit un garage à vélos ou vélomoteurs, également un parking pour votre véhicule personnel si vous souhaitez adopter ce mode de transport. Quant à votre bureau nous vous l'avions décrit sommairement lors de notre précédent entrevue. Votre bureau est donc ce joli bureau paysager que vous pouvez apercevoir de la baie vitrée et qui se trouve au fond du couloir à droite après avoir pris la petite porte qui descend sur la gauche. Il me reste donc à vous souhaiter une très bienvenue et un bon courage.
Employee Et bien merci monsieur le directeur du personnel, je suis ravi d'appartenir maintenant à cette entreprise prestigieuse. Merci.

accueillir to welcome
au nom de on behalf of
bientôt soon
ce sujet this subject
un horaire timetable
une coupure autorisée
   official break
le repas meal
bénéficier de to benefit from

préciser to point out
modifier to modify
(se) terminer to end
le congé annuel annual leave
le mois d'août the month of August
évoqué (here) touched on
évoquer to evoke
les transports collectifs
   group transportation

(Continued on next page.)

se déplacer to move around	**apercevoir** to see / make out
vos propres moyens your own means	**la baie vitrée** bay window
le cas case	**au fond de** at the end of
à votre disposition at your disposition	▶ **le couloir** corridor
un vélo cycle	**la petite porte** little door
souhaiter to wish	**descendre** to go down / descend
▶ **décrire** to describe	**appartenir** to belong to
joli pretty	**prestigieux** (**prestigieuse**) prestigious

▶ **Je suis très heureux de vous revoir** I am very happy to see you again. Remember the similar phrase **Je suis ravi(e) de...** 'I'm delighted to...' **Heureux** (f. **heureuse(s)**) is the ordinary word for 'happy'. Re- as in **revoir** can be prefixed to many verbs to convey the idea of 'again', e.g. **refaire** 'to redo', **revenir** 'to come back', etc. So **à nouveau** 'again' is superfluous here.

Votre candidature a eu une suite positive is a rather formal way of saying you've got the job. **A eu** 'has had' is a past tense form of **avoir** 'to have'.

▶ **je vous rappelle** I remind you

vous êtes amené à travailler. The verb **amener** normally means 'to bring'. Here it is used in an idiomatic formal sense to get over the idea of 'required'.

▶ **pour vous permettre de** to allow you to. A useful construction which can be used in various ways. **Pour me permettre de** means 'to allow me to'; **pour nous permettre de** 'to allow us to'. **Permettre** is linked to *to permit*.

bien qu'il n'y a pas grande chose although there isn't very much. **Bien que** means 'although' and **grande chose** (lit. great thing) is an idiomatic way of saying 'very much'.

▶ **se trouve sur le site** is located on the site (lit. finds itself on the site). **Se trouver**, like **se situer** in Unit 2, means 'to be located / situated'.

▶ **vous savez que le repos hebdomadaire** you know that the weekly break. **Savez** comes from **savoir** 'to know'. Remember **Je ne sais pas** 'I don't know'. Although **hebdomadaire** is a difficult word it is nevertheless the usual way of saying 'weekly'.

▶ **a lieu le samedi.** From **avoir lieu** 'to take place'. When using days of the week, particularly in the context of a regular occurrence, the French use the definite article **le**. So 'on Fridays' would be **le vendredi**. (Note that Sundays are also free.)

▶ **j'ai oublié de** I have forgotten to. **Oublier** means 'to forget'.

en ce qui concerne is a useful phrase which means 'as far as ... is concerned'.

▶ **L'entreprise est fermée** The firm is closed. **Fermer** 'to close'. The opposite of **fermé(e)** is **ouvert(e)** 'open'.

▶ **ni... ni...** neither... nor... **Ni le directeur, ni sa secrétaire** means 'Neither the director nor his secretary'.

▶ **ce qui veut dire** which means. **Veut dire** comes from **vouloir dire**, literally 'to want to say'. It is a bit cumbersome, but it is the standard way of translating 'to mean': **Je ne sais pas ce que vous voulez dire** is 'I don't know what you mean'.

▶ **quant à votre bureau** as for your office. **Quant à votre salaire** 'as for your salary', etc.

lors de on the occasion of

▶ **un bureau paysagé** an open-plan office

▶ **Il me reste donc à vous souhaiter une très bienvenue** It just remains for me to wish you a big welcome. **Vous êtes la bienvenue** means 'You are welcome'.

bon courage literally means 'good courage', but it is frequently used idiomatically when somebody is setting out to do something. It has the idea of 'good luck'.

Practise what you have learned

9 As dialogue 4 is rather difficult, with a lot of new vocabulary, here are a few of the key phrases again. Translate them into French. (Answers on p. 108.)

(a) I am very happy to see you again.

_____

(b) I welcome you on behalf of our managing director.

_____

(c) You have an official break of one hour.

_____

(d) You can also take advantage of our company restaurant.

_____

(e) The weekly meeting is taking place on Friday.

_____

(f) As regards annual leave...

_____

(g) Which means that there is no public transportation.

_____

(h) He works in an open-plan office.

_____

10 You are being asked to take a message about terms of employment. Read through dialogue 4 again and then switch on the recording.
(Answers on p. 108.)

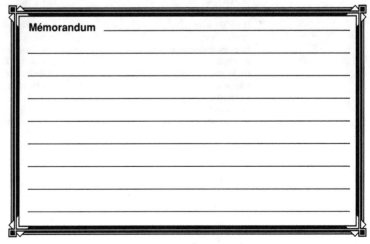

Mémorandum _____

11 In this speaking exercise you will be taking part in a conversation about the working week, facilities and holidays (vacations). You might like to check the section on telling the time on pp. 103-4 before you start.

Key words and phrases

la planification	planning
une semaine	week
un jour	day
un mois	month
voir	to see
demain	tomorrow
le lendemain	following day
hier	yesterday
avant-hier	day before yesterday
vers 10 heures	at about 10 o'clock
tout le monde	everybody
personne ne ...	nobody
évaluer	to evaluate/consider
peut-être	perhaps
par exemple	for example
quand même	nevertheless
se lever	to get up
je suis débordé(e)	I'm swamped (with work)
trouver	to find
un agenda	diary
l'informatique	computing
un banquier	banker
supprimer / annuler	to cancel
remettre	to postpone
Ça pose un problème	That poses a problem
recevoir	to receive
Je ne sais jamais	I never know
durer	to last
le comité de direction	management committee
essayer	to try
un industriel	industrialist
installer	to install / set up
J'ai entendu parler de ...	I have heard about ...
participer à	to participate in
expliquer	to explain
il suffit que ...	it is sufficient that ...
travailler	to work
la prochaine réunion	next meeting
attendre	to wait for / expect
de la part de	on behalf of
rappeler	to call back / remind
entendu	agreed (lit. heard)
arranger	to arrange
Je suis très heureux de ...	I am very happy to ...
un horaire	timetable
permettre	to allow/permit
se trouver	to be located
hebdomadaire	weekly
avoir lieu	to take place
oublier	to forget
le congé annuel	annual leave
fermé(e)	closed
ni... ni...	neither... nor...
vouloir dire	to mean
en voiture	by car
quant à	as for
un bureau paysagé	open-plan office
descendre	to go down / descend / get off
Vous êtes la bienvenue	You are welcome

Grammar

Telling the time

The 24-hour clock   The 24-hour clock is frequently used in France. To give the time you simply say **il est** followed by the hours o'clock, e.g. **Il est vingt-et-une heures** 'It's 21 hours (9 p.m.)'. In between the hours you simply add the number of minutes: **Il est douze heures cinq** (12.05), **Il est dix-sept heures vingt-trois** (17.23), **Il est vingt-trois heures treize** (23.13). You don't need to add **minutes** (minutes).

The 12-hour clock   The basic format still applies, e.g. **Il est dix heures vingt** (10.20), **Il est trois heures quinze** (3.15). You also quite often find the equivalent of 'twenty to six', etc. This is expressed in French by saying it is 'six o'clock less (**moins**) twenty', i.e. **Il est six heures moins vingt**, etc. The quarter hours can be expressed either by using **quinze** or **quart**: **Il est six heures et quart** means 'It is a quarter past six', **Il est dix heures moins le quart** means 'It is a quarter to six' (notice the **le** before **quart** in this case!).

For the half hour you can use **trente**, e.g. **Il est six heures trente**, or you can say **et demie**, e.g. **Il est six heures et demie** 'It is half past six'. Noon is **midi**, e.g. **Il est midi et quart** is 'It is a quarter past twelve (noon)'. Midnight is **minuit**, e.g. **Il est minuit moins dix** is 'It is ten to twelve (midnight)'.

Have a look at the two clocks below.

Il est neuf heures cinq
Il est neuf heures et quart
Il est neuf heures vingt
Il est neuf heures vingt-cinq

Il est trois heures moins cinq
Il est trois heures moins dix
Il est trois heures moins le quart
Il est trois heures moins vingt-cinq

Other useful words   Here are a few more useful words to use when describing your weekly schedule:

aujourd'hui	today		
demain	tomorrow	**le lendemain**	the day after
hier	yesterday	**avant-hier**	the day before yesterday

You may have noticed two different ways of saying 'day', 'morning' and 'evening':

le jour	**la journée**
le matin	**la matinée**
le soir	**la soirée**

(Continued on next page.)

Le jour, le matin, le soir tend to be used when you are thinking of them in the sense of a specific time, e.g. **Nous allons terminer dans deux jours** 'We'll finish in two days'; **Il doit venir ce matin** 'He should come this morning'.

La journée, la matinée, la soirée are used when you are thinking more of what you are going to do or have done, e.g. **Bonne journée!** 'Have a good day!' or **Nous avons eu une soirée magnifique** 'We had a fabulous evening'.

12   When you've understood this section on time, listen to the recording. You'll be given some times to fill in on the clocks below. (Answers on p. 108.)

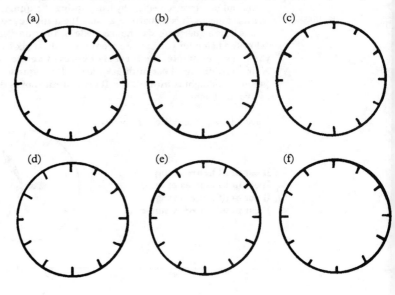

Read and understand

13 Many hotels offer conference and seminar facilities to business people. Below is an extract from the brochure prepared by the Présidence hotel. In providing an English translation, somebody at the printers has slipped up and mixed up the order of the English version. Try to sort out the problem. (Answers on p. 108.)

FRENCH VERSION	YOUR VERSION	PRINTER'S VERSION
Occultation de jour pour projections	4	1 Sound equipment on request
Nombreuses prises électriques (220 volts)		2 Stage
Disposition des tables selon votre désir (U, V, etc)		3 Numerous electrical points
Possibilité de podium		4 Black-out for slide/film projection
Sonorisation sur demande		5 Flexible seating arrangements
Écran 3m x 2m		6 Super 8 sound projector
Paperboards à feuilles volantes (0,65 x 0,95)		7 Overhead projector (800w)
Crayons feutre		8 Closed-circuit TV
Blocs personnalisés au nom de chaque participant		9 Photographer
Crayons		10 16mm sound projector
Lutrin		11 Personalized writing pads
Machine à écrire		12 Tape recorder
Magnétophone		13 Lectern
Projecteur diapositives 24 x 36 automatique		14 Flip charts
Sonorisation		15 35 mm sound projector
Traduction simultanée		16 Reprographic facilities for documents and transparencies
Projecteur super 8 sonore		17 Shorthand typists
Projecteur 16 mm sonore		18 Simultaneous translation
Projecteur 35 mm sonore		19 Felt-tip pens
Télévision intérieure		20 Hostesses
Magnétoscope VHS... avec caméra...		21 Automatic slide projector
Reportage photo		22 Typewriter
Rétroprojecteur 800 W polarisant		23 Interpreters
Reproduction de documents et transparents		24 VHS video and camera
Des sténodactylographes		25 Sound equipment
Des traducteurs		26 Pencils
Des hôtesees d'accueil		27 Screen 3m x 2m

14 Here's a bit of practice with days of the week and months. Answer the following questions about guided visits around the mediaeval town of Sarlat. (Answers on p. 108.)

VISITES COMMENTÉES

DORDOGNE - PÉRIGORD

SARLAT
Ville d'Art et d'Histoire

GUIDES CONFÉRENCIERS AGRÉÉS par la
CAISSE NATIONALE
DES MONUMENTS HISTORIQUES
ET DES SITES

	Juin	Juillet-Août	du 15/07 au 15/08	Septembre
Lundi Mardi Mercredi Jeudi Vendredi	10 h 30 22 h 00	10 h 30 15 h 00 22 h 00	10 h 30 15 h 00 18 h 00 22 h 00	10 h 00 21 h 30
Samedi	15 h 00 22 h 00	15 h 00 22 h 00	15 h 00 18 h 00 22 h 00	15 h 00 21 h 30
Dimanche	22 h 00	10 h 30 22 h 00	10 h 30 22 h 00	10 h 30 21 h 30

Prix de la visite : (durée 1 h 30)
Adultes : 18 F — Enfants - Étudiants : 10 F

Toute l'année sur réservation pour groupes
Possibilité de billets jumelés avec le Musée Aquarium

BILLETS - RÉSERVATIONS - DÉPART DE LA VISITE :

OFFICE DU TOURISME
Hôtel de Maleville, place de la Liberté - Tél. 53.59.27.67

Dans la mesure du possible, et pour faciliter le service, veuillez prendre vos billets à l'avance

(a) In what period do visits take place on a Monday? _____

(b) When is the first visit on Wednesdays in September? _____

(c) How many tours are there on Saturday mornings? _____

(d) When is the last tour on Sundays in September? _____

(e) Can you take a tour on Thursday afternoon's in June? _____

(f) In which months are there three visits every weekday? _____

(g) How long does each tour last? _____

(h) In which months of the year can groups book visits? _____

Did you know?

Setting up a business in France

According to French law, a company exists once it has been given a registration number. For this, the Articles of Association (**les statuts**) have to be drawn up and the capital (**le capital initial**) must be deposited with a bank or other authorized depository. Once the shareholders (**les actionnaires**) have signed the Articles, the board (**le conseil**) and chairman (**le président**) are elected, and the constitution and the name of the company must be publicized in one of the legal journals. The shareholders and board of the company must then file a declaration with the Clerk of a Commercial Register. Once the Clerk has issued a Certificate of Entry, the capital may be withdrawn and used for the business. Notification must then be sent to the fiscal and social authorities, and registration taxes paid.

A non-EC national setting up a business in France has to obtain a Business Certificate (**la Carte de Commerçant Etranger**). This card is not required for EC nationals but the Treasury may seek proof of residence in the EC. A potential EC investment in France must in principle be declared to the French Ministry of Finance, which has a period of fifteen days to refuse the investment. Non-EC investors need to make a formal declaration to the Treasury for any investment and then have to obtain an authorization from the Treasury before starting any business operations in France. Foreign investment likely to create jobs is encouraged.

A direct investment in France is defined as (i) the purchase, creation, or expansion of a business in France, and/or (ii) any operation leading to the holding by non-French residents of a controlling interest in a French company, that is 20% of its capital or voting rights if the company is listed on the Stock Exchange and 33% of its capital or voting rights if the company is unlisted.

Foreign-controlled businesses are required to have a bank account in France. They are subject to the same regulations and have the same access to finance as French companies.

Information on markets and on other issues relating to the establishment of a business can be obtained through the French Chambers of Commerce, which run good data bases on local economies. Chambers of Commerce also provide legal and general advice and facilitate business contacts.

Your turn to speak

15 Try to describe your own working day – what time you have to get up, what you have for breakfast, how you get to work, your working hours, your holidays (vacations). Start with **je me lève vers** (I get up at about). When you've described your day aloud, listen to the recording and see what Philippe had to say.

Answers

Practise what you have learned

Exercise 1 *Receptionist:* (c), (e), (f), (g), (h); *Businessman:* (a), (b), (d), (g)

Exercise 2 (a) mardi, le 25 (b) à quelle heure? (c) peut-être (d) il vient (e) sa secrétaire (f) rester (g) un dîner de gala (h) tout le monde (i) sera

Exercise 4 *Managing director:* Wednesday a.m. computer programmer, p.m. meeting with Comolog; banker. Thursday late p.m. Management Committee. Friday a.m./p.m. seminar.
Janick: Tuesday a.m./p.m. away at conference. Thursday a.m. Work Inspector, late p.m. Management Committee. Friday, an interview with a job applicant.

Exercise 5 (a) an interview with a job applicant (b) 25 June (c) she's on her way back from Paris (d) meeting with English agent (e) the budget (f) lunch with a new client (g) 16.00 Wednesday to 11 o'clock Friday (h) she can't be cancelled (i) Friday afternoon 14.00

Exercise 7 (a) J'ai entendu parler de votre entreprise (b) Je serais intéressé d'arranger une réunion (c) Pourriez-vous m'expliquer comment...? (d) Il suffit que vous veniez mercredi (e) Nous travaillons beaucoup avec les entreprises américaines (f) Charles est absent pour le moment (g) C'était de la part de qui? (h) Pourriez-vous rappeler en début d'après-midi? (i) Il n'y a pas de message

Exercise 8 (a) vendredi, le 26 janvier, 20.00 (b) mardi, le 10 mars, 14.30 (c) lundi, le 8 avril, 19.30 (d) jeudi, le 14 mai, 13.00 (e) mercredi, le 17 juin, 13.45 (f) lundi, le 3 juillet, 19.45 (g) jeudi, le 30 septembre, 17.15 (h) samedi, le 11 novembre, 10.30

Exercise 9 (a) Je suis très heureux de vous revoir (b) Je vous accueille au nom de notre directeur général (c) Vous avez une coupure autorisée d'une heure (d) Vous pouvez aussi bénéficier de notre restaurant d'entreprise (e) La réunion hebdomadaire a lieu vendredi (f) En ce qui concerne les congés annuels... (g) Ce qui veut dire qu'il n'y a pas de transports publics (h) Il travaille dans un bureau paysagé

Exercise 10 Le nouvel employé doit travailler de 7 heures 30 à 16.45 de lundi à jeudi. Une coupure de 45 minutes est autorisée pour les repas. Vendredi la journée se termine à 13 heures. Le congé annuel est en août et l'entreprise est fermée.

Grammar

Exercise 12 (a) 8 o'clock (b) 10.20 (c) 10.45 (d) 12.10 (e) 7.40 (19.40) (f) 9.40 (21.40)

Read and understand

Exercise 13 The order should be: 4, 3, 5, 2, 1, 27, 14, 19, 11, 26, 13, 22, 12, 21, 25, 18, 6, 10, 15, 8, 24, 9, 7, 16, 17, 23, 20

Exercise 14 (a) June – September (b) 10.00 (c) none (d) 21.30 (e) no (f) July and August (g) 1½ hours (h) all year round

7 | ON THE PHONE

You will learn

- to understand a variety of typical responses from telephone operators
- to state the reasons for your call
- to leave messages

and you will be given information about post and telecommunications in France

Study guide

To help you keep a check on your progress, you could mark off the various tasks as you complete them.

Dialogue 1 + Practise what you have learned
Dialogue 2 + Practise what you have learned
Dialogue 3 + Practise what you have learned
Dialogue 4 + Practise what you have learned
Ensure you know the **Key words and phrases**
Study the **Grammar** section
Do the exercises in **Read and understand**
Did you know? Post and telecommunications in France
Your turn to speak

Dialogues

 1(a) *Expecting a call from the States*

Hotelier	Bonjour monsieur. Passé une bonne nuit?
Guest	Bonjour monsieur. Oui très bonne nuit, merci. La chambre est très agréable. J'ai un petit problème. On doit m'appeler aujourd'hui ou demain des Etats-Unis, mais je n'ai pas le numéro de téléphone. Pouvez-vous me donner ça?
Hotelier	Bien sûr monsieur. Le numéro de téléphone c'est le 35 84 14 12.
Guest	Alors 35 94.
Hotelier	Non 35 84.
Guest	35 84.
Hotelier	14 12.
Guest	14 12.
Hotelier	Voilà monsieur.
Guest	Merci.

 1(b) *Wrong numbers are still quite common*

Receptionist	Allô.
Caller 1	Allô, Marie-Françoise?
Receptionist	Non, monsieur. Vous devez faire erreur de numéro, je pense. Je ne comprends pas. Je n'ai personne de ce nom.
Caller 1	Françoise? Marie-Françoise?
Receptionist	Non, je ne connais pas.
Caller 1	Mme Durand?
Receptionist	Non plus.
Caller 1	Vous n'avez pas de Mme Durand?
Receptionist	Non, je n'ai personne de ce nom là.
Caller 1	Ah! bon.
Receptionist	Je suis désolée.
Caller 1	J'ai dû me tromper de numéro. Excusez-moi.
Receptionist	Je vous en prie.
Caller 1	Au revoir.
Receptionist	Au revoir monsieur.
Receptionist	Entreprise des Jardins bonsoir.
Caller 2	Allô. C'est l'Institut Consulaire?
Receptionist	Non, monsieur. C'est l'Entreprise des Jardins à l'appareil.
Caller 2	Ah! J'ai dû me tromper de numéro, excusez-moi.
Receptionist	C'est pas grave. Bonsoir.
Caller 2	Au revoir.

agréable pleasant/nice	
des Etats-Unis from the USA	
◆ **donner** to give	
◆ **connaître** to know	

◆ **Excusez-moi** I'm sorry	
le jardin garden	
l'institut (m.) institute	
consulaire of the council	

◆ **Passé une bonne nuit?** Short for **Avez-vous passé une bonne nuit?** 'Have you had (lit. passed) a good night?' **Passer** is often used to ask how something went. **C'est bien passé?** 'Did it go well?'

On doit m'appeler One way of saying 'I'm expecting a call' (lit. one should me call). Remember **devoir** to should/must/ought': **Je dois partir** 'I must go'.

C'est le... It is usual to add **le** (the) before a number.

- **Vous devez faire erreur de numéro** You must be making a mistake in the number. **Faire erreur** means 'to make a mistake'.
- **Je ne comprends pas** I don't understand. From **comprendre** 'to understand'.
- **Je n'ai personne de ce nom** I have nobody of that name. **Ce, cette** can mean both 'this' and 'that'; **cette entreprise** (f.) 'this/that firm'. **Ne...personne...** 'nobody'. **Il n'y a personne dans le bureau** means 'There's nobody in the office'.

  Non plus Nor that. A standard rejoinder when you are repeating you don't know something or somebody.
- **Je suis désolé(e)**. A commonly used phrase meaning 'I'm really sorry' (lit. desolated).
- **J'ai dû me tromper de numéro** I must have made a mistake in the number. **J'ai dû** also comes from **devoir**. This time it is the past tense. **Me tromper** comes from **se tromper** 'to make a mistake' (see grammar section, p. 121).
- **Je vous en prie**. A common phrase meaning 'Don't mention it'. It can be used instead of **pas de quoi** (see p. 113).
- **à l'appareil** on the line. **Qui est à l'appareil? Henri Beaumont à l'appareil.**

  C'est pas grave It's not important / It doesn't matter. Although 'not' is correctly translated by **ne... pas...**, the **ne** very often gets left out when you're speaking.

Practise what you have learned

1 Use the clues to fill in the grids with some of the key words from the dialogue. They will unveil a vertical word relevant to this unit. (Answers on p. 126.)

(a) **Faire erreur = se** ___*tromper*___

(b) **Chaque téléphone a son** _____

(c) **On doit m'**_____ **des Etats-Unis.**

(d) **Mme Michelot le regrette beaucoup. Elle est** _____

(e) **Il n'y a pas de monde. Il n'y a** ___*personne*___

(f) **Vous y dormez.**

(g) **La première chose que vous entendez.** (1b)

(h) **20**

(i) **Pas de quoi. Je vous en** _____

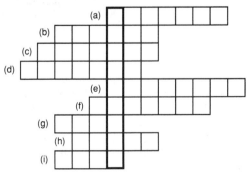

2 Back to the recording for a speaking exercise to give you an opportunity to get somebody to take a message. **Est-ce que je peux laisser un message?** 'May I leave a message?'

Dialogues

2 *A telephonist at the company switchboard*

Telephonist	Allô.
Caller 1	Allô.
Telephonist	Oui, bonjour monsieur.
Caller 1	Oui, bonsoir madame, c'est bien l'Institut Consulaire?
Telephonist	Oui, c'est bien ça.
Caller 1	Oui, pouvez vous me passer monsieur Jean-Claude Moyen s'il vous plaît?
Telephonist	Qui dois-je annoncer monsieur?
Caller 1	Antoine Delavigne.
Telephonist	Ne quittez pas, je vous le passe.
Caller 1	Merci.
Telephonist	Institut Consulaire de Dieppe, bonsoir.
Caller 2	Oui bonsoir madame, pourriez-vous me passer Monsieur Martin s'il vous plaît?
Telephonist	Connaissez-vous son numéro de poste, s'il vous plaît?
Caller 2	Oh! ça doit être le 1124, je crois.
Telephonist	Ne quittez pas monsieur, je vous le passe.
Caller 2	Merci.

Telephonist	Institut Consulaire de Dieppe, bonsoir.
Caller 3	Oui bonsoir madame, pourrais-je parler à Monsieur Rambaut s'il vous plaît?
Telephonist	Monsieur Rambaut est absent.
Caller 3	Ah, bon?
Telephonist	Souhaitez-vous rappeler ou laisser un message ou bien qu'il vous rappelle?
Caller 3	Oui, qu'il me rappelle alors.
Telephonist	A quel numéro monsieur?
Caller 3	Au 35 82 33 00.
Telephonist	Je lui laisse le message.
Caller 3	Je vous remercie.
Telephonist	Au revoir monsieur.
Telephonist	Institut Consulaire de Dieppe, bonsoir.
Caller 4	Bonsoir madame. Pourrais-je parler à Monsieur Renfort s'il vous plaît?
Telephonist	Monsieur Renfort n'est pas là, tout de suite, il est en réunion.
Caller 4	Ah, quand est-ce que je peux rappeler pour être sûr de l'avoir?
Telephonist	Essayez demain matin.
Caller 4	Demain matin?
Telephonist	A ... vers huit heures.
Caller 4	D'accord. Merci.
Telephonist	De rien. Au revoir monsieur.
Caller 4	Au revoir.

je crois I think	**absent** not here
laisser to leave	◆ **tout de suite** immediately / at the moment
quand when	**en ligne** on the line

C'est bien l'Institut Consulaire? It is the council institute? The caller thinks he's right but he uses the construction **C'est bien...?** to get confirmation.

Pouvez-vous me passer...? Can you put me through to...?

Qui dois-je annoncer? Who shall I say it is? Lit. 'Who must I announce?'

◆ **Ne quittez pas**. Lit. 'Don't leave', but it's the usual telephone phrase for 'Could you hold on a moment?'

- **Connaissez-vous son numéro de poste?** Do you know his extension number?

Ça doit être... That/it must be...

Pourrais-je parler à...? Could I speak to...?

Souhaitez-vous rappeler? Do you wish to call back? You also hear quite often **Souhaitez-vous patienter?** 'Do you want to hold on / wait?'

- **Ou bien qu'il vous rappelle?** Or rather that he calls you back?

Qu'il me rappelle. Instead of saying **Pourrait-il me rappeler?** (Could he call me back?), you can, as here, just repeat the phrase **qu'il me rappelle**, literally 'that he calls me back'.

A quel numéro? On what number?

- **Il est en réunion** He's in a meeting

pour être sûr de l'avoir in order to be sure of getting (lit. having) him

- **Essayez demain matin** Try tomorrow morning. **Essayer** means 'to try'.

de rien is another polite way of saying **pas de quoi / je vous en prie** 'don't mention it'. **Rien** means 'nothing' and, like **ne...pas...**, **ne... personne...** and **ne...jamais**, it is normally used with **ne**, e.g. **Je ne comprends rien** 'I understand nothing'.

Practise what you have learned

3 Sort out from the series of telephone dialogues, the questions or statements that are missing. (Answers on p. 126.)

(a) _____ **Qui dois-je annoncer?**

(b) **Connaissez-vous son numéro de poste?** _____

(c) **Pourrais-je parler à M. Rambaut?** _____

(d) _____ **A quel numéro, monsieur?**

(e) _____ **M. Renfort est en réunion.**

(f) _____ **Essayez demain matin.**

4 Listen now to a similar exchange on the recording and then answer the questions below. Remember that **revenir** is 'to return'. (Answers on p. 126.)

(a) How do you know it is late afternoon/evening?

(b) What does the caller want to know about M. Rambaut?

(c) Has he? If not, where is he?

(d) What are the two choices the telephonist gives the caller?

(e) Which does he choose?

(f) What does the telephonist say to show she will do what the caller wants?

5 Switch on your recording for a chance to practise some of the most important telephone vocabulary. **Immobilier Bonoron** is the Bonoron (Real) Estate Agency.

Dialogues

3 *Leaving messages and getting information*

Secretary Bonjour, monsieur, je suis la secrétaire de Monsieur Esperce. M. Esperce ne pourra pas se rendre à votre rendez-vous, vendredi dix-sept. Pouvez-vous me rappeler pour un autre rendez-vous? Vous avez notre numéro. Je vous remercie. Au revoir, monsieur.

Mlle Dupont Je suis Mlle Dupont. J'ai vu votre annonce dans *Le Monde*. Je serais intéressée. Pourriez-vous m'envoyer, s'il vous plaît, quelques détails de cet emploi? Mon nom est Marie Dupont. Mon adresse est 14 Rue de la Voûte, 12100 Millau.

Telephonist Institut Consulaire de Dieppe, bonsoir.
Customer Oui, bonsoir madame. Je cherche un renseignement, je ne sais pas si vous pouvez me passer quelqu'un. C'est un problème de logiciel que j'ai avec du matériel que j'ai appris à utiliser chez vous.
Telephonist Ne quittez pas, monsieur, je vais vous passer Monsieur Rambaut qui est le responsable du centre informatique.
Customer Monsieur...
Telephonist Monsieur Rambaut.
Customer D'accord, merci.
Telephonist Je vous le passe. Au revoir monsieur.
Customer Au revoir.

Mlle Durand Je serais intéressée par un téléphone dans ma voiture. J'ai vu votre annonce. Pourriez-vous, s'il vous plaît, m'envoyer une documentation. Mon nom est Mlle Durand, Sylvie, 33 rue du Vent, 34000 Montpellier.

♦	**un autre** another	♦	**quelqu'un(e)** someone
♦	**envoyer** to send		**chez vous** at your firm/place
	les détails (m.) details		**quitter** to leave
♦	**un emploi** job/post	♦	**la voiture** car
	passer to pass		

---

ne pourra pas se rendre à votre rendez-vous [He] will not be able to get to your meeting. **Pourra** is a future form from **pouvoir** 'to be able to'.

♦ **J'ai vu votre annonce dans *Le Monde*** I have seen your ad in *Le Monde*. **Vu** comes from **voir** 'to see'.

Je serais intéressée Lit. 'I would be interested'. Here the caller is using **serais** in the sense of 'might be interested'. **Serais**, remember, is the conditional (*would*-) form from **être** 'to be'.

♦ **Je cherche un renseignement** I'm looking for some information. **Chercher** means 'to look for'. **Je cherche une nouvelle voiture** 'I'm looking for a new car'. **Un renseignement** is a single or specific piece of information, as opposed to **informations** or **renseignements**, meaning 'information' in general.

♦ **C'est un problème de logiciel** It's a software problem. **Logiciel** (m.) is the usual word for 'software'.

♦ **j'ai appris à utiliser** I learned to use. **Utiliser** is a common way of translating 'to use'. **Appris** comes from **apprendre** 'to learn'. **J'apprends le français** 'I'm learning French'. **J'ai appris le français** 'I (have) learned French'.

♦ **le responsable** the person in charge / responsible

♦ **le centre informatique** the computing centre. **Il est dans l'informatique** means 'He is in computing'. Note also **un(e) informaticien(ne)** 'computer scientist'.

une documentation refers to publicity material

Practise what you have learned

6 Here are a number of phrases based on the recordings you've just heard in dialogue 3. First of all translate them, then put a ✓ by the three that are actually used. (Answers on p. 126.)

(a) **M. Cartier ne pourra pas revenir ce soir.**

_____ ☐

(b) **Est-ce que vous avez un autre numéro?**

_____ ☐

(c) **Pourriez-vous m'envoyer une documentation?**

_____ ☐

(d) **Ma secrétaire cherche un autre emploi.**

_____ ☐

(e) **C'est un problème de logiciel.**

_____ ☐

(f) **Je vais vous passer le responsable du centre informatique.**

_____ ☐

(g) **Je serais intéressée par un emploi chez vous.**

_____ ☐

7 Listen to the conversation on the recording a couple of times and then, using your pause control to give you more time, decide whether the following statements are **vrai** (true) or **faux** (false). (Answers on p. 126.)

	vrai	faux
(a) **C'est Mme Tardieux qui téléphone.**		✓
(b) **Elle devait avoir un rendez-vous demain.**		✓
(c) **Il veut décider les détails d'une annonce.**	✓	
(d) **Elle a un problème avec un de ses employés dans le centre informatique.**		✓
(e) **Elle va rappeler pour trouver une nouvelle date.**	✓	
(f) **La documentation est bien arrivée.**	✓	
(g) **Le monsieur a un téléphone de voiture.**	✓	
(h) **Le numéro de l'agence est le 45 53 12 19.**		✓

8 In the speaking exercise, you're going to practise leaving a couple of messages.

Dialogues

4 *The telephone system in France*

A French person answers the question: **C'est facile à utiliser?** *'Is it easy to use?'*

Telephonist — Oui, c'est très facile et c'est très modernisé. Nous n'avons plus besoin d'indicatifs. Chaque département a un numéro approprié. Un exemple – l'Aveyron, c'est le numéro soixante-cinq. Nous établissons six numéros et nous mettons le soixante-cinq devant ces six numéros. Pour la région parisienne, nous avons besoin de faire le numéro un.

Pour les cabines téléphoniques nous avons besoin d'argent, ou d'une carte téléphonique.

Par contre les hommes d'affaires ont leur téléphone dans la voiture et nous avons également le Minitel. C'est un genre de petit ordinateur à la disposition de tout foyer dont le but principal était de faciliter la recherche d'un numéro téléphonique en dehors du département sans passer par l'intermédiaire des renseignements.

Aujourd'hui le Minitel est utilisé très fréquemment. Il offre un grand nombre de facilités et de passe-temps. Vous avez toutes sortes de rubriques selon vos intérêts. Vous avez la possibilité de passer une annonce ou une publicité. Le Minitel a une multitude d'autres services.

Mais, si j'ai un conseil d'ami à vous donner, ne vous amusez pas trop longtemps sur cette machine car ce n'est pas gratuit. Le seul service que France Télécom offre est la recherche d'un numéro téléphonique.

- **facile** easy
- **une cabine téléphonique** public phone box/booth
- **l'argent** (m.) money
- **moderniser** to modernize
- **une carte téléphonique** phone card
- **avoir besoin de** to need
- **par contre** on the other hand
- **un exemple** example
- **en dehors de** outside
- **établir** to establish
- **utiliser** to use
- **devant** in front of
- **fréquemment** frequently
- **une rubrique** heading/listing
- **une multitude** multitude
- **car** because/for/since
- **gratuit** free of charge

Nous n'avons plus besoin d'indicatifs We no longer need area codes (**l'indicatif** is 'area code'). There have already been several examples of constructions with **ne**. For example: **ne...personne** 'nobody'; **ne...pas** 'not'; **ne...jamais** 'never'. **Ne...plus** follows the same pattern and means 'no longer'.

Chaque département a un numéro approprié Each department (roughly equivalent to an English county or US state) has an appropriate (i.e. its own) number

nous mettons we put. From **mettre** 'to put'.

les hommes d'affaires businessmen. A businesswoman is **une femme d'affaires**.

Nous avons également le Minitel We also (lit. equally) have Minitel. An advanced data-retrieval system now well-established in France.

C'est un genre de petit ordinateur It's a sort of mini-computer. Two important words to note here: **un genre** 'a sort/type' and **l'ordinateur** (m.), the everyday word for 'computer'.

à la disposition de tout foyer available to (lit. at the disposition of) every household

dont le but principal était de faciliter la recherche of which the main purpose was to help in finding. **La recherche** is linked to **chercher** 'to look for'.

sans passer par l'intermédiare des renseignements without going through the intermediary of directory enquiries (information). In fact France Télécom offer this as a free service obtainable nationwide by keying in the number 11 on Minitel.

◆ **Il offre un grand nombre de facilités et de passe-temps. Offrir** is 'to offer' and **un passe-temps** is literally 'pastime'.

◆ **selon vos intérêts** according to your interests. 'According to your salary' would be **selon votre salaire**.

une annonce ou une publicité. Both words mean 'ad', but **une annonce** is usually associated with smaller ads whereas **publicité** is more often used in the context of a marketing campaign or large ad.

◆ **si j'ai un conseil d'ami à vous donner** if I have a (piece of) friendly advice to give you. **Le conseil** is linked to **conseiller** 'to advise'.

◆ **Ne vous amusez pas trop longtemps** Don't amuse yourself for too long. To give an instruction or to make a firm suggestion, you just use the **vous**-form of the verb, e.g. **Venez ici!** 'Come here!' **Donnez-moi!** 'Give me!' **Amusez-vous!** 'Amuse yourself! / Have a good time!

◆ **le seul service** the only service. Similarly, **le seul produit** 'the only product'; **la seule banque** 'the only bank', etc. **Seul** can also mean 'alone', e.g. **Je travaille seul(e)** 'I work alone'.

Practise what you have learned

9 In the left-hand column are words and phrases. On the right are a number of clue definitions – but they are in a different order. Match the words and definitions together. (Answers on p. 126.)

(a)	**indicatif**	(i)	**Vous les demandez quand il y a quelque chose que vous ne comprenez pas.**
(b)	**le numéro un**	(ii)	**Vous y utilisez soit de l'argent soit une carte téléphonique.**
(c)	**une cabine téléphonique**	(iii)	**la recherche d'un numéro par Minitel**
(d)	**Minitel**	(iv)	**un genre de petit ordinateur**
(e)	**des renseignements**	(v)	**On n'en a plus besoin en France.**
(f)	**un service gratuit**	(vi)	**Vous le mettez devant le numéro que vous appelez à Paris.**

(Continued on next page.)

10

On the recording you will hear some instructions on how to telephone abroad from France. The transcript of those instructions is given below, with a few gaps. Select the correct word from the box to complete the text. (Answers on p. 126.)

France Télécom est ——(a)—— de vous offrir ce guide du téléphone international. Nous——(b)—— qu'il facilitera vos contacts avec votre ——(c)—— , vos ——(d)—— et vos relations ——(e)—— . C'est ——(f)—— d'appeler l'——(g)—— en automatique de la plupart des téléphones ——(h)—— , des bureaux de postes et des hôtels.

● Décrochez le combiné et attendez la——(i)——

● Composez le——(j)—— et attendez la seconde tonalité.

● Composez ensuite——(k)—— du pays désiré, puis l'indicatif de la ville——(l)—— le zéro, et le numéro de votre correspondant.

C'est moins cher pendant les——(m)—— à tarifs réduits (heure française).

● Tous les jours de——(n)—— pour tous les pays de la Communauté Européenne.

● De 22 heures à 10 heures pour le Canada et les——(o)——

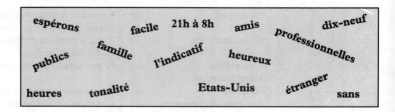

espérons   facile   21h à 8h   amis   dix-neuf

publics   famille   l'indicatif   heureux   professionnelles

heures   tonalité   Etats-Unis   étranger   sans

Key words and phrases

passer	to pass
une bonne nuit	a good night
donner	to give
faire erreur / se tromper	to make a mistake
comprendre	to understand
ne...personne...	nobody
Je suis désolé(e)	I'm really sorry
Je vous en prie	Don't mention it
à l'appareil	on the line
Excusez-moi	Excuse me / I'm sorry
Ne quittez pas	Hold on / Hold the line
connaître	to know
le numéro de poste	extension number
rappeler	to call back
tout de suite	immediately
Il est en réunion	He's in a meeting
essayer	to try
un autre	another
une annonce / publicité	ad
envoyer	to send
un emploi	job/post
chercher	to look for
un renseignement	piece of information
quelqu'un(e)	someone
logiciel (m.)	software
apprendre	to learn
le/la responsable	person responsible
le centre informatique	computing centre
facile/difficile	easy/difficult
moderniser	to modernize
l'argent (m.)	money
une carte téléphonique	phone card
gratuit	free of charge
mettre	to put
un homme / une femme d'affaires	businessman/woman
un genre / une sorte	a type/sort
un ordinateur	computer
à la disposition de tout foyer	available to every household
offrir	to offer
le passe-temps	pastime
selon vos intérêts	according to your interests
un conseil d'ami	piece of friendly advice
s'amuser	to amuse oneself / have a good time
seul	only/alone
la tonalité	the dialling tone
décrocher	to pick up (the receiver)

Grammar

Modal verbs

This is the name given to verbs such as **pouvoir** 'to be able to', **vouloir** 'to want / like', **devoir** 'to have to / ought to / should'. They are usually linked to another verb which is always in its full (i.e. infinitive) form.

Je peux comprendre.	I can understand.
Voulez-vous sortir?	Do you want to go out?
Il doit rappeler.	He should / ought to call back.

Here are the irregular present tenses of these key verbs:

	pouvoir	**vouloir**	**devoir**
je	peux	veux	dois
tu	peux	veux	dois
il	peut	veut	doit
elle	peut	veut	doit
nous	pouvons	voulons	devons
vous	pouvez	voulez	devez
ils	peuvent	veulent	doivent
elles	peuvent	veulent	doivent

They are often used in forms other than the present tense, and it is important at least to be able to recognize them. Here are a few examples:

Elle a pu venir.
She has been able to come. (simple past tense)

Elle pourra venir.
She will be able to come. (future tense)

Elle pourrait venir.
She would be able to come. (conditional tense)

Il a voulu téléphoner.
He wanted to telephone. (simple past)

Il voudra téléphoner.
He will want to telephone. (future tense)

Il voudrait téléphoner.
He would like to telephone. (conditional tense)

Il a dû patienter.
He has had to wait. (simple past)

Il devra patienter.
He will have to wait. (future)

Il devrait patienter.
He would have to wait. (conditional)

These verbs have been introduced here because different forms have already cropped up several times and it is important to begin to recognize at least the basic meaning. You are not expected at this stage to know all the various tenses. There will be more on this later (see the grammar sections in Units 11 and 12). Be warned!

Possessives

These are little words such as 'my', 'his', 'your', etc. They have cropped up several times, so it is appropriate to take the opportunity of pulling them together. Basically, there are three forms of each word, depending on whether the noun to which it is linked is masculine singular, e.g. **mon ordinateur** (my computer); feminine singular, e.g. **ma voiture** (my car); or plural, e.g. **mes ordinateurs** (my computers), **mes voitures** (my cars). Here's a table for reference:

	masculine singular	*feminine singular*	*plural*
my	**mon**	**ma**	**mes**
your (familiar)	**ton**	**ta**	**tes**
his	**son**	**sa**	**ses**
her	**son**	**sa**	**ses**
our	**notre**	**notre**	**nos**
your (polite)	**votre**	**votre**	**vos**
their	**leur**	**leur**	**leurs**

Note When 'my', 'your (familiar)', 'his' or 'her' are linked to a feminine noun that starts with a vowel, the **ma** becomes **mon**, the **ta** becomes **ton** and the **sa** becomes **son**, e.g. **mon entreprise** (f.), **ton arrivée** (f.), **son annonce** (f.).

Reflexive verbs

These are quite a feature of the French verb scene but the name makes them seem worse than they are. In English we have a number of reflexive verbs, *I wash myself, he amuses himself, we stop ourselves,* and so on. The slight problem is that in French they are not always used in ways that can be directly translated back into English. In this unit, for instance, the following reflexive verbs have cropped up: **s'appeler** 'to be called'; **se tromper** 'to make a mistake'; **se rendre** 'to get to'; **s'amuser** 'to have a good time'. In a dictionary, reflexive verbs are always listed in the **se** form of the infinitive. Here's an example of the full present tense of a typical reflexive verb **se tromper** 'to make a mistake':

je me trompe	**nous nous trompons**
tu te trompes	**vous vous trompez**
il se trompe	**ils se trompent**
elle se trompe	**elles se trompent**

All the other reflexive verbs behave in the same way: **me** is associated with **je**; **te** with **tu**; **se** with **il, elle, ils, elles,** and so on. You might like to look back through some of the earlier units and spot a few reflexive verbs.

Read and understand

11 France Télécom offers a number of additional services. Below are the names and definitions of some of these services – see if you can match them up. (Answers on p. 126.)

(a) **le signal d'appel**

(b) **la conversation à trois**

(c) **le transfert d'appel**

(d) **le mémo appel**

(e) **la facturation téléphonique détaillée**

(f) **les répondeurs téléphoniques**

(g) **télégramme**

(i) telephone answering machines

(ii) telegram (still available in France; cheap, fast and easy to use)

(iii) hold facility which alerts the user to an incoming call

(iv) alarm call

(v) itemized phone bill

(vi) transfer facility which allows you to receive calls on other phones

(vii) three-way conversation enables a third person to be brought in

12 Here is a description of **la carte pastel international,** the international service card offered by France Télécom. Read it through and answer the questions below. The following words may help you: **lorsque** 'when'; **à partir de** 'from'; **d'outre mer** 'overseas'; **n'importe quel poste** 'any phone'. (Answers on p. 126.)

LA CARTE PASTEL INTERNATIONALE

La Carte Pastel Internationale est le service que FRANCE TELECOM met à votre disposition pour simplifier vos communications téléphoniques :
– avec la France, lorsque vous séjournez à l'étranger,
– avec l'étranger, lorsque vous appelez de France.
Avec la Carte Pastel Internationale :

– vous établissez, à partir de la France Métropolitaine et des départements français d'Outre Mer, vos communications en direction de l'étranger :
  • directement à partir des nouvelles cabines équipées d'un publiphone à carte,
  • à partir de n'importe quel poste à touches musicales, en composant le 3610 (accès par voie automatique),
  • à partir de tout autre poste (accès par un opérateur de FRANCE TELECOM) en composant le :
    – 3650 pour les communications nationales
    – 19 33 + indicatif du pays, pour les communications internationales.
– vous appelez la France à partir de plus de 50 pays :
  • en utilisant les services d'un opérateur local,
  • de façon simplifiée, grâce au service de France Direct au départ de 11 pays (voir page 4),
Vous n'avez plus à payer le coût de votre communication en monnaie locale, il vous sera automatiquement débité plus tard sur votre compte téléphonique en France.

(a) Why has France Télécom introduced the card?

(b) What are the two main uses?

(c) What are the two types of phone from which you can use the card without an operator?

(d) From how many countries can you phone France using the card?

(e) Do you have to pay the cost in local money?

(f) How are you billed?

PAP   *Professionels à Professionels*

This is a business directory which has one national and eight regional editions. Businesses are listed free of charge and some 835,000 copies are issued annually.

Le PAP est adressé aux décisionnaires en matière: il est envoyé, dans les entreprises, aux fonctions suivantes: Direction Générale, Service Achats, Service Commercial, Service Technique, Service Administratif.

The contents page looks like this:

	PAGES
Mode d'emploi du PAP	1
En savoir plus sur le PAP	5
Comment annoncer dans le PAP	6
FRANCE TELECOM au service de l'entreprise	11
Index alphabétique	25
Index par secteurs d'activités	43
Liste des entreprises	63
Index des annonceurs	517

Note: **annoncer** means 'to advertise'.

Did you know?

Post and telecommunications in France

The postal and telephone services in France were until recently run by the PTT (**Postes, Télégraphes, Téléphones**). The telephone is now the responsibility of France Télécom. PTT has around 17,200 post offices dispersed throughout the country. The automated sorting operations within France depend on the five-digit postcodes. The first two digits are the number of the appropriate department, and the remaining three identify the local sorting office. Certain large cities such as Paris, Lyon and Marseille are divided into several numbered **arrondissements** or districts, and in such cases the number of the **arrondissement** forms the last three digits of the postcode (75013). Organizations and businesses which receive large quantities of mail belong to the **CEDEX (Courrier d'Entreprise à Distribution Exceptionnelle)** system, which operates in large towns and cities in order to speed up sorting and delivery. (An example of an address with code and CEDEX is: Chambre de Commerce et d'Industrie de Paris, 27 Avenue de Friedland, 75382 Paris CEDEX 08). There are also express services such as **Chronopost** which can guarantee speedy delivery in France and abroad. Within France and the EC, **Chronopost** delivers letters or parcels up to 25kg within 24 hours, and within 72 hours for most other countries. This form of quick delivery is increasingly being used.

Financial services are also provided by post offices: **la Caisse Nationale d'Epargne**, a savings bank with more than 18 million accounts, and the **Comptes Courants Postaux**, the current postal accounts, with more than 8 million accounts.

The telephone system in France has received massive investments and is now automated and internationally linked. It has been converted to an eight-digit numbering system, with the area code included in the telephone number. This is with the exception of Paris, for which 1 must be prefaced to the eight-digit number if you are phoning from outside the city. If you are phoning from Paris to somewhere outside the city, the number must be prefaced by a 16.

The most important success achieved in recent years by the French telecommunications industry was the introduction of **Minitel** in 1985. **Minitel** is the name of a range of computer terminals linked to a telephone which provide the subscriber with a nationwide phone directory service, as well as some 6,000 other services from information providers. Thus, in addition to access to the electronic telephone directory (**l'annuaire électronique**), subscribers can also consult a range of commercial information services (**le service télétel**), such as banks, hotels, trains, planes, programmes of events, road information, sports centres, language learning, etc. **Minitel** has also connected homes to catalogue databases, with credit-card payment systems facilitating purchasing from home.

Your turn to speak

13 In the final speaking section you're going to have another opportunity to leave messages. Use the vocabulary from the unit to think up how you would leave the following messages.

(a) You have seen the ad in the paper for software. You are interested and want more details and documentation. Leave your name, address and telephone number.

(b) You are unable to get to a meeting. Give the reason and ask to be called back in order to fix a new date.

When you've spoken your version aloud, switch on the recording and see what Philippe and Brigitte said. Bonne Chance!

Answers

Practise what you have learned

Exercise 1 (a) tromper (b) numéro (c) appeler (d) désolée
(e) personne (f) chambre (g) allô (h) vingt (i) prie

Exercise 3 (a) Pouvez-vous me passer M. J.-C. Moyen, s'il vous plaît?
(b) Ça doit être le 1124, je crois (c) M. Rambaut est absent
(d) Qu'il me rappelle, alors (e) Pourrais-je parler à
M. Renfort, s'il vous plaît? (f) Quand est-ce que je peux
rappeler pour être sûr de l'avoir?

Exercise 4 (a) The telephonist says 'bonsoir' (b) If he has returned
(c) No. He's in a meeting (d) Call back or leave a message
(e) Call back (f) D'accord

Exercise 6 (a) M. Cartier will not be able to return this evening
(b) Do you have another number (c) Could you send me
some details ✓ (d) My secretary is looking for another job
(e) It's a software problem ✓ (f) I'll put you through to the
person in charge of the computer centre ✓ (g) I'd be
interested in a job with your firm

Exercise 7 *Vrai:* (c), (e), (f), (g); *faux:* (a), (b), (d), (h)

Exercise 9 (a) v (b) vi (c) ii (d) iv (e) i (f) iii

Exercise 10 (a) heureux (b) espérons (c) famille (d) amis
(e) professionnelles (f) facile (g) étranger (h) publics
(i) tonalité (j) 19 (k) l'indicatif (l) sans (m) heures
(n) 21h à 8h (o) Etats-Unis

Read and understand

Exercise 11 (a) iv (b) vii (c) vi (d) iii (e) v (f) i (g) ii

Exercise 12 (a) it simplifies phone communications (b) to phone
France when you're abroad; to phone abroad from France
(c) new boxes equipped with the publiphone card; any
phone with musical touch buttons (d) 50 (e) no
(f) automatically debited on your phone bill at a later date

You will learn

- to understand and ask about facilities on offer in a region
- to ask and answer questions about other companies
- to show visitors around your firm
- to explain what you could offer a French company
- about aspects of the legal framework within which French industry operates

and you will be given information on the French education system

Study guide

To help you keep a check on your progress, you could mark off the various tasks as you complete them.

Dialogue 1 + Practise what you have learned
Dialogue 2 + Practise what you have learned
Dialogue 3 + Practise what you have learned
Dialogue 4 + Practise what you have learned
Ensure you know the **Key words and phrases**
Study the **Grammar** section
Do the exercises in **Read and understand**
Did you know? Education in France
Your turn to speak

Dialogues

1 *A Mayor talks about education, medical and leisure facilities*

Mayor Pour la scolarité, nous commençons donc à accueillir les enfants aux environs de deux, trois ans dans une école maternelle qui passe pour être une des plus jolies de la région. Nous y avons actuellement près de quatre-vingt-dix enfants et puis nous avons ensuite une école primaire qui permet donc de poursuivre la scolarité jusqu'au moment où les enfants sont en âge de partir au collège.

Visitor Ceci dans votre commune?

Mayor Dans notre commune. Alors, à partir du collège, eh bien, les enfants ont à leur disposition les collèges Dieppois et les lycées Dieppois tant professionnels que lycées de culture générale et là, nous avons donc, un service de cars qui, matin et soir assurent la desserte de ces établissements sans aucun problème.

Visitor Oui.

Mayor Donc, un service très complet au niveau de la scolarité. Pour ce qui est des services médicaux, nous avons un médecin sur la commune et nous avons donc tous les autres établissements de soins de Dieppe qui se trouvent à peine à trois kilomètres, avec l'hôpital, les deux cliniques et tous les services paramédicaux qui s'y rattachent. Et puis alors, pour les loisirs, bien, on a une situation un petit peu privilégiée puisque nous sommes à la fois urbains mais également ruraux. C'est-à-dire nous avons la mer à trois kilomètres, la forêt à trois kilomètres, et une ... des équipments de loisirs qui permettent de faire du tennis, du basket, du football et tout ceci, de manière vraiment tout à fait, tout à fait conviviale. Il y a un bon état d'esprit associatif dans la commune. Voilà.

donc then/so (a filler word)
aux environs de around
➧ **joli (e/s/es)** pretty/nice
près de close to
puis/ensuite then
en âge de at the age of
une commune district
➧ **un médecin** doctor
➧ **se trouver** to be located
➧ **complet** complete
à peine barely/hardly
➧ **l'hôpital** (m.) hospital
paramédical (paramédicaux) paramedical (here plural)
puisque because/since
rural (ruraux) rural (here plural)
➧ **c'est-à-dire** that is to say
la campagne countryside
➧ **autour de** around about
la mer sea
➧ **la forêt** forest
le basket basketball

➧ **Nous commençons à accueillir** we begin to accept children. Although **accueillir** means 'to welcome', it is sometimes used in the more general sense of 'to accept'. **Commencer** is 'to begin'.

une école maternelle qui passe pour être. The system of **écoles maternelles** is highly developed in France. They are like kindergartens or play groups. **Qui passe pour être** is a modest way of saying 'which is accepted as being' (lit. which passes to be).

➧ **nous y avons actuellement** we have there at the moment. **Y** comes before the verb and means 'there'. **J'y vais** 'I'm going there'. **Actuellement** does *not* mean 'actually'. The adjective **actuel(le)** means 'present/current', e.g. **la situation actuelle** 'the present situation'.

une école primaire qui permet donc de poursuivre la scolarité a primary school which enables the children to continue their education. **Permettre** means 'to permit/enable'.

➧ **jusqu'au moment où** until the moment when. **Où** normally means 'where' but in some expressions of time it is used idiomatically to translate *when*.

les collèges and **les lycées** are types of secondary school. **Un lycée** is generally more academic, **un collège** more vocationally orientated.

tant...que... as much...as...

un service de cars qui assurent a coach service which provides/assures

la desserte is linked to **desservir**, a verb meaning 'to provide a transportation service'. **La SNCF dessert tout la France** 'SNCF provides a transportation service for the whole of France'.

sans aucun problème without any (lit. no) problem. A useful phrase.

au niveau de. Lit. 'at the level of'. The phrase is often used to convey the sense of 'as far as ... is concerned'.

les établissements de soins. Lit. 'the establishments of caring'. A common phrase to cover the full range of medical and social services.

qui s'y rattachent which are attached to them. This is another idiomatic use of **y** – here it means 'to it / to them'.

▶ **nous sommes à la fois** we are at one and the same time. **La fois** means 'time' or 'instance' when associated with the concept of number, e.g. **trois fois** 'three times', **chaque fois** 'each time'. **Le temps** is used in the sense of 'time spent', e.g. **un bon temps** 'a good time'.

des équipements de loisirs leisure facilities

de manière conviviale in a convivial manner. The mayor is searching for the right phrase and perhaps doesn't quite succeed.

Il y a un bon état d'esprit associatif There's a good community spirit

Practise what you have learned

1 Before doing this exercise have a look at the grammar explanation on adjectives (p. 138). It's time to focus on how they work. Below is a list of adjectives. Look back through the transcript of dialogue 1 and find the noun or pronoun with which they are associated. (Answers on p. 142.)

(a) **maternelle** _ecole_   (f) **privilégiée** _____
(b) **professionnels** _lycées_   (g) **urbains/ruraux** _____
(c) **générale** _culture_   (h) **conviviale** _manière_
(d) **complet** _____   (i) **associatif** _esprit_
(e) **médicaux** _____

2 Now a listening activity where you can eavesdrop on two French people talking about their own town. Below is a list of twelve phrases. Listen and mark off the seven that are actually used in the conversation. (Answers on p. 142.)

(a) **qui passe pour être une des plus jolies de la région**   ✓
(b) **elle accueille des enfants de la région parisienne**
(c) **nous avons un service de cars qui assurent la desserte des écoles**   ✓
(d) **les enfants y restent jusqu'au moment où**   ✓
(e) **c'est un lycée tant professionnel que de culture générale**   ✓
(f) **au niveau des services médicaux**
(g) **pour la plupart**
(h) **compétents et sympathiques**   ✓
(i) **nous sommes à la fois urbains et ruraux**   ✓
(j) **tout autour du centre**
(k) **la mer se trouve à 13 kilomètres**
(l) **il existe un esprit assez convivial**   ✓

3 You're thinking of establishing a small firm in France. Switch on the recording and you'll be able to take part in a conversation with the local mayor.

Dialogues

2 *Is it possible to visit Penly power station?*

M. André C'est tout à fait possible. Nos portes sont grandes ouvertes pour l'ensemble des visiteurs. Comment ça se passe? Nous accueillons les groups dans la salle de conférence où nous leur faisons un exposé sur la façon dont on travaille et la façon dont on a construit l'installation. Et ensuite pendant à peu près 2 heures, ils vont visiter le site.

Organizer C'est sûrement très intéressant. Maintenant s'ils vous posent des questions portant, par exemple, sur la sûreté, est-ce-que ça va être gênant pour vous?

M. André Ce n'est absolument pas gênant. Au contraire vous savez qu'on a développé un aspect sûreté important dans nos installations, donc nous sommes prêts à répondre à toutes les questions à ce sujet.

Organizer Bien et pendant la visite elle-même ils ne courent aucun danger corporel.

M. André Il n'y a aucun danger corporel vis-à-vis de l'énergie nucléaire.

Organizer Bien, merci beaucoup.

M. André Merci.

tout à fait certainly/absolutely	◆ **au contraire** on the contrary
pendant during	**donc**
le site site	◆ **ce sujet** this subject
sûrement for sure	**elle-même** itself (f.)
par exemple for example	**corporel** of the body / physical
la sûreté security	◆ **l'énergie** (f.) **nucléaire**
gênant embarrassing/inconvenient	nuclear energy

◆ **Nos portes sont grandes ouvertes** is a common but idiomatic way of saying 'Our doors are wide open'.

pour l'ensemble des visiteurs. You usually come across **ensemble** meaning 'together', e.g. **Nous allons ensemble** 'We are going together'. Here it has the sense of 'the whole of visitors', i.e. 'all visitors'.

◆ **Comment ça se passe?** Lit. 'How that happens?' **Se passer** is 'to happen'. Here, 'How do we organize it?'

◆ **Nous leur faisons un exposé** We give them a presentation. The phrase literally means 'We to them make a presentation' and it is another example of how the verb **faire** is often used idiomatically.

la façon dont on travaille the way in which we work. The phrase is repeated in **la façon dont on a construit** 'the way in which we have built'. **Construit** is from **construire**, 'to build'.

s'ils vous posent des questions if they put questions to you

portant sur la sûreté touching on security

◆ **Nous sommes prêts à répondre** We are ready to reply. **Je suis prêt(e) à investir** 'I am ready to invest'.

◆ **Ils ne courent aucun danger.** Lit. 'They are not running any danger'. **Courir** also means 'to run' in the more usual sense.

Practise what you have learned

4 Using the transcript and notes work out the French equivalent of the following phrases. (Answers on p. 142.)

(a) Our doors are wide open.

_____

(b) We welcome visitors.

_____

(c) There is a presentation in the conference room.

_____

(d) the way in which we have constructed the installation

_____

(e) He wants to visit the nuclear site.

_____

(f) It's not embarrassing at all.

_____

(g) We are ready to reply to all the questions.

_____

5 Listen to the conversation on the recording, then match up the questions (a)–(g) and the answers (i)–(vii). Use the grid below. (Answers on p. 142.)

(a) **Bonjour, je peux vous aider?**
(b) **Il y a combien de personnes dans le groupe?**
(c) **Vous voulez que nous essayons d'organiser un petit programme?**
(d) **Bon, normalement nous commençons avec un exposé dans la salle de conférence. Ça vous va?**
(e) **Combien de temps vous avez?**
(f) **Et voulez-vous visiter toute l'installation nucléaire?**
(g) **Ils ne vont courir aucun danger. Quand est-ce que vous voulez venir?**

(i) **Parfait.**
(ii) **Mercredi matin vers 10 heures, si ça vous convient.**
(iii) **Une dizaine.**
(iv) **A peu près deux heures et demie.**
(v) **Merci beaucoup. Ça serait très gentil.**
(vi) **Ah oui merci. J'ai un groupe d'hommes et de femmes d'affaires qui voudrait visiter votre entreprise.**
(vii) **Oui, s'il n'y a pas de danger corporel.**

(a)	(b)	(c)	(d)	(e)	(f)	(g)

6 Your turn to speak. On the recording you will be invited to help organize a visit from some French industrialists.

Dialogues

3 *An agent for the Provincial Bank tries to get a new client at a branch of Renault Alpine.*

M. Tomas	Je viens vous voir parce que je suis en train de visiter toutes les entreprises importantes de la région et Alpine est une des plus importantes. Je sais que vous faites dans les 900 millions de chiffre d'affaires par an.
M. Thétiot	C'est exact.
M. Tomas	Si je ne me trompe.
M. Thétiot	C'est exact.
M. Tomas	Vous avez 180 millions de capitaux permanents.
M. Thétiot	C'est toujours vrai, c'est exact.
M. Tomas	Vous avez un endettement très faible.
M. Thétiot	Faible.
M. Tomas	C'est pourquoi, je pense que nous pourrions peut-être travailler ensemble. Je souhaiterais pouvoir financer vos investissements futurs.
M. Thétiot	C'est à étudier. C'est selon les conditions que vous pourrez faire.
M. Tomas	Oui, je peux vous proposer des financements de long terme, de moyen terme, des crédits à l'exportation ou enfin si vous voulez des crédits de trésorerie.
M. Thétiot	Nous cherchons actuellement des concours bancaires pour financer nos projets d'investissements de véhicules futurs donc vous arrivez donc à point.
M. Tomas	Ah bien.

souhaiter to want/wish		**enfin** finally	
♦ **l'investissement** (m.) investment	♦	**un véhicule** vehicle	
♦ **le financement** financing		**futur** future	

♦ **Je viens vous voir** I've come to see you (lit. I come to see you).

♦ **je suis en train de visiter** I am visiting. **En train de** emphasizes that you are in the act of doing something. **Je suis en train d'étudier** 'I'm (in the act of) studying'.

une des plus importantes (**entreprises**) one of the most important (firms).

♦ **Je sais que vous faites dans les 900 millions de chiffre d'affaires par an** I know that you have a turnover of 900 million per year. **Nous faisons un chiffre d'affaires de 3**
♦ **millions** 'We have a turnover of 3 million'. **Par semaine** 'per week'; **par mois** 'per month'.

♦ **Si je ne me trompe** If I am not mistaken. **Se tromper** is 'to make a mistake'. In speech the **pas** in **ne...pas** (not) is omitted.

180 millions de capitaux permanents 180 millions of capital (fixed) assets.

♦ **Capitaux** is the plural form of **le capital** 'capital'. **Capital initial** is 'start-up capital'.

♦ **un endettement très faible** a very low debt liability. **Un endettement** is 'debt'; **faible** basically means 'feeble' but is often used to mean 'low/small' in a financial context.

♦ **C'est pourquoi, je pense que...** That's why I think that... **Penser**, like **croire** means 'to think'.

♦ **Je souhaiterais pouvoir financer vos investissements futurs** I would like to be able to finance your future investments

C'est à étudier. It literally means 'It is to study', and it's a good way of saying 'I'll think about it'.

C'est selon les conditions que vous pourrez faire. Lit. 'It is according to the conditions that you will be able to do'. Another example of **faire** being used idiomatically.

Je peux vous proposer Lit. 'I can to you propose' **Proposer** often means 'to offer' or 'to suggest'.

♦ **de long terme, de moyen terme** long term. medium term. Also **de court terme** 'short term'.

♦ **des crédits à l'exportation** export credits. **Exporter** is the verb for 'to export'.

> des crédits de trésorerie cash credits. Also des difficultés de trésorerie 'cash-flow problems'.
>
> Nous cherchons actuellement... We're at the present time looking for...
>
> des concours bancaires assistance from a bank. Concours can also mean 'competition'.
>
> ♦ Vous arrivez donc à point You have arrived at just the right moment

Practise what you have learned

7 Listen again to the dialogue and look through the transcript. Make a list of all the words or phrases (not numerals) that have to do with finance and put your translation alongside. There are about 10 key phrases. (The answers are given on p. 142. If you do not understand them, check back in the notes and vocabulary of dialogue 3.)

_____   _____

_____   _____

_____   _____

_____   _____

_____   _____

_____   _____

_____   _____

8 On the recording you will hear a similar discussion between the same two people. Below, to help you, is a transcript of the discussion. Listen through a couple of times then, using the transcript and your pause control, compare it with dialogue 3 and see if you can find how the same idea was expressed in slightly different ways in this second recording. Underline any difference you find. There are no answers for this exercise.

M. Thomas	Je rends visite actuellement à toutes les entreprises importantes de la région et naturellement Alpine en fait partie. C'est pourquoi je suis venu vous voir. Je crois que vous faites dans les 900 millions de chiffre d'affaires par an.
M. Thétiot	C'est exact.
M. Thomas	Vous avez 180 millions de capitaux permanents et un endettement financier très faible.
M. Thétiot	Hum exact.
M. Thomas	Donc, je souhaiterais pouvoir financer vos investissements futurs.
M. Thétiot	C'est à étudier. Ça dépend à quelles conditions vous pourriez le faire.
M. Thomas	Eh bien. Je peux vous proposer des financements de long terme, de moyen terme, des crédits à l'exportation, enfin des crédits de trésorerie.
M. Thétiot	Nous cherchons actuellement des concours bancaires de moyen terme pour financer nos projets d'investissements de véhicules futurs. Vous arrivez donc à point.

Dialogues

4 *The production manager of Alcatel Business Systems explains their use of robots and how printed circuitboards are made*

Interviewer Nous voici maintenant devant une nouvelle machine. Pourriez-vous me dire à quel stade de la fabrication nous en sommes?

Production manager Eh, bien, cette machine sert à déposer des micro-composants sur des cartes électroniques. Approchez-vous plus près, vous verrez en effet que chaque tête vient déposer des composants sur la surface de la carte. Les voyez-vous?

Interviewer Ah! En effet, je vois mieux.

Production manager Lorsque les composants sont tous déposés la carte est ensuite emmenée dans le four de manière à ce que la colle soit polymerisée.

Interviewer Vous voulez dire que la colle va sécher?

Production manager Absolument.

> ▸ **nouvelle** (f.sing.) new
> ▸ **nouveau** (m.sing.) new
> **le micro-composant** micro-component
> **électronique** electronic
>
> **en effet** in fact / actually
> ▸ **chaque** each
> ▸ **la tête** head
> **le four** oven
> **sécher** to dry

Nous voici Here we are

à quel stade de la fabrication nous en sommes what stage of the production we are at. **La fabrication** is linked to **fabriquer** 'to produce'.

cette machine sert à déposer. Lit. 'this machine serves to deposit'. **Servir à** is 'to serve to', as in **L'ordinateur sert à faciliter la communication** 'The computer serves to facilitate communication'.

Approchez-vous plus près Come closer. The **vous**-form of the present tense is used to give a command or a firm suggestion. Other examples are: **Venez!** Come!; **Allez!** Go! Here the **vous** is added because **s'approcher** is a reflexive verb (see grammar p. 121).

vous verrez you will see. **Je verrai, tu verras, il/elle verra, nous verrons, vous verrez, ils/elles verront** is the irregular future tense of **voir** 'to see'. For more on the future tense see the grammar section in Unit 12.

Les voyez-vous? Do you see them? Similarly, **Le comprenez-vous?** 'Do you understand it?'

Je vois mieux I see better. **Mieux** often crops up in a variety of contexts.

la carte est ensuite emmenée the card/board is then taken away. **Emmener** means 'to take (something) away'. **La carte** refers to the printed circuitboard, **le circuit imprimé**.

de manière à ce que is one way of conveying the idea of 'so that'

la colle soit polymerisée the glue is polymerized. Don't worry about **soit** as the translation of 'is'. There's a complicated grammatical explanation, but for now just be able to recognize it.

Vous voulez dire que...? You mean that...?

Practise what you have learned

9 Work out the French for the following phrases. (Answers on p. 142.)

(a) Here we are now... _____

(b) Could you tell me what stage of the production we are at?

_____

(c) Come closer! _____

(d) Can you see them?_____

(e) You mean that...? _____

10 See if you can glean enough from the recording to answer these questions. Some new key words are **l'atelier** 'the workshop'; **le clavier** 'the keyboard/touchpad'; **l'emballage** 'packaging'; **les boîtes de carton** 'cardboard boxes'. (Answers on p. 142.)

(a) Which workshop are they in? _____

(b) What is produced there? _____

(c) What are the shells made of? _____

(d) What is connected to the touchpad? _____

(e) What is used to see that the finished _____
product is working well?

(f) Where does the packaging take place? _____

(g) What are the assembled units packed in? _____

(h) Where are they loaded onto pallets? _____

11 First fill in the gaps below, choosing the right phrase from the box. Then switch on the recording and check your answers by taking part in a conversation in which you play the role of a visitor.

(a) _____ ?
Les robots posent de la colle pour les circuits imprimés.

(b) _____ ?
Il y a quatre robots en tout.

(c) _____ ?
Cette nouvelle machine sert à déposer des micro-composants sur des cartes électroniques.

(d) _____ .
Approchez-vous plus près, vous verrez mieux.

(e) _____ ?
Absolument. La colle se sèche après à peu près 20 minutes.

> **Combien de robots y a-t-il?   Je ne peux rien voir.**
>
> **Pourriez-vous m'expliquer ce qui se passe?**
>
> **Vous voulez dire que la colle va se sécher?**
>
> **Pourriez-vous me dire à quel stade de la fabrication nous en sommes?**

Key words and phrases

joli(e/s/es)	pretty/nice
actuellement	at the present time
jusqu'au moment où	until the moment when
nous sommes à la fois	we are at one and the same time
près de	close to
complet	complete/full
le médecin	doctor
l'hôpital (m.)	hospital
se trouver	to be located
c'est-à-dire	that is to say
autour de	around about
la fôret	forest
commencer	to begin/start
Nos portes sont grandes ouvertes	Our doors are wide open
Comment ça se passe?	How does that happen / come about?
un exposé	presentation
construire	to construct/build
par exemple	for example
gênant	embarrassing
courir	to run
le sujet	subject
au contraire	on the contrary
prêt à	ready to
l'énergie (f.) nucléaire	nuclear energy
recevoir	to receive
nouveau (m.)	new
nouvelle (f.)	new
voir	to see
je suis en train de visiter	I am (in the act of) visiting
un(e) des plus important(e)s	one of the most important
Je sais que...	I know that...
le chiffre d'affaires	turnover
par an/mois/jour/semaine	per year/month/day/week
se tromper	to make a mistake
le capital	capital
un endettement	debt/liability
Je pense que...	I think that...
financer	to finance
l'investissement (m.)	investment
le financement	financing
de long/moyen/court terme	long/medium/short term
des crédits à l'exportation	export credits
le véhicule	vehicle
Vous arrivez à point	You've arrived at just the right time
expliquer	to explain
remarquer	to notice
le circuit imprimé	printed circuitboard
chaque, chacun(e)	each / each one
servir à	to serve to
s'approcher	to approach
le composant	component
la tête	head
mieux	better
Vous voulez dire que...?	You mean that...?

Grammar

Object pronouns

Pronouns that are the object of the verb – *I see him, we gave them to her,* etc. – need a bit of explanation. All the object pronouns go before the verb in French, e.g. **je les vois** 'I see them', **il me dit** 'he tells me', etc. Here is a list of the object pronouns. The difficulties come with 'to him', 'to her' and 'to them'.

me	me / to me
te	you / to you (familiar)
le/l'	him / it (m.)
la/l'	her / it (f.)
lui	to him / to her★
nous	us / to us
vous	you / to you (polite)
les	them (m./f.)
leur	to them (m./f.)★

★Note   **lui** is also used to translate English *him* or *her* whenever it means 'to him' or 'to her', as in *I gave (to) her the book.* **Leur** is also used for English *them* when it means 'to them', as in *We're going to offer (to) them the contract,* **Nous allons leur offrir le contrat**.

Switch on the recording and see how the following sentences are pronounced:

Je ne le sais pas.
I don't know it.

Il ne me connaît pas.
He doesn't know me.

Elle nous donne les composants.
She gives us the components.

Vous l'avez remarqué?
Did you notice it/him?

La banque va les financer.
The bank is going to finance them.

Nous allons leur proposer un nouveau projet.
We're going to propose a new project to them.

12   Now see if you can translate the following sentences. (Answers on p. 142.)

(a)   He sees me each day.

_____

(b)   I'm going to give (to) them the contract.

_____

(c)   Do you see her? (polite)

_____

(d)   They find it embarrassing.

_____

(e)   He is explaining to her how it happens.

_____

Adjectives

Descriptive words are obviously very important and in all the units there are quite a lot of them. Some examples here are **joli**, **gênant**, **complet** and **nucléaire**. In dictionaries, they are always listed in their masculine form, but when they are used in sentences, they have to 'agree' with the noun to which they are linked. This means that for a feminine singular you add an -**e** (e.g. **la campagne est jolie**) unless the base adjective already ends in -**e**. For masculine plural you add an -**s** (e.g. **les projets complets**) and for feminine plural you add -**es** (e.g **les petites boîtes**).

Remember that some of the most common adjectives precede the noun (see the grammar section in Unit 5). Certain adjectives are a bit irregular. For instance, all adjectives ending in -**al**, such as **capital**, form their masculine plural in -**aux** (**les projets capitaux**). The feminine forms of -**al** adjectives are regular (**les dettes capitales**).

There are also a few adjectives that are irregular in nearly all their forms. Here are two of the most useful ones:

nouveau (m.), **nouvelle** (f), **nouveaux** (m.pl.), **nouvelles** (f.pl.) – 'new'
vieux (m.), **vieille** (f.), **vieux** (m.pl.), **vieilles** (f.pl.) – 'old'

Look through the dialogues again and see how many adjectives you can spot. Notice how they agree with the various nouns to which they are linked

Read and understand

13 This is how SNCF, the French Railway Company, advertises one of its new services for business people. Read it through to get the gist then try to find the French phrases which correspond to those listed below in English. (Answers on p. 142.)

Businesspass la nouvelle dimension du train

Businesspass : des conditions financières préférentielles

BUSINESSPASS procure aux entreprises des réductions tarifaires substantielles tant sur le voyage lui-même que sur les locations de voiture et de chambre d'hôtel.

☐ Une réduction de 15 % à 25 % sur les parcours SNCF* en 1ʳ et 2ᵉ classe, toute l'année, sur tous les trains.

☐ Une réduction de 20 % sur les locations de voitures auprès d'"AVIS Train + Auto".

☐ Une réduction de 10 à 20 % dans 150 hôtels de 2 à 4 étoiles.

BUSINESSPASS, le bon calcul pour ceux qui ont le sens des affaires.

* et dès le 1ᵉʳ novembre également vers l'Allemagne !

Businesspass : utilisable par l'ensemble de vos collaborateurs

Tous les membres de votre entreprise peuvent voyager avec BUSINESSPASS car les coupons ne sont pas nominatifs.

BUSINESSPASS, la solution souplesse par excellence.

Businesspass : disponible à tout moment

Avec BUSINESSPASS vous disposez instantanément d'un titre de transport. Vous pouvez choisir entre deux formules "FRANCE ENTIÈRE" ou "PARCOURS DÉTERMINÉS".

Renseignez-vous auprès du chargé de voyage de votre entreprise, il vous aidera à déterminer la solution la mieux adaptée.

BUSINESSPASS, la destination liberté.

SNCF

(a) preferential financial conditions ___des conditions financière préférentielle___

(b) substantial price reductions ___réductions tarifaires substantielle___

(c) the business sense ___le sens des affairs___

(d) usable by all your colleagues _____

(e) the coupons are not named _____

(f) always available _____

(g) the whole of France _____

(h) pre-defined routes _____

(i) get the information _____

(j) the most appropriate solution _____

14 A good way of advertising a company's products is to insert ads in PAP, Professionnels à Professionnels (see p. 123). Study the selection below and see if you can answer the questions. (Answers on p. 142.)

Service porte à porte rapide et fiable, de vos documents et paquets à destination des USA et de plus de 100 pays dans le monde

Aéroport Lille Lesquin
zone de fret BP 446
59810 Lesquin - - - - - - - - - - - 20 87 58 50

CGI

CREDIT GENERAL INDUSTRIEL
DIVISION ENTREPRISES

Des formules de financement simples, rapides et aux meilleures conditions
Crédit-bail, location longue durée, crédit, crédit immatériel, enveloppe-investissement, affacturage.

Pour en savoir plus,
service Minitel : 3614 Code CGI

Parc club des Prés
8 rue Papin
59650 Villeneuve d'Ascq

114 CGI (Credit General Industriel)
59 Villeneuve d'Ascq   20 67 01 10

Entreprise Balavoine

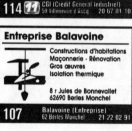

Constructions d'habitations
Maçonnerie - Rénovation
Gros œuvres
Isolation thermique

8 r Jules de Bonnevallet
62690 Berles Monchel

107 Balavoine (Entreprise)
62 Berles Monchel   21 22 02 91

LEON DESMARETS ets

BELGIQUE

Notre spécialité : les éléments préfabriqués en béton sur mesure en petites et moyennes séries tous matériaux de construction
44 rue de Ten-Brielen
07780 Comines BELGIQUE
19.32 56 55 50 71

43 Desmarets
59 Lille   20 55 92 26

World Science Technology Trade Business Compagny

Traducteurs spécialisés

Your partner in Brussels

Traductions techniques juridiques et commerciales
Service d'interprètes de et vers toutes langues
Télex : LYDIA 652238 Télécopie : 19.32 24 68 24 30
124 av Charles Quint 1080 Bruxelles BELGIQUE 19.32 24 65 91 62

336 WSTIBC
Bilxes Belgique 19.32 24 65 91 62

electricite generale
bernard dache

installations industrielles
installations particulières
chauffage électrique
pompe à chaleur
alarme incendie
maintenance d'usine
dépannage rapide
automatisation

Siège social :
2, rue Ribot 60100 Creil
44 25 84 58

Atelier - Bureaux :
28, rue Jean Jaurès 60100 Creil
44 55 52 32

132 Dache (Bernard)
60 Creil   44 25 84 58

Déménagements

LEVOYE

PIERRE LEVOYE

Location monte-meuble

Partout on le voit
Dunkerque, Lille

route Nationale - 59232 Vieux Berquin

Crédit aux   **28 42 72 77**   Devis
allocataires   **20 47 47 77**   gratuit

121 Déménagements Levoye
59 Vieux Berquin   28 42 72 77

Pour développer vos ventes, annoncez dans le PAP

Contactez l'ODA

N°VERT 05 04 04 03

ODA

Régisseur de la publicité dans les annuaires officiels de FRANCE TELECOM
7 avenue de la Cristallerie
92317 Sèvres Cedex
(1) 46 23 30 00

(a) Who can you go to for technical, legal and commercial translations? _____

(b) Which company delivers documents and parcels door to door to the USA? _____

(c) How can you develop your sales? _____

(d) What is the French word for 'removals'? _____

(e) What do you consult if you want to know more about loans and credits? _____

(f) Where is Leon Desmarets' headquarters? _____

(g) What number do you ring if you want to see a display of electrical equipment? _____

(h) If you want a new house, who can help you? _____

Did you know?

Education in France

Primary and secondary

Education in France is compulsory from six to sixteen. More than 80% of children go to state schools, where education is free. These schools are run by the Ministry of Education, which sets their curricula. There are also private schools that are primarily run by the Roman Catholic Church. An attempt by the socialist government in 1984 to integrate Catholic schools into the state system failed since many viewed it as an attack on the freedom of choice.

Primary education comprises nursery schools (**les écoles maternelles**) for children under six, and primary schools for children from six to eleven. At eleven, pupils are directed to secondary schools (usually a **collège d'enseignement secondaire** or a **lycée**), where teaching is divided into two cycles. The first lasts four years and leads to the **Brevet des Collèges** (roughly equivalent to GCSEs). In the second secondary cycle, pupils spend three years studying for the **Baccalauréat**. This exam is usually taken at the age of 18 or 19 and all those who pass it are eligible to go on to university. It is roughly equivalent to A-levels (or SAT in the US). There are various categories of the **Baccalauréat**, such as A (literature), B (economics), C (mathematics and physics), D (mathematics and natural sciences), E (agriculture), F (technology), G (administration, management and business), H (computing). The majority of children, however, still leave school at sixteen to take up jobs or apprenticeships or to enter technical colleges for special courses.

Higher

The possibilities offered in Higher Education fall into two broad groups. There are short study courses on technology and business administration offered by Institutes of Technology (**Instituts Universitaires de Technologie, IUT**), by the technical departments of **lycées**, and by specialist higher colleges for the paramedical and social sectors. These colleges attract 40% of **Baccalauréat** holders. Universities and the **Grandes Ecoles** offer longer study courses taking three or more years.

There are 71 universities with a student population of over one million. These universities are multi-disciplinary and offer a wide variety of courses. The long study courses are basically divided into three successive stages, each lasting two years. The first stage, which leads to the **DEUG** (**Diplôme d'études universitaires générales**), prepares students for longer periods of studies. The second stage introduces more in-depth study and a higher level of specialization. It leads to a **Licence** degree in three years, to a **Maîtrise** degree in four years or to an engineering degree in five years. The third stage trains students in research, and leads to a **Diplôme d'études supérieures specialisées** (**DESS**) or to a **Doctorat**. There is currently considerable debate over standards, over funding and over the length of courses.

The **Grandes Ecoles** prepare students for managerial positions in industry, commerce and administration. The **Baccalauréat** is not enough for admission to these schools. Prospective students must also sit a competitive entrance examination which requires two or three years' study in special classes at a **lycée**, university or at the **Grandes Ecoles** themselves (**classes préparatoires**). Top **Grandes Ecoles** include **l'Ecole Polytechnique, l'Ecole Centrale, l'Ecole des Hautes Etudes Commerciales, l'Ecole des Mines, l'Ecole des Ponts et Chaussées** and **l'Ecole Nationale d'Administration**, a postgraduate institution training senior civil servants.

Your turn to speak

15 See if you can make up eight sentences or questions using each of the eight words listed below. Say them aloud and then switch on the recording and see what Brigitte and Philippe came up with.

joli	pretty/nice	**en train de**	in the act of
se trouver	to be located	**je sais que**	I know that
commencer à	to start to	**expliquer**	to explain
se passer	to happen	**vous voulez dire**	you mean

Answers

Practise what you have learned

Exercise 1   (a) une école (b) lycées (c) culture (d) un service (e) des services (f) une situation (g) nous (h) manière (i) esprit

Exercise 2   The phrases that appear are (a), (d), (e), (g), (h), (i), (l)

Exercise 4   (a) Nos portes sont grandes ouvertes (b) Nous accueillons les visiteurs (c) Il y a un exposé dans la salle de conférence (d) la façon dont nous avons construit l'installation (e) Il veut visiter le site nucléaire (f) Ce n'est absolument pas gênant (g) Nous sommes prêts à répondre à toutes les questions

Exercise 5   (a) vi (b) iii (c) v (d) i (e) iv (f) vii (g) ii

Exercise 7   un chiffre d'affaires; le capital permanent; un endettement très faible; financer; investissements futurs; des financements de long terme; de moyen terme; des crédits à l'exportation; des crédits de trésorerie; des concours bancaires

Exercise 9   (a) Nous voici maintenant... (b) Pourriez-vous me dire à quel stade de la fabrication nous en sommes? (c) Approchez-vous! (d) Les voyez-vous? (e) Vous voulez dire que...?

Exercise 10   (a) assembly workshop (b) telephones (c) plastic (d) printed circuitboards (e) automated testing machines (f) at the end of the workshop, right at the back (g) cardboard boxes (h) behind the door at the back

Grammar

Exercise 12   (a) Il me voit chaque jour (b) Je vais leur donner le contrat (c) La voyez-vous? (d) Ils/elles le trouvent gênant (e) Il lui explique comment ça se passe

Read and understand

Exercise 13   (a) des conditions financières préférentielles (b) des réductions tarifaires substantielles (c) le sens des affaires (d) utilisable par l'ensemble de vos collaborateurs (e) les coupons ne sont pas nominatifs (f) disponible à tout moment (g) la France entière (h) parcours déterminés (i) renseignez-vous (j) la solution la mieux adaptée

Exercise 14   (a) WSTTBC (b) Federal Express (c) advertise in PAP (d) déménagements (e) CGI (Minitel) (f) Belgium (g) 44 55 52 32 (h) Entreprise Balavoine

You will learn

- how to make enquiries about products
- to 'sell' your company and its products
- how to purchase products
- how to establish agencies
- how to raise finance in France

  and you will be given some information on money, banking and finance in France

Study guide

To help you keep a check on your progress, you could mark off the various tasks as you complete them.

Dialogue 1 + Practise what you have learned
Dialogue 2 + Practise what you have learned
Dialogue 3 + Practise what you have learned
Dialogue 4 + Practise what you have learned
Ensure you know the **Key words and phrases**
Study the **Grammar** section
Do the exercises in **Read and understand**
Did you know? Money, banking and finance in France
Your turn to speak

Dialogues

1 *M. Gedeon from Alcatel Business Systems describes his firm's products*

M. Gedeon Alcatel Business Systems est une société qui fabrique et commercialise des produits qui servent à la communication d'entreprise. Ainsi notre établissement fabrique des terminaux téléphoniques, ce que nous appelons des terminaux d'abonnés.

Mme Coste Pourriez-vous me dire plus précisemment ce que vous livrez à vos clients?

M. Gedeon Alors nous-mêmes, nous travaillons sur deux marchés: un marché pour France Télécom et un marché pour le privé. Pour France Télécom, nous fabriquons divers produits tel que l'Alto et tel que le Fidelio. L'Alto est un produit simple qui sert à téléphoner et qui n'a aucune autre fonctionnalité. Par contre le Fidelio est un poste beaucoup plus complexe, puisque nous retrouvons entre autres fonctions, des mémoires et une écoute amplifiée.

Mme Coste Pourriez-vous me donner quelques renseignements sur vos cadences de production?

M. Gedeon Actuellement, nous sortons 15,000 terminaux d'abonnés par jour de nos lignes de fabrication. En fait, notre fabrication se divise en deux grands ateliers: un atelier d'équipment des cartes électroniques, c'est-à-dire que sur ces cartes, nous venons déposer des composants électroniques, nous soudons ces composants et, ensuite, nous amenons les cartes dans le second atelier qui est l'atelier d'intégration.

Je tiens également à vous préciser que actuellement, nous sommes 700 salariés dans cet établissement et nous répartissons en plusieurs catégories professionnelles différentes: nous avons 3% d'ingénieurs et cadres, 3% d'agents de maîtrise, 12% de techniciens, 63% d'ouvriers spécialisés et 11% d'agents administratifs.

Mme Coste Merci pour toutes ces informations qui je crois m'ont permis de mieux connaître Alcatel Business Systems.

ainsi thus/so
un terminal (pl. **terminaux**) terminal(s)
♦ **livrer** to deliver
♦ **le privé** the private sector
par contre on the other hand
le poste unit (usually 'post')
retrouver to find
entre among/between
une ligne de fabrication production line
en fait in fact
♦ **souder** to solder
également equally
♦ **préciser** to point out
♦ **un(e) salarié(e)** salaried person
♦ **des agents de maîtrise** supervisory staff
♦ **un ouvrier spécialisé** specialist worker
♦ **je crois** I think

qui fabrique et commercialise which manufactures and sells

ce que nous appelons des terminaux d'abonnés. M. Gedeon defines his product as terminals for (telephone) subscribers – **un abonné** is 'a subscriber'.

alors nous-mêmes well, we ourselves. Also: **moi-même** 'myself', **toi-même** 'yourself', **lui-même** 'himself', **elle-même** 'herself', **vous-même** 'yourself', **eux-mêmes** 'themselves' (m.) and **elles-mêmes** 'themselves' (f.).

Nous travaillons sur deux marchés We work in (lit. on) two markets

divers produits tel que diverse/various products such as

qui sert à téléphoner which serves to make phone calls / which is used for making phone calls. From **servir à** 'to serve to'.

et qui n'a aucune autre fonctionnalité and which has no other function. **Ne...aucun(e)...** means 'no': **J'ai n'ai aucune idée** 'I have no idea'.

beaucoup plus complexe much more complex. **Beaucoup de produits** means 'many products'.

des mémoires et une écoute amplifiée – the Fidelio has memory and amplified listening. **Une écoute** is related to **écouter** 'to listen to'.

quelques renseignements sur vos cadences de production. Remember **renseignements** like **informations** is normally used in the plural. She asks him for 'some information on your production rates'.

nous sortons 15,000... Generally **sortir** means 'to go out', e.g. **Est-ce que vous sortez ce soir?** 'Are you going out this evening?' Here he means 'we send out'. You may also need **la sortie** 'the exit'.

notre fabrication se divise our production line is split. **Se diviser** is 'to divide/split'.

un atelier normally means 'a workshop'. Here it is more like 'a production unit'.

nous venons déposer we place. **Déposer** means 'to place'. **Venir** 'to come' is sometimes used idiomatically to stress the continuity of an action. In English it can often be left untranslated.

Nous amenons les cartes dans l'atelier d'intégration We take (away) these cards to the assembly unit

Je tiens également à vous préciser.... I'd also like to point out to you... **Je tiens à** is an idiom which means 'I'm anxious to / I'd like to'.

Nous nous répartissons en plusieurs catégories We are divided up into several categories. **Se répartir** is another word for 'to divide up / share out'.

un cadre is a term often found in French organizations. It refers to somebody in a position of responsibility in management.

qui m'ont permis de mieux connaître. Lit. 'which to me have permitted to better know'. In French you permit *to* somebody to do something. **Je lui ai permis de visiter le centre** 'I allowed (to) him to visit the centre'.

Turn over for the exercises based on this dialogue.

Practise what you have learned

1 Using the transcript and the notes of dialogue 1, work out the French equivalent of the following sentences. (Answers on p. 162.)

(a) Alcatel Business Systems manufactures and sells many products.

(b) Do you deliver to your clients?

(c) There is no other product on the market.

(d) Could you give me some information on your firm?

(e) We have two production lines.

(f) I would like to (I am anxious to) point out that we have 700 salaried employees.

(g) I know the engineers better than the administrators.

2 Listen carefully to the conversation on the recording (it's Mme Coste and M. Gedeon again), then fill in the gaps in the transcript below. Use the jumbled list at the bottom if you're not sure how to spell the words. (Answers on p. 162.)

Mme Coste   M. Gedeon, bonjour. Tout d'abord, je _Tiens_ (a) vous remercier de nous avoir accueillis. Vous _rep_ (b) donc Alcatel Business Systems. Est-ce que vous _pourriez_ (c) en quelques mots me brosser un portrait de votre _entre_ (d) ?

M. Gedeon   Eh bien, bonjour madame. En effet, donc vous êtes _____ (e) Alcatel Business Systems. ABS est une société qui est _spéc_ (f) dans la communication d'entreprise et notre _établis_ (g) tout particulièrement conçoit et _fab_ (h) des terminaux d'abonnés; _c'est-à-dire_ (i) des téléphones. L'établissement de Saint Nicolas est un établissement qui _emploie_ (j) actuellement 768 salariés, ces 768 salariés étant répartis dans des catégories _prof_ (k) différentes: ouvriers, techniciens, agents de maîtrise ainsi qu'ingénieurs et _cadres_ (l) .

> c'est-à-dire   fabrique   emploie   représentez
> cadres   établissement   chez   pourriez
> tiens à   spécialisée   entreprise   professionnelles

3 In the speaking activity you'll be asking some questions to establish whether or not you want to trade with a company.

Dialogues

2 *Didier asks about the easiest ways of transporting raw materials and finished goods*

Didier Moi, je voudrais vous demander également donc pour les dessertes aussi bien pour l'arrivée de mes matières premières que pour ensuite le retour des matières fabriquées. Quels sont les moyens les plus faciles de transport?

M. Le maire Eh bien, ils sont de deux types: tout d'abord au niveau des transports routiers, nous sommes ici, sur notre zone d'activité au cœur de l'ensemble routier de desserte de la région Dieppoise avec, à chaque extrémité de la zone, un échangeur qui nous permet donc de recevoir les flux routiers du nord de la France et à l'autre extrémité ceux qui viennent de la région Rouennaise et de la région Parisienne et également même de la basse Normandie ou du Havre.

Didier C'est ça.

M. Le maire Donc une excellente desserte routière qui jouit d'autre part des interventions de l'équipment lorsqu'il y a des intempéries d'hiver et d'autre part alors, une desserte ferroviaire avec la gare de triage, la plateforme ferroviare qui permet une excellente desserte également par voie ferrée.

Didier Tout à fait et pour cette chose là, il faut que je me mette en rapport avec la SNCF je pense.

M. Le maire Voila, oui, c'est notre société des chemins de fer qui traite ce problème à la gare de Dieppe.

Didier Très bien, je vous remercie beaucoup.

> **la desserte** transportation system
> **le type** type
> **chaque extrémité** each end
> **un échangeur** (traffic) interchange
> **le flux** flow
> ♦ **du nord** from the North
> **même** even
> **d'autre part** in addition
> ♦ **la gare** station
> **la gare de triage** marshalling yard
> **la plateforme** platform (in goods yard)
> **le quai** platform (for passengers)
> **la chose** thing/matter

Turn over for the notes to this dialogue.

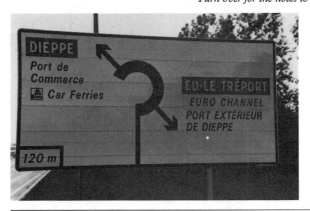

je voudrais vous demander également I would also like to ask you. **Demander** means 'to ask' (not 'to demand').

aussi bien pour...que pour... both for...and for... **Aussi bien que** means 'as well as'.

- **l'arrivée des matières premières** the arrival of raw materials
- **le retour des matières fabriquées**. Lit. 'the return of the finished goods'.
- **Quels sont les moyens les plus faciles...?** What are the easiest means...?

tout d'abord first of all

au niveau des transports routiers. Lit. 'at the level of road transportation'. Here, 'as far as road transportation is concerned'.

au cœur de l'ensemble routier de desserte at the heart of the whole road network

- **ceux qui viennent de...** those who come from... It is *ceux* **qui** because 'those' refers to **les flux**, which is masculine plural. If 'those' had been referring to a feminine noun the word used would have been *celles* **qui**.

la basse Normandie. The mayor is describing the lower southern part of Normandy – **bas(se)** literally means 'low'. **Les Pays-Bas** are 'the Low Countries', i.e. Holland.

qui jouit des interventions de which benefits from the deployment of. **L'intervention** is sometimes used idiomatically.

- **lorsqu'il y a des intempéries d'hiver** when there are winter storms.
- **D'hiver** means 'of winter'. 'Of summer' is **de l'été**, 'of autumn' **de l'automne** and 'of spring' **du printemps**.

une desserte ferroviaire railway network

par voie ferrée by rail (lit. by track of iron). **Le fer** is 'iron'; **ferré(e)** 'of iron'. You often come across **le chemin de fer**, lit. 'the iron way', i.e. 'the railway'.

- **Il faut que je me mette en rapport avec...** It is necessary for me to get in contact with... **Il faut**, 'it is necessary', cropped up earlier; **se mettre en rapport avec** is one way of saying 'to get in contact with'.

la SNCF stands for **la Société Nationale de Chemins de Fer Français**, i.e. the French national railway company

qui traite ce problème which deals with this problem. **Traiter** is 'to handle' or 'to deal with'.

Practise what you have learned

4 Fill in the crossword below. All the clues should produce key words that appeared in dialogue 2. The vertical word has something to do with roads. (Answers on p. 162.)

   (a) **le contraire de 'départ'**
   (b) **une _____ d'activité**
   (c) **Chaque personne en a pour faire circuler le sang** (blood).
   (d) **Le Nord et le Sud sont les deux _____ du monde.**
   (e) **Il fait froid en _____**
   (f) **On peut y trouver des trains.**
   (g) **de la voie ferrée**

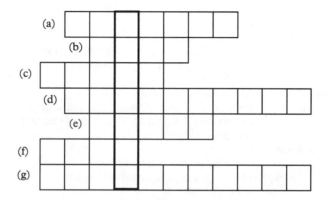

5 Here are a number of questions, but they have got detached from the answers. See if you can match them up, then check your version with the recording. You'll notice there are two sets of boxes in the grid below: one for the first attempt before listening, the other for after you have heard the recording. (Answers on p. 162.)

   (a) **Et les matières fabriquées, elles arrivent comment?**
   (b) **Pourquoi? C'est le moyen le plus facile?**
   (c) **Il y a un échangeur près d'ici?**
   (c) **Vous n'avez pas de problème en hiver?**
   (d) **Vous n'utilisez jamais les transports ferroviaires?**

   (i) **Juste à l'extrémité de la zone il y en a un.**
   (ii) **Si, surtout pour le retour des matières fabriquées. Il y a une gare de la SNCF à 2 kilomètres d'ici.**
  (iii) **Normalement nous utilisons des transports routiers.**
  (iv) **Quelquefois, mais l'équipement intervient très rapidement.**
   (v) **Oui, parce que nous sommes au cœur de l'ensemble routier de la région.**

	(a)	(b)	(c)	(d)	(e)
1st attempt					
2nd attempt	(a)	(b)	(c)	(d)	(e)

Dialogues

3 *M. Grandchamp is interested in buying some document folders from*
M. Leroy

M. Grandchamp	Bonjour. Monsieur Leroy. Nous nous sommes rencontrés hier à la foire exposition de Rouen. Je suis très intéressé par l'achat de vos pochettes plastiques, mais vous avez oublié de me donner le prix de cet article. Je souhaiterais les acheter par 500 et par 1000 et dans le même temps si vous pouviez me donner les frais de sérigraphie pour ces mêmes quantités cela m'intéresserait beaucoup. Veuillez me rappeler au 364 27 32. Merci.

M. Grandchamp	Oui, allô.
M. Leroy	Monsieur Grandchamp?
M. Grandchamp	Ah bonjour monsieur, oui Monsieur Grandchamp à l'appareil.
M. Leroy	Oui, bonjour Monsieur Grandchamp. Je suis euh Monsieur Leroy au téléphone.
M. Grandchamp	Ah bonjour, M. Leroy.
M. Leroy	Euh, j'ai reçu votre message téléphonique concernant votre demande de prix pour les pochettes plastiques que nous fabriquons. Bien nos prix pour 500?
M. Grandchamp	Oui.
M. Leroy	(Le prix) est de 13 francs 50.
M. Grandchamp	Oui, je prends note, ne quittez pas.
M. Leroy	S'il vous plaît.
M. Grandchamp	Voilà je suis à vous.
M. Leroy	Voilà, alors le prix pour 500 est de 13 francs 50 hors taxes.
M. Grandchamp	Oui.
M. Leroy	Sans publicité.
M. Grandchamp	Donc, vierge hein?
M. Leroy	Vierge oui.
M. Grandchamp	Très bien.
M. Leroy	Pour 1000?
M. Grandchamp	Oui.
M. Leroy	11 francs 80.
M. Grandchamp	11 francs 80 oui toujours vierge.
M. Leroy	Toujours vierge oui. Nos prix sont départ région parisienne.
M. Grandchamp	Ah, d'accord, bien. Bon ça va aller. En ce qui concerne la sérigraphie, parce que là c'est le prix du produit nu, j'aurais aimé savoir combien coûtait l'inscription d'une marque ou d'un logo sur la pochette plastique.
M. Leroy	Alors concernant la sérigraphie, nous avons fait un prix forfaitaire deux couleurs.
M. Grandchamp	Oui.
M. Leroy	Il est de 1 franc 60 unitaire pour petite quantité.
M. Grandchamp	Pour petite quantité, c'est-à-dire pour 50 ou 100 ou...
M. Leroy	50 euh 100 euh 50.
M. Grandchamp	Et pour 500 produits du même type avec la même marque vous descendez à combien là?
M. Leroy	Et bien, écoutez, il faudrait que vous nous indiquiez vos quantités et nous étudierons un prix par quantités.

- **la foire exposition** trade fair exhibition
  une pochette folder
- **oublier** to forget
- **donner** to give
- **sans** without
  publicité publicity (logo, etc.)
  nu naked (here 'basic')
  une marque design/brand
  la couleur colour
  unitaire per unit
- **écouter** to listen to
- **étudier** to study

- **nous nous sommes rencontrés** we met. This is the past tense from the verb **se rencontrer** 'to meet (each other)'.

- **Je suis très intéressé par l'achat...** Lit. 'I am very interested by the purchase...' – a normal way of saying 'I'm very interested in buying'. **Acheter** means 'to buy'.

  dans le même temps at the same time

- **les frais de sérigraphie.** Remember **les frais**, it is an important word meaning 'costs' or 'charges'; **la sérigraphie** is 'silk-screen printing'.

- **Veuillez me rappeler** is a short but polite way of saying 'Would you be kind enough to call me back'.

  Monsieur Grandchamp à l'appareil. This is the normal way of answering the phone. **L'appareil** means more generally 'apparatus' but it also has the specific meaning of 'phone'.

  J'ai reçu votre message téléphonique I have received your telephone message. **Reçu** comes from **recevoir** 'to receive'.

  concernant votre demande de prix concerning your request about (the) price

  le prix est de... is the slightly idiomatic way of saying 'the price is'; **de** stands for 'at the level of / at an amount of'.

  Je prends note, ne quittez pas I'm noting that down, don't hang up (lit. 'don't leave' from **quitter** 'to leave')

- **Voilà je suis à vous** can mean 'OK, I'm all yours' but in a formal situation a better translation would be 'I'm with you'.

  hors taxes before tax (lit. without taxes). An important point to make. **Taxes** usually refers to VAT, which in French is called **Taxe à la Valeur Ajoutée (TVA)**. **Ajouter** is 'to add'.

  vierge. The dictionary translation is 'virgin' but it is used to mean 'without any additions or trimmings'.

- **en ce qui concerne** is another way of saying **concernant**

  J'aurais aimé savoir combien coûtait... Lit. 'I would have liked to know how much ... costed?' He could more simply have said **Je voudrais savoir combien coûte...** 'I would like to know how much ... costs?'

- **un prix forfaitaire** an inclusive price

  Vous descendez à combien? How much will you go down to?

  Il faudrait que vous nous indiquiez vos quantités. M. Leroy does not want to be drawn into detailed negotiations. He says 'You should let us know the numbers you want' (lit. It would be necessary that you to us point out your quantities).

Turn over for the exercises based on this dialogue.

Practise what you have learned

6 If necessary listen to dialogue 3 again, or, if you prefer, read through the transcript. Below are a number of sentences from the dialogues but they have got mixed up. Match the two halves of each sentence together. (Answers on p. 162.)

(a) **Nous nous sommes rencontrés hier**

(b) **Si vous pouviez me donner les frais**

(c) **Concernant votre demande de prix**

(d) **Alors le prix pour 500**

(e) **J'aurais aimé savoir combien coûtait**

(f) **Concernant la sérigraphie**

(g) **Pour 500 produits du même type avec la même marque**

(h) **Il faudrait que vous nous indiquiez vos quantités**

(i) **est de 13 francs 50 hors taxes.**

(ii) **l'inscription d'une marque ou d'un logo.**

(iii) **et nous étudierions un prix par quantité.**

(iv) **à la foire exposition de Rouen.**

(v) **nous avons fait un prix forfaitaire.**

(vi) **pour les pochettes plastiques que nous fabriquons.**

(vii) **de sérigraphie pour ces mêmes quantités cela m'intéresserait beaucoup.**

(viii) **vous descendez à combien là?**

7 On the recording is a discussion similar to the one you have just heard, but with some differences. Listen to it and answer the questions below. (Answers on p. 162.)

(a) What was the telephone message requesting?

(b) What has to be paid on top of the 13 francs 50?

(c) What does **vierge** mean in this context?

(d) Work out the difference in price per unit between purchasing 500 and 1000.

(e) What is the region mentioned?

(f) What do you have to pay 1 franc 60 per unit for?

(g) When will he call back?

(h) And why?

8 In the speaking exercise you'll be invited to negotiate a price for a computer.

Dialogues

4 *A recorded message followed by a discussion about setting up an agency*

Agent Ah, bonjour. J'ai vu votre publicité dans la revue *Moniteur*. Je suis distributeur de produits similaires à ceux que vous fabriquez et je souhaiterais vous représenter en France. Avez-vous déjà un agent? Si oui, pouvez-vous m'en donner l'adresse? Si non, je serais intéressé pour vous représenter dans le quart Nord-Ouest de la France et plus spécialement en Normandie. Pouvez-vous me rappeler au 362 27 55. Je rappelle le numéro 362 27 55, afin que nous établissions un premier contact. Merci, monsieur.

Agent Alors Monsieur Leroux, Vinco 76 a déjà un distributeur en Angleterre?

M. Leroux Pas encore, mais nous envisageons dans le proche avenir d'en avoir un.

Agent Et si ça pouvait se faire, ça m'intéresse personnellement. Quelles seraient vos conditions grosso modo hein?

M. Leroux Nos conditions sont fonction du chiffre d'affaires sur lequel vous vous engagez avec nous par an.

Agent Mettons dans un premier temps un chiffre d'affaires annuel de 200,000 francs.

M. Leroux Pour 200,000 francs nous accordons des remises de 30% sur le tarif public. Le tarif public c'est le tarif disons de facturation au consommateur final.

Agent Oui de combien?

M. Leroux 30%.

Agent Et puis, si j'arrivais mais j'aimerais bien arriver à un million de chiffre d'affaires annuel au bout de mettons 3 ans?

M. Leroux Un million de chiffre d'affaires annuel, actuellement nos conditions, nos remises sont de 45%.

Agent Bon, d'accord.

- **la revue** magazine
- ◆ **le distributeur** distributor
- ◆ **le produit** product
- **déjà** already
- **le quart** quarter (here 'area')
- **le Nord-Ouest** North West
- **le Nord-Est** North East
- **envisager** to envisage
- **personnellement** personally
- **par an** per year
- ◆ **annuel** annual
- **au bout de** at the end of

Turn over for the notes to this dialogue.

J'ai vu votre publicité I saw your publicity. **J'ai vu** (lit. I have seen) comes from **voir** 'to see'.

similaires à ceux que vous fabriquez similar to those that you produce. **Ceux que** (those that) is used because it is referring to the plural of a masculine noun (**le produit**). When referring to the plural of a feminine noun (e.g. **pochettes**) use **celles que**.

Je souhaiterais vous représenter I would like to represent you

Pouvez-vous m'en donner l'adresse? En is a rather difficult word which is often slipped in. It means 'of it/them/him', etc.

plus spécialement en Normandie more precisely/specially in Normandy

Je rappelle le numéro I'll remind you of the number

afin que nous établissions un premier contact in order that we (might) establish an initial contact. **Afin que**, like **pour**, means 'in order to'. Given a choice, use the simpler **pour**.

dans le proche avenir in the near future

d'en avoir un to have one of them. Note **en** meaning 'of them'.

Si ça pouvait se faire is another idiomatic way of using the verb **faire** 'to do'. Here **se faire** has the sense of 'to come about' or 'to materialize'. Lit. 'If that could itself do'.

Quelles seraient vos conditions grosso modo? Lit. 'What they would be your conditions broadly speaking'. **Je vous explique ça grosso modo** means 'I'll explain the broad outlines to you'.

fonction du chiffre d'affaires. Lit. 'a function of the turnover', i.e. 'relate to the turnover'.

sur lequel vous vous engagez avec nous on which you are engaged with us. **S'engager** is 'to be engaged / taken on'.

Mettons dans un premier temps un chiffre d'affaires... Let's put the turnover initially... **Dans un premier temps** 'at first / initially'. Remember the use of the **nous**-form of the verb to say 'let's do something'. 'Let's see' would be **Voyons**; 'Let's go down' **Descendons**, etc.

Nous accordons des remises de 30% We allow/grant a discount of 30%. **Une remise**, 'a discount/reduction', is a useful word.

le tarif de facturation au consommateur the gross price to the consumer. **La facturation**, 'billing', is linked to **la facture** 'the bill/invoice'. So, here, he means a reduction on the gross price to the consumer, **le consommateur**.

Practise what you have learned

9   Here are some key words. Look back at dialogue 4 and find the phrases in which they appear and write them down. (Answers on p. 162.)

(a) _____ **votre publicité** _____

(b) _____ **similaires à ceux que** _____

(c) **Je serais intéressé** _____

(d) _____ **nous envisageons** _____

(e) _____ **fonction du** _____

(f) _____ **dans un premier temps** _____

(g) _____ **le tarif public.**

10   On the recording you will hear a message left on an answer phone. Listen through a couple of times, then, using your pause control, see if you can write it down. (Answer on p. 162.)

Message:

_____

_____

_____

_____

_____

_____

_____

_____

11   In the speaking exercise you're going to enquire about becoming an agent in Canada.

Key words and phrases

un abonné	subscriber
livrer	to deliver
le marché	market
le privé	private sector
retrouver	to find
des renseignements (m.) ⎫ des informations (f.) ⎭	information
une ligne de production/fabrication	production line
l'atelier (m.)	workshop
préciser	to point out
un(e) salarié(e)	salaried person
un cadre	member of management team
des agents de maîtrise	supervisory staff
un ouvrier (spécialisé)	(specialized) worker
croire	to believe/think
permettre	to allow/permit
les matières (f.) premières	raw materials
les matières (f.) fabriquées	finished goods
Quels sont les moyens les plus faciles...?	What are the easiest means...?
le Nord, le Sud	the North, the South
l'Est, l'Ouest	the East, the West
ceux qui viennent de	those who come from
l'hiver, l'été	winter, summer
l'automne, le printemps	autumn (fall), spring
la gare	station
se mettre en rapport/contact avec	to get in touch/contact with
le chemin de fer	railway
nous nous sommes rencontré(e)s	we met
la foire	trade fair
l'exposition (f.)	exhibition
Je suis très intéressé par l'achat...	I'm very interested in buying...
oublier	to forget
donner	to give
les frais	costs/charges
Veuillez me rappeler	Would you be so kind as to call me back
en ce qui concerne / concernant	concerning
Je suis à vous	I'm with you (i.e. paying attention)
hors taxes	before tax
TVA (Taxe à la Valeur Ajoutée)	VAT (Value Added Tax)
Combien coûte...?	How much does...cost?
un prix forfaitaire	inclusive price
descendre le prix	to lower the price
écouter	to listen to
étudier	to study
un ordinateur	computer
la publicité	ad
la facture	bill
le consommateur	consumer
la remise	discount
le distributeur	distributor
le produit	product
annuel	annual

Grammar

Comparatives and superlatives

How to say: 'bigger', 'biggest', 'younger', 'youngest', etc. This is not too much of a problem in French. Look at these examples:

Comparative
Le directeur est plus grand que moi.
The director is bigger (lit. more big) than me.

Le prix final est plus intéressant.
The final price is more interesting.

Cette exposition (f.) est plus internationale.
This/that exhibition is more international.

So, the way to say 'bigger', 'more interesting', 'more international' is simply to put **plus** in front of the adjective.

Superlative
Here are some examples of the superlative:

La plus haute tour du monde.
The highest tower in the world.

L'entreprise la plus dynamique en France.
The most dynamic firm in France.

Les plus grandes remises possibles.
The biggest discounts possible.

So, the superlative is formed by putting the definite article (**le, la, les**) + **plus** in front of the adjective.

In the grammar section in Unit 5 it was noted that some adjectives come in front of the noun and some after it. This rule holds good in the comparative and superlative.

'Better' and 'best'
Incidentally, 'better' as an adjective is **meilleur**, e.g.:

Il est meilleur que moi.
He is better than me.

C'est une meilleure solution.
It is a better solution.

Similarly, 'best' is **le meilleur**:

Le meilleur train de la journée.
The best train of the day.

Les meilleurs agents parlent français.
The best agents speak French.

If you want to use 'better' as an adverb, i.e. to describe the verb and not the noun, use **mieux**:

Pour mieux connaître la situation.
In order to better know the situation.

Ce serait mieux de venir aujourd'hui.
It would be better to come today.

12 Try to translate these phrases. (Answers on p. 162.)

(a) He is younger than me.

Il est plus jeune que moi.

(b) the best solution

(c) the lowest tarif ('low' is **bas**)

(d) the most interesting markets

(e) The turnover is bigger. ('big' is **élevé** here)

(f) the most difficult thing

(g) the best clients

(h) the most specialized market

Read and understand

13 Minitel has established itself as a major force in the world of data presentation and retrieval. Thousands of companies use it to advertise their services and products. **Eurodefi** has a range of language-related services. Read through their product range (opposite) then see if you can fill in the gaps in the English translation. (Answers on p. 162.)

Eurodefi _____(a)_____ you everything about Europe.

- _____(b)_____ the facts and figures on Europe: tax systems, costs of

  social programmes, _____(c)_____ , finance...

- _____(d)_____ translations using Minitel (English). Response in less

  than half _____(e)_____

- _____(f)_____ opportunities. Ads for agents, for _____(g)_____ and
  for partners.

- Specialist _____(h)_____

- Linguistic service in 8 _____(i)_____

14 In a completely different sector, this is how P&O try to persuade French people to use their ships to cross over to Britain. Read through the text (opposite), then answer the questions below. (Answers on p. 162.)

(a) What do P&O no longer have to prove?

(b) The French word for 'the Channel' is

(c) Their ships are spacious, comfortable and

(d) How are their prices described?

(e) On what two things are there no restrictions?

(f) Where is lead-free petrol (gasoline) available?

(g) What do the French and Belgium ports have?

(h) Who is transported by Jetfoil?

(i) What sort of connections are there by train for London?

Foreign exchange

Studying the list of currencies available at the Banque de France is a good way of learning the adjectives relating to the major countries. **Billets** are 'bank notes' and **chèques de voyage** 'travellers' cheques'.

BANQUE DE FRANCE

DIEPPE

LES OPÉRATIONS DE CHANGE AUX MEILLEURES CONDITIONS SANS COMMISSION DE GUICHET

Valeurs courantes disponibles sur place :

BILLETS

BILLETS ÉTRANGERS :

DOLLAR U. S.	MARK ALLEMAND	FRANC BELGE
LIVRE STERLING	FRANC SUISSE	DOLLAR CANADIEN
LIVRE DE JERSEY	FLORIN NÉERLANDAIS	ESCUDO PORTUGAIS
LIVRE DE GUERNESEY	PESETA ESPAGNOLE	SCHILLING AUTRICHIEN
LIVRE IRLANDAISES	LIRE ITALIENNE	DRACHME GREC

BILLETS DE LA ZONE FRANC :

FRANC C. F. A. (Afrique centrale)
FRANC C. F. A. (Afrique de l'Ouest)
FRANC C. F. A. (Polynésie)

Sur commande, nous pouvons également vous approvisionner en quelques jours dans la plupart des autres monnaies étrangères.

CHÈQUES DE VOYAGE

FRANC FRANÇAIS	PESETA ESPAGNOLE	FRANC SUISSE
DOLLAR U. S.	LIVRE STERLING	DOLLAR CANADIEN
MARK ALLEMAND		

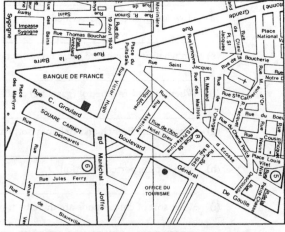

BANQUE DE FRANCE - 4, rue C. Groulard à DIEPPE
☎ 35 82 83 84
Guichets ouverts du mardi au samedi
de 8 h. 45 à 11 h. 55 et de 13 h. 30 à 15 h. 45

Published with special permission from the Bank of France

Did you know?

Money, banking and finance in France

The French currency is the franc. It is monitored and regulated by **la Banque de France** (Central Bank). France belongs to the European Monetary System, which regulates the rates of most EC countries within fixed limits and contributes to currency stabilization.

The **franc zone** is another monetary system to which France belongs. It was created in 1945 and includes the Overseas Departments and Territories, as well as thirteen African countries (former colonies). Currencies are exchanged on a fixed basis within this zone and transfers are facilitated.

The banking system is under the supervision of **la Banque de France**, which has the usual central banking functions and plays an important role in defining monetary and credit policies. It issues bank notes and manages France's gold and foreign-currency reserves. It acts as the intermediary between the Ministry of Finance and the banks, regulating and supervising the latter. **La Banque de France** is the banker's bank, providing clearing and collection services. Examinations of the banks are carried out by **la Commission Bancaire**, whose examiners are representatives of **la Banque de France** and are entitled to have access to all relevant books and records. Application to establish a bank must be made to the **Comité des Etablissements de Crédit** through the **Association Française des Banques**, the professional association of commercial banks.

The commercial banking sector ranges from the large commercial banks with nationwide branch networks to small, specialist institutions. The major commercial banks are the **Banque Nationale de Paris**, the **Crédit Lyonnais**, and the **Société Générale**. All three have subsidiaries in consumer credit, leasing, factoring, venture capital and merchant banking. In addition, the mutual agricultural credit banks such as **Crédit Agricole** have expanded rapidly and compete with the big commercial banks. Originally, **Crédit Agricole** was established solely for farmers and rural communities. Since 1982, it has been allowed to operate as a normal retail bank and lends to companies in any sector.

The commercial banking sector also includes banks such as:

- **le Crédit Mutuel,** which to some extent offers a similar service to the **Crédit Agricole**

- **la Banque Populaire**, another co-operative mutual bank specializing in small and medium-sized industries, craftsmen and professionals

- **le Crédit Foncier de France**, the main source of mortgages in France, particularly for commercial loans

- **la Banque Française du Commerce Extérieur**, useful for overseas trading activities

There are also savings banks, which comprise essentially the Post Office Savings Bank and **les Caisses d'Epargne**. In addition, there are about 150 foreign-owned banks operating in France.

Your turn to speak

15 For the final speaking exercise compose an answer-phone message explaining that you would like to become the agent for a French firm. Try to bring in how you know there might be a position free, which part of the country you want to represent, perhaps even why the French firm should be interested in you. End the message by asking the person you are trying to contact to call you back. When you've thought up a message and *spoken it out aloud*, switch on and see what Caroline said.

Answers

Practise what you have learned

Exercise 1   (a) ABS fabrique et commercialise beaucoup de produits   (b) Est-ce que vous livrez à vos clients?   (c) Il n'y a aucun autre produit sur le marché   (d) Pourriez-vous me donner quelques renseignements/informations sur votre société?   (e) Nous avons deux lignes de fabrication   (f) Je tiens à vous préciser que nous avons 700 salariés   (g) Je connais les ingénieurs mieux que les agents administratifs

Exercise 2   (a) tiens à   (b) représentez   (c) pourriez   (d) entreprise   (e) chez   (f) spécialisée   (g) établissement   (h) fabrique   (i) c'est-à-dire   (j) emploie   (k) professionnelles   (l) cadres

Exercise 4   (a) arrivée   (b) zone   (c) cœur   (d) extrémités   (e) hiver   (f) gare   (g) ferroviaire

Exercise 5   (a) iii   (b) iv   (c) i   (d) iv   (e) ii

Exercise 6   (a) iv   (b) vii   (c) vi   (d) i   (e) ii   (f) v   (g) viii   (h) iii

Exercise 7   (a) the price of plastic folders   (b) tax (TVA)   (c) without publicity   (d) 1 franc 70   (e) the Paris region   (f) silk-screen printing   (g) next week   (h) to arrange a meeting

Exercise 9   (a) J'ai vu votre publicité dans la revue *Moniteur*   (b) Je suis distributeur de produits similaires à ceux que vous fabriquez   (c) Je serais intéressé pour vous représenter dans le quart Nord-Ouest de la France   (d) Pas encore, mais nous envisageons dans le proche avenir d'en avoir un   (e) Nos conditions sont fonction du chiffre d'affaires   (f) Mettons dans un premier temps un chiffre d'affaires annuel de 200,000 francs   (g) Pour 200,000 francs nous accordons des remises de 30% sur le tarif public

Exercise 10   Bonjour. J'ai vu votre publicité dans le journal. Je suis un distributeur de produits similaires à ceux que vous fabriquez. Je souhaiterais vous représenter aux Etats-Unis, plus spécialement dans le Sud. Si vous n'avez pas déjà un distributeur, pouvez-vous me rappeler au 89 25 86 10. Je voudrais bien établir contact. Merci et au revoir.

Grammar

Exercise 12   (a) Il est plus jeune que moi   (b) la meilleure solution   (c) le tarif le plus bas   (d) les marchés les plus intéressants   (e) Le chiffre d'affaires est plus élevé   (f) la chose la plus difficile   (g) les meilleurs clients   (h) le marché le plus spécialisé

Read and understand

Exercise 13   (a) tells (b) all (c) energy (d) rapid (e) a day (f) business (g) suppliers (h) dictionaries (i) languages

Exercise 14   (a) their reputation   (b) la Manche   (c) have the most up-to-date equipment   (d) competitive (**intéressants**)   (e) weight of baggage and the number of souvenirs brought back   (f) throughout the country (i.e. Britain)   (g) excellent rail links   (h) pedestrians   (i) immediate

You will learn

● how to bargain and negotiate
● how to discuss prices politely
● the language of business plans
 and you will be given information about business structures in
 France

Study guide

To help you keep a check on your progress, you could mark off the
various tasks as you complete them.

Dialogue 1 + Practise what you have learned

Dialogue 2 + Practise what you have learned

Dialogue 3 + Practise what you have learned

Dialogue 4 + Practise what you have learned

Ensure you know the **Key words and phrases**

Study the **Grammar** section

Do the exercises in **Read and understand**

Did you know? Forms of business structure in France

Your turn to speak

Dialogues

1   *Arrangements for a business trip to the town of Tours*

Organizer   M. Liçois, bonjour. Je suis heureux de vous retrouver puisque vous représentez Dieppe Voyage. Nous avons déjà travaillé ensemble et nous en étions très satisfaits. Alors cette fois-ci, comme je vous l'avais écrit dans ma dernière lettre, nous allons donc envoyer une vingtaine de personnes à Tours.

M. Liçois   C'est ça. Mardi prochain.

Organizer   Mardi prochain c'est un...

M. Liçois   C'est un groupe, la délégation d'industriels du Middlesex.

Organizer   Tout à fait, tout à fait. Ces gens arrivent au ferry de 15 heures à Dieppe.

M. Liçois   15 heures direction Tours.

Organizer   Oui.

M. Liçois   Où vous souhaitez un hébergement?

Organizer   Oui.

M. Liçois   Et donc je vais m'occuper de ça pour vous, et retour le lendemain pour le ferry de minuit.

Organizer   C'est ça, c'est ça.

M. Liçois   Donc je vous ai fait la cotation, enfin le devis pour l'autocar. Donc je vous donne comme ça oralement et si vous le souhaitez, je peux vous le donner, faire ça par écrit.

Organizer   Ah oui, j'aimerais bien que vous nous confirmiez tout ça par écrit. Bien une facture pro-forma peut-être?

M. Liçois   Très bien. Mais, je vais vous envoyer ça. Donc, le prix je l'ai établi à 5200 francs sur lesquels je vous ai fait une ristourne de 10% puisque nous avons déjà travaillé ensemble.

puisque since/because		**les gens** people	
ensemble together		**direction Tours** heading for Tours	
◆ **dernier (dernière)** last		**le retour** return	
◆ **la lettre** letter		**C'est ça** That's correct	
◆ **envoyer** to send		◆ **le devis** estimate	
◆ **prochain** next		**l'autocar (le car)** coach (bus)	
◆ **un industriel** industrialist		**donner** to give	

Je suis heureux de vous retrouver 'I'm happy to see you again' (lit. to find you again)

Nous en étions très satisfaits We were very satisfied. **En** meaning 'with it' (i.e. our previous work together) crops up again here.

cette fois-ci. The **ci** added to the noun just gives emphasis to 'this'. 'This plan' would be **ce plan-ci**. Similarly, if you add **-là** it conveys the idea of 'that'. 'That time' **cette fois-là**; 'that plan' **ce plan-là**.

Où vous souhaitez un hébergement? Where you are wanting accommodation? **Héberger** is one verb for 'to accommodate'.

Donc je vais m'occuper de ça pour vous So, I'll look after that for you. The verb **s'occuper de** means 'to take care of something / to get on with something'. It is very useful. **Il s'occupe de l'administration** means 'He looks after the administration'.

Je vous ai fait la cotation I've prepared (lit. done) the quotation for you

Je peux vous faire ça par écrit I can do it for you in writing. From **écrire** 'to write'.

j'aimerais bien que vous nous confirmiez. Lit. 'I would very much like that you to us confirm'. **Confirmer** is 'to confirm'.

Une facture pro-forma peut-être? A pro-forma invoice perhaps? **Une facture** 'a bill'.

le prix, je l'ai établi... the price, I have established it... **Etablir** is 'to establish'.

sur lesquels je vous ai fait une ristourne de 10% on which I have made you a discount of 10%. **Sur lesquels** because the 'on which' is referring back to francs (masculine plural).

Practise what you have learned

1 Using the transcript and the notes, translate the following short sentences into French. (Answers on p. 180.)

(a) I am happy to work together.

(b) We are satisfied by your last letter.

(c) The industrialists are arriving next Wednesday.

(d) We are wanting to find accommodation in Dieppe.

(e) She looks after the quotations.

(f) Can you confirm in writing?

(g) I'm going to send you the bill.

2 On the recording is a conversation about a proposed visit to England by a group from a French Chamber of Commerce. Listen through a couple of times and then answer the following questions in English.
(Answers on p. 180.)

(a) Who gave her blessing to the visit?

(b) Is it the first time they have worked together?

(c) When are they arriving in England and what day of the week are they returning? _78_ _13h_ _11/3_

(d) When will she make the arrangements? _Today_

(e) There will be quite a lot of people in the group. What does the organizer want from the hotel? _Discount 10 - 15%_

(f) From whom will she get quotations? _2 - 3 Comp_

(g) In what form should all the details be presented? _In writing._

(h) Where will the invoice be sent?

3 Your turn to take part in a discussion arranging a visit to your company. Switch on when you're ready.

Dialogues

2 *Arranging a reception for a visiting delegation*

Organizer	Monsieur Deligne bonjour.
M. Deligne	Bonjour monsieur.
Organizer	Ecoutez, j'ai eu un contact avec mes amis anglais qui doivent venir là, la semaine prochaine.
M. Deligne	Oui.
Organizer	Et au lieu de faire un apéritif un soir, pourriez-vous leur proposer une dégustation de vin?
M. Deligne	Ah tout à fait monsieur, c'est tout à fait dans mes coordonnées puisque j'étais moi-même professeur d'oenologie. On va vous faire si vous voulez une dégustation à l'aveugle; vous proposer trois vins blancs et trois vins rouges au choix et on essaiera ensemble de retrouver ces vins avec un petit commentaire technique sur l'oenologie.
Organizer	Et nous continuerons le repas après.
M. Deligne	Et par la suite le repas du soir.
Organizer	Ce sera très intéressant ça.
M. Deligne	Oui tout à fait, tout à fait.
Organizer	Parfait.
M. Deligne	Si ça vous convient monsieur vous me dîtes, vous me précisez la date et on vous prépare cela.
Organizer	Mercredi prochain.
M. Deligne	Mercredi prochain d'accord monsieur.

blanc	white	**ce sera**	it will be
rouge	red	**parfait**	perfect
après	after(wards)		

▸ **Ecoutez** Listen! It sounds less abrupt in French than in English.

J'ai eu un contact avec... I have had contact with... **Eu** is the irregular past from **avoir**.

▸ **au lieu de faire un apéritif** instead of offering (lit. doing) an aperitif. **Au lieu de** is the usual way of saying 'instead of', e.g. **au lieu de téléphoner, au lieu de moi**, etc.

▸ **Pourriez-vous leur proposer une dégustation de vin?** The words **proposer** and **dégustation de vin** (wine tasting) are often found together. **Déguster** is the rather inelegant verb for 'to taste'. **Voulez-vous déguster?** means 'Do you want to taste? (not disgust!). **Leur**, remember, means 'to them'.

C'est dans mes coordonnées. Normally **coordonnées** is associated with 'whereabouts', e.g. **Pouvez-vous me donner vos coordonnées?** 'Can you tell me how to get in touch with you?' Here the organizer is using it idiomatically to mean that it's within his competence.

l'oenologie oenology (the study of wine). Important and much respected in France.

▸ **j'étais professeur** I was a teacher. When talking about professions, you don't need 'a' (**un/une**). 'I'm a doctor', for example, is **Je suis médecin**.

une dégustation à l'aveugle a blind tasting. **Aveugle** means 'blind'.

trois vins au choix. You often find **au choix** on signs in shops, meaning you can choose from a selection of what is on offer. **Le choix** is 'the choice'.

▸ **On essaiera ensemble** We will try together. **Essaiera** is the (slightly irregular) future form from **essayer** 'to try'. See p. 214 for information on the future tense.

un commentaire technique a technical commentary

Nous continuerons le repas We will continue the meal

par la suite is a slightly formal way of saying 'next' or 'then'. More usual is **puis** or **ensuite**.

Vous me précisez la date. The verb **préciser** means 'to confirm' or 'to give'.

Practise what you have learned

4 In the word grid below there are thirteen words from the dialogue. See if you can spot them, then check the context in which each word appears. Some are written horizontally, some vertically. (Answers on p. 180.)

_____   _____   _____

_____   _____   _____

_____   _____   _____

_____

e	u	c	v	a	ç	u	u	t
p	r	o	c	h	a	i	n	e
u	a	n	b	f	g	d	e	o
i	d	t	r	è	s	r	d	o
s	n	a	v	e	u	g	l	e
q	u	c	i	p	x	e	h	i
u	k	t	n	o	u	s	d	a
e	l	s	s	o	i	r	t	

5 Match up the phrases in the jumbled list below with the gaps in the sentences. When you have done that, say the completed sentences out loud, then switch on the recording to see if you got the gaps correctly filled and to check on your pronunciation.

(a) **Nous ne pouvons décider qu'après leur arrivée** _____

(b) _____ **m'occuper toute la journée de l'administration, je voudrais visiter nos partenaires en France.**

(c) **Je préfère savoir ce que je vais boire au lieu de participer à**

_____

(d) **J'ai trouvé**_____ **très utile et intéressant.**

(e) _____ **je vais arriver lundi le 16 et repartir jeudi le 19.**

(f) **Pouvez-vous me** _____ **les détails de la cotation que vous m'avez envoyée avant-hier?.**

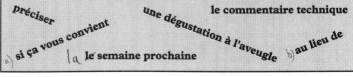

préciser   une dégustation à l'aveugle   le commentaire technique

si ça vous convient   la le semaine prochaine   b) au lieu de

Dialogues

3 *M. Pasquier, the owner of a construction company, explains how he can help with a client's housing problem*

Client Bon bref, j'ai cette maison où il n'y a pas de toilettes ni dedans ni dehors. Le jardin est dans un triste état et il n'y a pas de chemin d'accès. Monsieur Pasquier que pouvez-vous faire pour moi?

M. Pasquier Nous pouvons vous faire tout ce qui est installation sanitaire à l'extérieur de la maison. C'est-à-dire le raccordement de votre maison au réseau ou la construction d'une fosse septique ou d'une mini-station d'épuration. Pour ce qui est du jardin nous pouvons vous apporter de la terre végétale, modeler le terrain.

Client Oui.

M. Pasquier Vous faire les plantations et l'engazonnement.

Client Bon, ben, d'accord. Mais alors il me faudrait un devis précis monsieur.

M. Pasquier Alors pour un devis précis il aurait fallu qu'on se rencontre sur le terrain. Votre jour sera le mien.

les toilettes (f.)	toilet	♦ **triste**	sad
l'état (m.)	state	**le chemin d'accès**	drive (lit. way of access)
sanitaire	sanitary	♦ **la maison**	house

♦ **ni dedans ni dehors** neither inside nor outside. **Ne...ni...ni...** is 'neither...nor...' **J'ai n'ai ni argent ni propriété** 'I have neither money nor property'.

Que pouvez-vous faire pour moi? What can you do for me?

nous pouvons vous faire is yet another example of an idiom with **faire**. Here it means 'we can do for you'.

tout ce qui est everything which is (relates to)

c'est-à-dire that is to say. A useful phrase.

le raccordement au réseau the connection to the network. **Réseau** is the general word for 'network', here meaning 'mains drainage'.

la construction d'une fosse septique the construction of a septic tank. **La fosse** is also the general word for 'pit'.

une mini-station d'épuration a small purifying unit. **Mini** can be put before a lot of nouns and it is not affected by the gender of the noun, e.g. **un mini-bar, une mini-voiture**, etc.

pour ce qui est du jardin as for the garden (lit. for that which is of the garden)

Nous pouvons vous apporter de la terre végétale We can bring you some earth rich in compost. **La terre** can mean 'ground' in general (**sur la terre** 'on the ground') or, as here, it can mean 'earth'. It also means 'earth' as opposed to **la lune** 'moon'.

(Nous pouvons vous) modeler le terrain (We can) landscape (lit. model) the area (for you). **Le terrain** is linked to the English word *terrain* and it is used in much the same way.

vous faire les plantations et l'engazonnement. You get the infinitive **faire** here because **nous pouvons** is understood. 'We can plant and turf the area for you'. **Le gazon** means 'turf', so **engazonnement** conveys the idea of 'turfing'.

Il me faudrait un devis précis I'd have to have a precise estimate

Il aurait fallu qu'on se rencontre sur le terrain. Don't worry about this – it's a grammatical minefield. Just accept that it means 'We would have to meet on site'. You use ♦ **se rencontrer** when there is no direct object; **rencontrer** alone is used when there is a direct object, e.g. **Je vais rencontrer M. Rambaut** 'I'm going to meet M. Rambaut'.

Votre jour sera le mien is a nice way of saying 'at your convenience' (lit. your day will be mine).

Practise what you have learned

6 Use the clues below to locate the appropriate word or phrase in the dialogue. (Answers on p. 180.)

(a) **On y habite.** _____

(b) **le contraire de dedans** _____

(c) **On y trouve des plantes et des fleurs.** _____

(d) **le contraire de heureux** _____

(e) **SNCF opère un** _____ **ferroviaire.**

(f) **un synonyme pour en dehors** _____

(g) **Avant de payer il vous faut un** _____

(h) **Souvent on va au bar pour** _____ **les gens.**

7 Listen now to a further stage in the bargaining between M. Pasquier and his client. They are discussing the estimate for laying the drive. You are not expected to understand every word, but see if you can get the gist and answer the following questions in English. (Answers on p. 180.)

(a) How much is the estimate for?

17,000. FF.

(b) Does the client think it is cheap or expensive?

(c) Is it M. Pasquier's final price?

No

(d) The price depends on the 'look', what you want to do with your property and on...?

Quality of Mats

(e) Does M. Pasquier have more expensive materials in his range (**sa gamme**)?

(f) What does the client decide to do?

Think about it.

(g) What does M. Pasquier offer to do if a different process is used?

quote again

8 Now it's your turn to take part in a discussion with a builder. Switch on the recording when you're ready.

Dialogues

4 *A businesswoman and a student discuss how to develop a business plan*

Student Alors, il faut connaître les marchés sur lesquels l'entreprise se situe?

Businesswoman Exactement. Il faut estimer le volume de ventes que l'on peut atteindre. On doit se demander qui sont les utilisateurs du produit – industriels, commerçants, collectivités ou gens particuliers? Puis, on doit considérer quelles évolutions du marché sont à prévoir dans les cinq années prochaines et comment on peut inciter les clients à acheter.

Student C'est difficile à établir des statistiques?

Businesswoman C'est difficile bien sûr, mais important. Vous devez vous demander quelles sont vos sources d'information; études de marché, contacts avec clients, organisations professionnelles, concurrents, fournisseurs, etc.

Student On doit, je suppose, étudier les sources d'approvisionnement?

Businesswoman Oui, les matières premières, les produits finis, les prix, la répartition géographique, les éventuelles contraintes politiques ou économiques. Tout ça fait partie de la connaissance nécessaire.

Student Et on doit analyser la concurrence?

Businesswoman Vous devez examiner vos principaux concurrents du point de vue des caractéristiques de leurs produits, du chiffre d'affaires et de leurs techniques de vente. C'est important aussi à considérer leurs avantages et leurs faiblesses. Est-ce qu'ils se comportent d'une façon aggressive ou accommodante? Est-ce que le matériel qu'ils fabriquent est de haute qualité? Est-ce qu'ils ont une bonne réputation?

Student Mmm. Je vous remercie beaucoup. Il faut que je refléchisse un peu sur tous ces points. Merci.

il faut it is necessary	◆ **fournir** to supply
◆ **estimer** to estimate/calculate	◆ **le fournisseur** supplier
◆ **la vente** sale	**l'approvisionnement** (m.) supply
◆ **atteindre** to reach/achieve	**les matières premières**
◆ **l'utilisateur** user	raw materials
un commerçant merchant/	**les produits finis** finished products
trader/shopkeeper	**la répartition** distribution
les collectivités conglomerates /	**la contrainte** constraint
large firms	◆ **la faiblesse** weakness
les gens particuliers individuals	**accommodant** accommodating

les marchés sur lesquels l'entreprise se situe the markets in which the firm is active (lit. the markets on which the firm situates itself)

◆ **on doit se demander** you have to ask yourself. **Demander** means 'to ask'. **Une demande** is 'a request' (*not* a demand).

Quelles évolutions du marché sont à prévoir? What developments in the market can be expected (lit. are to foresee)? **Prévoir** 'to foresee'.

inciter les clients à acheter to persuade (lit. incite) clients to buy

études de marché market surveys. From **étudier** 'to study'.

◆ **les concurrents** the competitors. An important word, as is **la concurrence** 'competition'.

◆ **les eventuelles contraintes** the possible constraints. **Eventuel(le/s)** does *not* mean
◆ 'eventual' but rather 'possible'. **Une éventuelle baisse des taux d'intérêt** is 'a possible reduction in interest rates'. **Le taux d'intérêt** is 'the interest rate'.

Est-ce qu'ils se comportent d'une façon aggressive? Do they behave aggressively?

Il faut que je refléchisse... I'll have to think about... **Refléchir** 'to reflect / think about'.

Practise what you have learned

9 List all the specifically business words in the dialogue and make sure you know what they mean. (A guide list is provided in the answers on p. 180.)

_____	_____
_____	_____
_____	_____
_____	_____
_____	_____
_____	_____
_____	_____
_____	

10 On the recording you will hear a number of sentences. Translate them into English. (Answers on p. 180.)

(a) _____

(b) _____

(c) _____

(d) _____

(e) _____

(f) _____

(g) _____

CHAMBRE
DE
COMMERCE
ET
D'INDUSTRIE

SECRETARIAT
COMPTABILITE
RELATIONS PUBLIQUES
COMMERCE EXTERIEUR

Key words and phrases

heureux (heureuse)	happy
satisfait	satisfied
ensemble	together
dernier (dernière)	last
la lettre	letter
envoyer	to send
prochain	next
un industriel	industrialist
un commerçant	merchant/trader/shopkeeper
s'occuper de	to look after / get on with
la cotation	quotation
le devis	estimate
par écrit	in writing
une facture	bill
écouter	to listen to
au lieu de	instead of
déguster	to taste/sample
essayer	to try
je suis...	I'm ...
médecin	a doctor
professeur	a teacher
industriel	an industrialist
au choix	your choice
la maison	house
ni dedans ni dehors	neither inside nor outside
triste	sad
rencontrer	to meet
estimer	to estimate/calculate
le volume de ventes	volume of sales
atteindre	to reach/achieve
l'utilisateur	the user
demander	to request / ask for
une étude de marché	market survey
le concurrent	competitor
la concurrence	competition
le fournisseur	supplier
fournir	to supply
les éventuelles contraintes (f.)	possible constraints
la faiblesse	weakness
se comporter	to behave (oneself)
par avion	by plane
la gamme	the product range

Grammar

The past tense

In this unit and in Unit 11, the grammar section will focus primarily on the past tense.

In English, two ways of expressing the past are to say, for example, *I have eaten* or *I ate; he has written* or *he wrote*. The past tense with *have/has*, etc. is called the perfect tense and it is this form that is most useful in oral communication. (For the other sort of past tense, the imperfect, see the grammar section in Unit 11.) As in English, the perfect tense in French is usually formed by taking 'to have', **avoir**, and adding the past participle of the main verb. Right through the course examples of the past have cropped up. Way back in Unit 1 we had **Vous avez fait bon voyage?** Other examples are **J'ai quitté Londres ce matin, Elle m'a demandé** (Unit 5); **Je n'ai pas évalué ce genre de choses** (Unit 6). There are many other examples that you can find if you flick back through the dialogues.

Most French verbs follow the pattern of these examples. To form the past tense, you use **avoir** plus the main verb ending in **-é**.

j'ai mangé	I have eaten
il a acheté	he has bought
nous avons commencé	we have begun
ils ont parlé	they have spoken

The **-é** ending is associated with verbs whose infinitives end in **-er**. This is the largest group, but some end in **-ir** (e.g. **finir, servir**). In this case the ending in the past tense is **-i** (e.g. **j'ai fini, j'ai servi**). The other group of verbs comprises those ending in **-re** (e.g. **vendre, répondre**). With **-re** verbs the ending in the past tense is **-u** (e.g. **j'ai vendu, j'ai répondu**).

It would be nice if that were the end of the story. Unfortunately it isn't. There are quite a lot of irregular past tenses that you do need to know because they are of fairly common verbs. Here are some of the main irregular past tenses you have come across:

j'ai fait	**faire** to do
j'ai dit	**dire** to say
j'ai écrit	**écrire** to write
j'ai mis	**mettre** to put
j'ai pris	**prendre** to take
j'ai compris	**comprendre** to understand
j'ai vu	**voir** to see
j'ai bu	**boire** to drink
j'ai reçu	**recevoir** to receive
j'ai ouvert	**ouvrir** to open
j'ai été	**être** to be
j'ai eu	**avoir** to have

Now try the exercise on the next page.

11 When you have understood the basic principles outlined on the previous page, have a go at translating the sentences below. (Answers on p. 180.)

(a) He has worked in France. (**travailler**)

_____

(b) I have spoken to his secretary. (**parler**)

_____

(c) We have finished the market survey. (**finir**)

_____

(d) I have sent a fax to the USA. (**envoyer**)

_____

(e) Have you received the letter? (**recevoir**)

_____

(f) They have said nothing. (**dire**)

_____

(g) I have done the plan. (**faire**)

_____

(h) Have you seen the products? (**voir**)

_____

Well that's enough for this unit. More on the past tense in Unit 11.

VINCO 76

Z.I. Louis Delaporte
Zone Marron
76370 Rouxmesnil-Bouteilles
Adresse Postale : BP 531
76370 Neuville-lès-Dieppe
Tél. 35 82 72 50
Télécopieur 35 82 73 32

BON DE COMMANDE 13896

Nom	Commande
Adresse : N° Rue	Date
Localité	Nom représentant
	Code représentant
Lieu de livraison	Conditions de paiement
	Banque
	Adresse banque
Date de livraison souhaitée	Echéance
Téléphone	Acompte C.C.P. Caisse
	Chèque N°

A rappeler dans la correspondance

Read and understand

12 Vinco is a large office furniture company which won the contract to supply the Winter Olympic Games in Albertville in 1992. This is how they introduce themselves in their brochure. Read it through then find the French equivalent of the English phrases below. (Answers on p. 180.)

Pour répondre à l'énorme marché des jeux olympiques d'hiver à Albertville en 1992, VINCO s'est engagé à livrer et installer plus de 10 000 bureaux sur les sites de Courchevel, Val d'Isère, Tignes, Les Arcs, La Plagne, Méribel, Les Ménuires, Les Saisies, et Pralognan en moins de 2 semaines.

Pour réaliser cette véritable performance olympique VINCO a conçu une ligne de mobilier à montage instantané.

Ces bureaux, tables, sièges, rangements, lampes aux lignes olympiques sont disponibles chez tous les concessionnaires VINCO.

Dans les années 80, pour avoir un vrai bureau il fallait une clé de 8, un tournevis, parfois une perceuse.

Il fallait aussi beaucoup de temps pour le montage et presque autant pour le démontage quand on déménageait...

Sans compter la perspective de tout recommencer la fois suivante.

Avec le mobilier J.O. on peut changer d'adresse ou seulement d'étage.

On peut même emporter son bureau chez soi.

ALBERTVILLE 92
FOURNISSEUR OFFICIEL

(a) to meet the needs of the enormous market _____

(b) to deliver and install _____

(c) to achieve this olympic performance _____

(d) Vinco has conceived/developed _____

(e) that can be assembled immediately _____

(f) these offices are available _____

And, should you want to order, you will need to complete Vinco's order form, a **bon de commande** (opposite). **Date de livraison souhaitée** is 'delivery date requested'; **échéance** 'expiry date'; **prévue** 'expected (foreseen)'; **cette case** 'this box'; **montant** 'total'.

13 In France a lot of money is invested in training. Here's how **Campus**, a national organization set up to help young graduates, describes its programme. Read it through then see if you can answer the questions. (Answers on p. 180.)

You may find the following definitions helpful: **préalable** 'preliminary'; **des fiches d'information** 'information sheets'; **les métiers** 'the professions'; **ces outils** 'the tools'; **PME** 'small or medium-sized enterprises (SME)'; **vos atouts** lit. 'your trump cards / your plus points'.

CAMPUS est la première structure nationale permanente qui organise le contact direct entre ENTREPRISES et JEUNES DIPLÔMÉS de l'enseignement supérieur.

L'efficacité du système réside dans une phase préalable, claire et objective, d'information sur les métiers.

Vous êtes Jeune Diplômé (Bac + 4).
Voici comment CAMPUS vous aide à préparer votre entrée dans le monde du travail :

1ʳᵉ étape : Une information objective.
En province ou à Paris, dans les permanences CAMPUS, vous pouvez consulter des fiches d'information très précises sur les grandes fonctions qui structurent l'entreprise et sur les métiers qui s'offrent à vous.

2ᵉ étape : La définition de votre projet professionnel.
Grâce à ces outils d'autodocumentation et à une session collective d'accompagnement, vous allez, petit à petit, vous situer dans un environnement professionnel puis définir et argumenter avec précision vos ambitions : "Ingénieur commercial dans une multinationale de l'agro-alimentaire ou cadre comptable dans une PME toulousaine"?...

3ᵉ étape : La validation de votre projet.
Celle-ci est réalisée par un consultant CAMPUS. Elle consiste à vérifier votre compréhension du métier choisi et la cohérence entre votre projet, vos atouts et les attentes des entreprises pour ce type de fonction. Cette validation représente, pour les entreprises CAMPUS, la garantie de votre motivation et du sérieux de votre démarche.

4ᵉ étape : Le contact avec les entreprises.
Si votre projet est validé et si vous ressentez le besoin d'une aide supplémentaire, CAMPUS peut vous aider à rencontrer des entreprises.

(a) What sort of structure is Campus?

(b) What is the essence of the first phase?

(c) What sort of information sheets are available?

(d) What is the essence of the second stage?

(e) What are the two examples of professions?

(f) Who evaluates your project?

(g) Why do the firms in the Campus scheme welcome the evaluation?

(h) What can Campus do for you in the fourth phase?

The Yellow Pages

Les Pages Jaunes is a very informative publication produced by France Télécom. In addition to the usual facts, figures and addresses, it publishes profiles of the major towns in France. Here's what it says about Le Havre:

Le Havre : premier port de conteneurs

Deuxième port français (53 millions de tonnes), Le Havre est devenu un grand port industriel. Bien que subissant le contrecoup de la politique nucléaire, Le Havre assure encore 40% des approvisionnements énergétiques de la France (pétrole, terminal d'Antifer, charbon).

La situation géographique, de mieux en mieux desservie par un réseau d'infrastructures nouvelles (autoroutes, pont de Normandie) le désigne comme un grand pôle européen du trafic de conteneurs (premier port français – près de 9 Mt, soit 900 000 conteneurs manutentionnés).

Le Havre contribue largement au commerce international de la France en s'appuyant sur des outils comme le centre de commerce international.

Ville portuaire, Le Havre a beaucoup développé, depuis 1930, sa fonction industrielle dans trois directions :

- la transformation des produits importés : pétrole, nickel, engrais...;
- l'industrie de main-d'œuvre : construction automobile (RNU Renault);
- l'industrie liée au port : réparation, construction navale, chaudronnerie, levage.

Sous-préfecture, sa fonction tertiaire est principalement orientée vers les transports et le négoce.

La création de l'université en 1984 a renforcé le pôle tertiaire havrais.

Did you know?

Forms of business structure in France

There are three basic forms of legal structure in French business: (i) **les Sociétés de Capitaux** (joint stock companies), which include the **Société Anonyme**, the **Société à Responsabilité Limitée** and the **Société en Commandité par Actions**; (ii) **les Sociétés de Personnes** (unlimited liability), which include the **Société en Nom Collectif** and the **Société Civile**; and (iii) other structures such as **le Groupement d'Intérêt Economique** (Economic Interest Group) and its European version, **le Groupement Européen d'Intérêt Economique**.

1 **La Société Anonyme (SA)** is very much like a corporation. The **SA** is set up with a minimum of seven shareholders. A non-French national can be part of an **SA** without holding a foreign trader's permit (**la carte de commerçant étranger**). The **SA** can be managed by either a board of between 3 and 12 directors (**le conseil d'administration**), headed by a chairman (**le président directeur général**), or alternatively, it may have a supervisory board (**le conseil de surveillance**) and an executive committee or a directorate (**le directoire**). Foreigners can be appointed directors. However, in certain specific activities such as banking, French law prohibits the appointment of foreign directors unless they are EC nationals or their appointment is specially authorized by the French authorities.

2 **La Société à Responsabilité Limitée (SARL)** is like a limited liability company. The **SARL** is the form of company most appropriate for small and medium-sized enterprises. It must have at least 2 and not more than 50 shareholders. The capital requirements are FF 50,000, compared with FF 250,000 for an **SA**. A **SARL** cannot be quoted on the stock market and its shares are not negotiable. Any transfer of shares must be by written agreement. This requires a registration fee of 4.8% of the price paid. There is no board of directors in a **SARL**. It is instead managed by one of several managing directors, appointed by an ordinary shareholders' meeting. A non-French national can be part of a **SARL** without holding a foreign trader's permit. However, a non-EC national must hold a foreign trader's permit to be designated as managing director.

3 **La Société en Commandité par Actions (SCA)** is like a limited partnership with shares. It is a form of commercial company which is established with two separate categories of partners: the general partners (**les commandités**) and the limited partners (**les commanditaires**). The **SCA** requires a minimum of 4 partners who can either be private individuals or legal entities. The **SCA** requires a minimum share capital of FF 250,000. The shares are freely negotiable. The **SCA** is managed by one or several managing directors who are appointed by the limited partners with the approval of all the general partners.

4 **La Société en Nom Collectif (SNC)**, corresponding to a general partnership, is the most common form of partnership, where each partner trades under the name of the **SNC**, and all partners are jointly and severally liable for the debts and obligations of the partnership. The **SNC** is set up with a minimum of 2 partners. The share capital of an **SNC** can be freely established (no compulsory limit) and paid up (no compulsory payment on issue). The **SNC** shares are not negotiable. Their transfer requires the unanimous consent of the partners and must be formalized in a written agreement. The **SNC** is managed by one or several managing directors.

5 **La Société Civile (SC)** is like a civil company and it is set up for purposes such as real-estate transactions, agricultural activities and professional activities. The **SC** is set up with a minimum of 2 shareholders and there is no minimum required share capital. The **SC** shares are not negotiable,

their transfer must be made by written agreement and with the unanimous prior consent of all shareholders. The **SC** is managed by one or several managing directors who do not need to be shareholders.

6 **Le Groupement d'Intérêt Economique (GIE)**, or the Economic Interest Group, is a legal structure enabling its members to merge their efforts in order to facilitate or develop their respective economic activities. The **GIE** is used for carrying out a joint action, the performance of which would be difficult individually, such as research services, marketing studies, publicity campaigns or the collective purchase of offices. The **GIE** must have at least 2 members with an economic activity. The **GIE** can be established without a share capital. In this case, it is financed by means of contributions and by the members. The **GIE** is managed by one or several managing directors who do not need to be members of the **GIE**.

7 **Le Groupement Européen d'Intérêt Economique (GEIE)**, or the European Economic Interest Group, has been instituted by the EC authorities in order to promote the establishment and co-operation of enterprises within the EC. The **GEIE**'s purpose is identical to that of the French **GIE**. A **GEIE** may set up its headquarters in France if its main administrative offices are located in France or if one of its members has its main administrative office in France.

Your turn to speak

 14 Here are some key words and phrases from the unit. Use them to make up some sentences of your own, then switch on the recording and see what Brigitte and Philippe came up with. If you wish, change the nouns from singular to plural, the adjectives from masculine to feminine (and/or singular to plural), and use any part of the verb.

(a) **votre dernière lettre**
(b) **heureux**
(c) **satisfait**
(d) **la cotation**
(e) **le devis**

(f) **au lieu de**
(g) **l'utilisateur**
(h) **une vente**
(i) **la concurrence**
(j) **s'occuper de**

Answers

Exercise 1 (a) Je suis heureux (heureuse) de travailler ensemble (b) Nous sommes satisfaits par votre dernière lettre (c) Les industriels arrivent mercredi prochain (d) Nous souhaitons trouver un hébergement à Dieppe (e) Elle s'occupe des cotations (f) Pouvez-vous confirmer par écrit? (g) Je vais vous envoyer la facture

Exercise 2 (a) the (female) managing director (b) no (c) 3 p.m, Monday 28 March; Thursday (d) today (e) a discount (f) one or two bus/coach companies (g) in writing (fax) (h) directly to the organizer

Exercise 4 eu, contact, prochaine, une, de, puisque, va, aveugle, vins, très, nous, ça, soir

Exercise 6 (a) une maison (b) dehors (c) le jardin (d) triste (e) réseau (f) à l'extérieur (g) devis (précis) (h) rencontrer

Exercise 7 (a) 12,000 francs (b) expensive (c) absolutely not (d) the quality of the materials (e) no (f) think about it (reflect on it) (g) produce another estimate

Exercise 9 Here are some of the words you might have in your list: les marchés, l'entreprise, le volume de ventes, les utilisateurs, le produit, industriels, commerçants, collectivités, clients, acheter, statistiques, études de marché, concurrents, fournisseurs, approvisionnement, matières premières, produits finis, les prix, la concurrence, chiffre d'affaires

Exercise 10 (a) You must know your markets (b) Can you estimate the volume of sales you can achieve? (c) We have lots of users for our products (d) How can you persuade clients to buy? (e) We have sources of information on our competitors (f) We must ask ourselves if there are some possible economic constraints (g) As for your competitors, you must study their turnover and their sales techniques

Exercise 11 (a) Il a travaillé en France (b) J'ai parlé à sa secrétaire (c) Nous avons fini l'étude du marché (d) J'ai envoyé une télécopie aux Etats-Unis (c) Avez-vous reçu la lettre? (f) Ils n'ont rien dit (g) J'ai fait le plan (h) Avez-vous vu les produits?

Exercise 12 (a) pour répondre à l'énorme marché (b) à livrer et installer (c) pour réaliser cette performance olympique (d) Vinco a conçu (e) à montage instantané (f) les bureaux sont disponibles

Exercise 13 (a) the first permanent and national structure (b) objective information (c) precise ones (d) you define your projects/ ambitions (e) commercial engineer in a multinational specializing in food and agriculture; financial manager in an SME in the Toulouse area (f) a Campus consultant (g) it provides a guarantee of your motivation and seriousness (h) put you in contact with firms

You will learn

- more on talking about the past
- how to outline your career
- how to complain when things go wrong
- how you might describe a typical week

  and you will be given information on employment regulations in France

Study guide

To help you keep a check on your progress, you could mark off the various tasks as you complete them.

Dialogue 1 + Practise what you have learned
Dialogue 2 + Practise what you have learned
Dialogue 3 + Practise what you have learned
Dialogue 4 + Practise what you have learned
Ensure you know the **Key words and phrases**
Study the **Grammar** section
Do the exercises in **Read and understand**
Did you know? Employment regulations in France
Your turn to speak

Dialogues

1 *Two people outline their careers for a CV* 〔first Worked〕

Alain   Je suis rentré chez Ford en 1970 et j'ai d'abord travaillé au siège à
Boulogne. Ensuite j'ai été muté en Normandie dans une usine
nouvelle qui démarrait près de Rouen. Je suis arrivé là en 1975 et
j'y suis resté sept ans jusqu'en 1982. Donc et à cette date je suis
parti démarrer une nouvelle usine du groupe Ford au Portugal près
de Lisbonne et là je suis resté jusqu'en 1985, après quoi j'ai
accompagné mon directeur de l'époque dans le sauvetage d'une
petite filiale qui était située dans, ... qui est située dans le nord de la
France et (c'est) là où je suis aujourd'hui depuis 1985.

Jean-Pierre   En ce qui me concerne, j'ai fait des études donc de linguistique en
France. A la suite de quoi je suis allé travailler dans un pays Anglo-
Saxon, l'Ecosse, pendant trois ans. Puis je suis allé en Amérique
Latine au Pérou où j'ai passé dix années en travaillant pour un
organisme culturel d'une part. Puis après trois années en basculant
dans l'administration et la gestion du personnel pour la société Fiat,
je suis rentré après dix ans en Europe pour participer à la
construction de nouvelles usines du groupe. Puis, en tant que
gestionnaire du personnel, j'ai demandé ma mutation en
Normandie où je viens d'arriver en assumant les mêmes fonctions
de responsable des ressources humaines.

     d'abord   at first
♦ **une usine**   factory
     jusqu'en   until
     accompagner   to accompany
♦ **le sauvetage**   rescue
♦ **sauver**   to save/rescue
     depuis   since
♦ **un pays**   country
     au Pérou   in/to Peru
     passer   to spend (time)
♦ **participer**   to take part in
♦ **la gestion**   management
♦ **le gestionnaire (la gestionnaire)**   manager
♦ **demander**   to request (*not* to demand)
♦ **la mutation**   transfer
     en assumant   assuming (i.e. taking up)
     les mêmes fonctions (f.)   the same functions

Je suis rentré chez Ford I joined Ford. In this unit you will notice a few examples of the past tense formed not with **avoir** but with **être** (see the grammar section in this unit). **Rentrer** here means 'to join a firm/organization'. It can also mean 'to come/go back', e.g. **Je suis rentré chez moi à 10 heures** 'I got back home at 10 o'clock'.

au siège at the headquarters (lit. at the seat). **Le siège** is 'the headquarters'. For 'headquarters' you might also find **la maison-mère**, lit. 'the mother house'.

J'ai été muté I was (lit. have been) transferred. You might notice a link between the English word *mutation* and **muter** 'to change/transfer'.

qui démarrait. The verb **Démarrer** has a nautical connotation meaning 'to cast off', but it is often used in the more general sense of 'to set out' or 'to get underway'. This form of the past tense is explained in the grammar section later in this unit.

J'y suis resté I stayed there. Note the use and position of **y** 'there'. Note also that **rester** is another verb that forms its past tense with **être** not **avoir**, as is **partir** in **je suis parti démarrer**.

après quoi after which. **Quoi** also means 'what' when used after a preposition, e.g. **A quoi pensez-vous?** 'Of what are you thinking?'

mon directeur de l'époque my director at that time. **L'époque** (related to the English word *epoch*) is often used to describe a period of time. **A cette époque j'étais...** means 'At that time I was...'

une filiale a branch of a company. A useful word.

qui était située...qui est située. Which was situated...which is situated. Here he corrects himself because the firm is still there.

En ce qui me concerne is a good phrase for starting off a description of what you do. It means 'as for me / as far as I'm concerned'.

j'ai fait des études. Lit. 'I have done some studies'. **Faires des études** and **étudier** are alternative ways of saying 'to study'.

à la suite de quoi... at the end of which...

je suis allé travailler I went to work. **Je suis allé** is another example of a past tense with **être** not **avoir**.

pendant trois ans for three years. **Pendant** normally means 'during', e.g **pendant la semaine** 'during the week'. When talking about the length of time you have spent somewhere, **pendant** is often used where in English you would say *for*. **J'ai étudié le français pendant cinq ans** 'I studied (lit. have studied) French for five years'.

en travaillant pour working for

en basculant. The verb **basculer** means 'to swing'. Here he is telling how he kept switching between administration and personnel management.

je suis rentré is an example of the more usual use of **rentrer**, meaning 'to go back'.

en tant que is a rather cumbersome idiomatic phrase meaning simply 'as'.

je viens d'arriver. Lit. 'I come from arriving'. To express the idea of having just done something you use **venir de**, e.g. **Nous venons de visiter Paris** 'We have just visited Paris'.

responsable des ressources humaines the person in charge of manpower (human resources). 'Responsible *for*' is **responsable de** not, as might be expected, **pour**.

Turn over for the exercises based on this dialogue.

Practise what you have learned

1 Look back over the two career descriptions in dialogue 1 and note down in the left-hand column the six examples of the past tense formed with **être** and not **avoir**. (Answers on p. 200.) Make sure you know what the words mean. (One verb occurs twice with two different meanings.)

Then use each verb to compose a short statement relating to yourself. There are no 'correct' answers for the second part.

(a) _____ _____

(b) _____ _____

(c) _____ _____

(d) _____ _____

(e) _____ _____

(f) _____ _____

2 Listen to the statements on the recording. Copy them down and check with dialogue 1 to see whether the information is **vrai** or **faux**.
(Answers on p. 200.)

	vrai	faux
(a)		
(b)		
(c)		
(d)		
(e)		
(f)		
(g)		
(h)		

3 On the recording you will be asked some questions about your own career.

Dialogues

2 *Two business friends talk about their week*

Sophie	Quelle semaine! J'ai été débordée de travail. Tu sais que lundi j'ai failli être renvoyée?
Paul	Non...vraiment?
Sophie	Oui, ils voulaient me transférer en Belgique pour travailler au siège.
Paul	Promotion?
Sophie	Non, pas du tout. C'est pour ça que j'ai refusé d'y aller. Ils voulaient une secrétaire bilingue, mais franchement, je suis très contente ici. J'ai beaucoup plus de responsabilité dans la filiale.
Paul	Qu'est-ce qui est arrivé alors?
Sophie	Bon, à la fin, je les ai convaincus que ça serait mieux pour tout le monde si je restais à Lyon...mais il y avait des moments difficiles.
Paul	Moi, j'ai eu une semaine pleine de réunions – réunions avec banquiers, agents, industriels, commerçants, avocats...
Sophie	Avocats?
Paul	Oui, nous avons des problèmes à résoudre avec des contrats pour la nouvelle construction en Côte d'Ivoire... Tu n'as jamais visité Abidjan?
Sophie	Non, jamais, et toi?
Paul	Pas encore, mais peut-être que j'aurai l'occasion d'y aller avant le commencement du travail, vers la fin de l'année.
Sophie	Tu as fini le rapport?
Paul	Quel rapport?
Sophie	Tu m'as dit que tu étais en train de préparer une étude sur l'utilisation de l'informatique.
Paul	Oui, c'est fait, mais je n'ai eu aucune nouvelle. Ça va durer un petit peu...

débordé(e) overwhelmed
transférer to transfer
en Belgique to Belgium
♦ **pas du tout** not at all
♦ **bilingue** bilingual
franchement frankly
content(e) happy
la responsabilité responsibility
♦ **la filiale** branch (of a firm)
à la fin in the end
rester to stay/remain
difficile difficult
♦ **un avocat** lawyer
le contrat contract
la Côte d'Ivoire Ivory Coast
le commencement start
c'est fait it's done

Turn over for the notes to this dialogue.

Quelle semaine! What a week! 'What a' is expressed by **quel** if it is linked to a masculine noun, **quelle** if the noun is feminine. **Quel homme!** 'What a man!' **Quelle journée!** 'What a day!'

J'ai failli être renvoyée I was almost fired. **Renvoyer** is 'to dismiss/fire someone'. The idiomatic use of **faillir** (lit. I have failed to be dismissed) is quite usual. **J'ai failli perdre le contrat** 'I almost lost the contract'.

J'ai refusé d'y aller I refused (lit. have refused) to go there. Note that **y** goes *before* the main verb.

Qu'est-ce qui est arrivé? What happened? **Arriver** can mean both 'to arrive' and 'to happen'. **Rien n'est arrivé** 'Nothing has happened'.

Je les ai convaincus I convinced (lit. have convinced) them. From **convaincre** 'to convince'.

Ça serait mieux pour tout le monde It would be better for everybody

Il y avait. Just as **il y a** means 'there is' or 'there are', **il y avait** can mean 'there was' or 'there were', e.g. **Il y avait beaucoup de gens** 'There were lots of people'.

pleine de réunions full of meetings. It is **pleine** and not **plein** because 'full' is referring to **une semaine**, a feminine noun.

des problèmes à résoudre problems to resolve. The past of **résoudre** incidentally is **résolu**: **Nous avons résolu le problème** 'We resolved (lit. have resolved) the problem'.

Tu n'as jamais visité Abidjan? Have you never visited Abidjan? Remember **ne…jamais…** means 'never'.

pas encore not yet

J'aurai l'occasion d'y aller I will have the opportunity to go there. **Occasion** is misleading – it means 'opportunity' *not* 'occasion', and it has other meanings: if you see **occasion(s)** in a shop window it means 'bargains', and outside a car salesroom it means 'secondhand'.

Tu as fini le rapport? Have you finished the report?

tu étais en train de préparer You were (in the act of) preparing. **Etais** is a past tense of **être**. (For more on this type of past tense see the grammar section in this unit.)

Je n'ai eu aucune nouvelle I have had no news. **Nouvelle** here is singular because it refers to one specific piece of news. **Ne…aucun(e)…** 'no'.

Ça va durer un petit peu is a useful idiomatic phrase meaning 'It will take some time' (lit. That is going to last a little bit). **Durer** is 'to last'. **Ça va durer longtemps?** 'Will it last long?'

Practise what you have learned

4 Using the transcript and the notes from dialogue 2, put the following phrases into French. (Answers on p. 200.)

(a) He has been overwhelmed with work.

_____

(b) I was almost fired.

_____

(c) We are refusing to go there.

_____

(d) There are 3 bilingual secretaries who work in the branch.

_____

(e) Nothing has happened.

_____

(f) There were lots of responsibilities.

_____

(g) The lawyer/solicitor has finished the new contract.

_____

(h) They have never worked in France.

_____

5 Use the framework below to have a go at describing your week. When you've finished, say your version aloud. (There are no 'correct' answers.) Then switch on the recording for some speaking practice using the same sort of phrases.

(a) **J'ai eu une semaine** _____

(b) **Lundi matin, j'ai parlé avec** _____

(c) **Mardi, j'ai travaillé** _____

(d) **Mercredi, j'ai commencé à** _____

(e) **Oui, jeudi, mon chef m'a dit que** _____

(f) **Vendredi, j'ai fini à** _____

(g) **Le weekend, j'ai visité** _____

Dialogues

3 *Two complaints: a short-fall in delivery and a tape recorder that won't record*

M. Lemoine Bon, ben écoutez, on a bien reçu votre colis là de trois cents pièces alors qu'on en a commandé cinq cents pièces. Alors, je ne comprends pas, il y a une disparité de deux cents pièces, on a commandé cinq cents pièces et il n'y en a que trois cents. Qu'est-ce que ça veut dire?

Employee 1 Oui et bien écoutez Monsieur Lemoine, nous nous en excusons, nous avons eu un problème de chaîne hier, ... et nous n'avons pu vous envoyer que trois cents pièces parce que c'étaient les seules disponibles et dès ce matin les deux cents complémentaires sont parties.

M. Lemoine On les aura quand alors?

Employee1 Je pense que vous les aurez dès demain...nous vous les avons envoyées en urgence et nous vous prions de nous en excuser.

M. Lemoine D'accord.

Client Alors, le magnétophone qu'on a reçu, il est bien mais il y a quelques problèmes. Il y a certaines fonctions qui ne marchent pas, apparement, je ne comprends pas, mais lorsqu'on appuie sur enregistrement par exemple, il y a des problèmes. Ça ne fonctionne pas.

Employee 2 Oui et ben, écoutez...je pense que vous...est-ce qu'un démonstrateur vous a presenté l'appareil correctement?

Client Euh. Non.

Employee 2 Bon, je pense que le plus intéressant pour vous ce serait que vous repassiez, on vous fera une démonstration, on y prendra le temps qu'il faut et je pense que vous pourrez donc en tirer toute satisfaction.

Client Ben...bientôt hein?

Employee 2 Oui, bien, vous passez quand vous voulez monsieur, nous sommes à votre disposition.

Client Moi, j'aimerais que vous passiez chez nous.

Employee 2 Que nous passions chez vous?

Client Ah, ben, oui.

Employee 2 Dès cet après-midi?

Client Entendu. Oui à quatorze heures?

Employee 2 Quatorze heures trente ça serait peut-être mieux.

Client Ah. Bon, d'accord.

Ecoutez! Listen!
♦ **votre colis** your package
une disparité disparity
complémentaires additional (pl.)
partir to leave
demain tomorrow
♦ **en urgence** urgently
♦ **le magnétophone** tape recorder
mais but
apparement apparently
un démonstrateur demonstrator
présenter to introduce/present
correctement correctly
bientôt soon
cet après-midi this afternoon
entendu agreed

- **on a bien reçu** we have indeed received. **Reçu** is the irregular past form from **recevoir** 'to receive'.

- **alors qu'on en a commandé** even though we ordered (lit. have ordered). **Commander** is 'to order'; **une commande** 'an order'. Note the use of **en** 'of them'.

Je ne comprends pas I don't understand

il n'y en a que. This can be broken down into **il y a** 'there is' or 'there are', **ne...que...** 'only' and **en**, which means 'of it' or 'of them'. So he is complaining that 'there are only (three hundred) of them'.

Qu'est-ce que ça veut dire? What does that mean? We have already had **vouloir dire** (to wish to say), which is the standard way of saying 'to mean'.

- **Nous nous en excusons.** The reflexive verb **s'excuser** is 'to apologize'. **Je m'excuse** 'I'm sorry'; **Il s'est excusé** 'He has apologized', etc. **En** keeps cropping up. Here it is translated as 'for that'.

Nous avons eu un problème de chaîne We have had a production problem. **Eu** is the past form from **avoir**, e.g. **j'ai eu** 'I have had'. **La chaîne** can mean 'the chain' but in an industrial context it means 'assembly/production line'.

Nous n'avons pu vous envoyer que... We have only been able to send you... **Pu** is the past form of **pouvoir** 'to be able to'. **Je n'ai pas pu le faire** 'I couldn't do it'. Note the use again of **ne...que...** meaning 'only'.

les seules disponibles the only (ones) available. **Disponible** means 'available'.

dès ce matin as from this morning

On les aura quand? We will have them when? **Aura** is the irregular future of **avoir**.

- **Nous vous prions de** is a very common polite way of saying 'we ask you to'.

- **fonctions qui ne marchent pas** functions which are not working. **Marcher** normally means 'to walk' but it is used also in the context of something working. **Ça marche?** 'Is it working?'

- **lorsqu'on appuie sur enregistrement** when you press record. **Appuyer** normally means 'to lean' but it is also used for 'to press (a button or control)'. **Appuyez sur le button** 'Press the button'. **Enregistrer/ l'enregistrement** mean 'to record / the recording'.

Ça ne fonctionne pas. He could just as well have said **Ça ne marche pas**. **Fonctionner** 'to function'.

- **le plus intéressant pour vous.** Here **intéressant** is used idiomatically to convey the idea of 'good'. **Une solution intéressante** is 'a good solution'; **un prix intéressant** 'a good price'.

que vous repassiez that you pass by again

On y prendra le temps qu'il faut We will take the time necessary for that

Vous pourrez donc en tirer toute satisfaction is simply a rather over-polite way of saying 'you'll be satisfied'.

- **Nous sommes à votre disposition** is an important phrase meaning 'We're at your service'.

J'aimerais que vous passiez chez nous I'd like you to come to us

Ça serait peut-être mieux That would be better perhaps

Turn over for the exercises based on this dialogue.

Practise what you have learned

6 On your recording you will hear a similar exchange to the second one in dialogue 3, this time about a Walkman with problems. Listen through a couple of times then fill in the gaps in the transcript below. (Answers on p. 200.) Here are a few words to help you understand it:

il s'arrête it stops   **s'arrêter** to stop
des piles neuves (brand) new batteries   **une pile** battery
dans un premier temps recently

Client   Oui, alors, _____(a)_____ ce modèle de Walkman que vous

m'avez _____(b)_____ en demonstration. Alors _____(c)_____

essayé ce Walkman là mais au bout d' _____(d)_____ il s'arrête.

Employee   Oui, _____(e)_____ des piles neuves d'abord dans un premier temps?

Client   Ah, bien sûr!

Employee   Bon, _____(f)_____ qu'à ce moment là, si c'est peut-être un

problème. Ecoutez, je pense que _____(g)_____ c'est que vous

passiez me voir. On regardera ça _____(h)_____ et la garantie pourra

_____(i)_____ fonctionner si c'est une anomalie dûe à l'appareil.

7 Complaining is an important subject so here's another example, this time to do with a machine which makes a strange noise, **un bruit étrange**. Listen through a couple of times, then, using your pause control, see if from the context you can match up the following French and English equivalents. (Answers on p. 200.)

(a) **lorsqu'on appuie sur**   (i)   it crackles
(b) **ça m'inquiète**   (ii)   when you press
(c) **dès le premier démarrage**   (iii) a manufacturing breakdown
(d) **ça grésille**   (iv) don't touch anything
(e) **ne touchez plus à rien**   (v)   as soon as you switch it on
(f) **un vice de fabrication**   (vi) it worries me

8 Your turn to speak. You'll have an opportunity to complain about a problem. Switch on when you are ready.

Dialogues

4 *An Algerian talks about his education and his management experience.*
(At that time the Algerian education system was much the same as the
French.)

Mohammed Alors, j'ai commencé bien sûr comme tout enfant par l'école
maternelle. Ça dure une année. Après l'école maternelle, j'ai été
envoyé dans une école primaire. A partir de là, nous passons un
examen national qui s'appelle la Sixième, qui, je crois, a disparu
maintenant. Après l'examen de sixième, nous sommes orientés
vers une école secondaire, un collège d'enseignement secondaire
parce que dans ma ville, à l'époque, il n'y avait pas de lycée. Donc,
j'ai fait le collège d'enseignement secondaire pendant quatre ans.

A la troisième, j'ai passé un examen national qui s'appelle le Brevet
d'Enseignement Général. Après cela, j'ai été envoyé dans un lycée
qui se trouve dans une autre ville à cent kilomètres de ma ville
natale. Dans le lycée, j'ai fait trois ans bien sûr, les classes
s'appellent la seconde, la première et la terminale.

Après le Bac, je suis allé à l'université. A l'université, j'ai fait des
études de sciences économiques avec spécialité gestion. La Licence
a duré quatre ans. Après ma Licence en sciences économiques,
spécialité gestion, j'ai commencé à travailler dans une entreprise
nationale de construction et j'avais commencé donc ma carrière
dans le département du personnel. Mais ça n'a pas beaucoup duré
parce que quelques mois après, j'ai eu une bourse et je suis venu en
Angleterre étudier le business. J'ai d'abord fait bien sûr six mois de
cours d'anglais et après cela, j'ai fait un diplôme en 'management
studies' suivi par un 'Master of Science' en 'recherche opérationnelle',
c'est-à-dire les modèles mathématiques appliquées à la gestion. Et
après cela en 1978, je suis revenu en Algérie et j'ai commencé à
enseigner à l'université d'Oran où j'enseignais la gestion et
l'organisation des entreprises.

J'ai parallèlement à mon travail à l'université, j'ai également travaillé
comme Chef de Département de Formation dans une entreprise
nationale qui avait pour mission l'importation des denrées
alimentaires et la distribution de ces produits alimentaires à travers
le territoire national.

commencer to start
durer to last
l'école maternelle (f.) kindergarten
une école primaire primary school
à l'époque at that time
‣ **ma carrière** my career
‣ **un cours** course
parallèlement in parallel
à travers across/throughout

Turn over for the notes to this dialogue.

bien sûr of course (lit. very sure). Here it is used as a filler.

j'ai été envoyé I was (lit. have been) sent

à partir de là is another way of saying 'after' or 'at the end of that'.

♦ **Nous passons un examen.** Note that **passer** means 'to take (an exam)' not necessarily to pass it (though he obviously did).

♦ **a disparu** (the exam) has disappeared. **Disparaître** means 'to disappear'.

nous sommes orientés vers. Lit. 'we are directed towards'. He uses the **nous**-form and the present tense because he is thinking here of what happens generally rather than what happened to him.

la sixième the sixth. Progression in education is described in reverse, i.e. pupils in **la sixième** would be about 11; **la première** 'the first' is where you get to at about the age of 17. Here **la sixième** is referring to an exam taken at the age of 11.

collège d'enseignement secondaire. For information on **CES** and **lycées** see the end of Unit 8. **Enseigner** is 'to teach'; **l'enseignement** 'teaching' or 'education'.

à cent kilomètres de ma ville natale 100 km away from my home town

le Bac is a common abbreviation for **le Baccalauréat** (see the end of Unit 8).

de sciences économiques avec spécialité gestion economics, specializing in management

♦ **la Licence** is roughly equivalent to a bachelor's degree (see the end of Unit 8).

quelques mois après a few months after

j'ai eu une bourse I had (got) a grant. **La bourse** is an interesting noun: it can mean 'purse', 'grant' or, with a capital B, 'the Stock Exchange'.

♦ **Je suis venu en Angleterre** I came to England. **Venir** means 'to come'.

suivi par un MSc en 'recherche opérationnelle' followed by an MSc in operational research

mathématiques appliquées applied maths (here as applied to management, **la gestion**)

je suis revenu en Algérie I returned to Algeria

♦ **Chef de Département de Formation** Head of the Training Department. **La formation** is a key word meaning 'education' or 'training'. **La formation professionnelle** 'professional training'.

qui avait pour mission is another way of saying that the firm 'was engaged in' the importation of foodstuffs – **l'importation des denrées alimentaires**. If you come across **alimentaire(s)**, it means something to do with food. Mohammed makes a slip here and says **élémentaires**.

Practise what you have learned

9   There are quite a lot of words describing various features of the education system. Find the French word(s) to match the English definition. (Answers on p. 200.)

(a)   what you get at the end of 3–4 years at university

_____

(b)   the very first school you go to

_____

(c)   the name of the exam which is roughly equivalent to GCSE

_____

(d)   two types of secondary school

_____

(e)   a general word for education or training

_____

(f)   the equivalent of 'A'-level (SAT)

_____

(g)   Mohammed had to follow one before he could study in England

_____

10   Listen to the job interview on the recording and then answer the questions below. (Answers on p. 200.)

(a)   What were the four types of school he attended?

_____

(b)   At what point did he go to the Lycée?

_____

(c)   And how long was he there?

_____

(d)   What was his speciality at Rouen?

_____

(e)   What sort of firm did he join after his degree?

_____

(f)   And in which department did he work?

_____

(g)   How long was he there and why did he leave?

_____

(h)   What did the firm in Peru do?

_____

(i)   What does he now want in France?

_____

Key words and phrases

Je suis rentré(e) chez Ford	I joined Ford
au siège	at the headquarters
muter	to transfer
une usine	factory
démarrer	to set out / start off
j'y suis resté(e)	I stayed there
je suis parti(e)	I left
de l'époque	at that time / of the time
à la suite de quoi	after / at the end of which
je suis allé(e)	I went
le sauvetage	rescue
sauver	to rescue
un pays	country
la gestion	management
participer	to take part in
le gestionnaire (la gestionnaire)	manager
demander	to request
la mutation	transfer
Je viens d'arriver	I have just arrived
le/la responsable de ressources humaines	the person in charge of manpower
J'ai failli être renvoyé(e)	I was almost fired / given the sack
pas du tout	not at all
bilingue	bilingual
la filiale	branch
Qu'est-ce qui est arrivé?	What has happened?
Je les ai convaincus	I convinced (lit. have convinced) them
convaincre	to convince
il y avait	there was / there were
un avocat	lawyer/solicitor
le commencement	start
J'aurai l'occasion d'y aller	I will have the opportunity of going there
Je n'ai eu aucune nouvelle	I have had no news
recevoir (j'ai reçu)	to receive (I have received)
le colis	package/parcel
commander	to order
Nous vous prions de...	We ask you to...
Ça marche?	Is it working?
le magnétophone/magnétoscope	tape/video recorder
appuyer sur le bouton	to press the button
Nous sommes à votre disposition	We are at your service
passer un examen	to take an exam
il a disparu	he/it has disappeared
la Licence	degree
la carrière	career
la bourse	purse/grant
la Bourse	Stock Exchange
Je suis venu(e) en Angleterre/France	I came to England/France
un cours	course
la formation	education/training

Grammar

The past tense (continued)

In Unit 10 the past tense was introduced. Just look back to familiarize yourself with what was said.

Here is something else to look out for with the perfect tense. You will have noticed that there are quite a few examples of verbs which form their past tense with **être** and not with **avoir**. In dialogue 1, for instance, we had **je suis rentré chez Ford, j'y suis resté** and **je suis allé**. These verbs tend to be associated with motion. Here is a list of the main ones you might meet. If you want an anagram to help you remember, the best I can do is 'EV'N MAD TRAMPS':

entrer	to enter	**je suis entré(e)**
venir	to come	**je suis venu(e)**
naître	to be born	**je suis né(e)**
mourir	to die	**il est mort / elle est morte**
arriver	to arrive	**je suis arrivé(e)**
descendre	to descend / get off	**je suis descendu(e)**
tomber	to fall	**je suis tombé(e)**
rester	to stay	**je suis resté(e)**
aller	to go	**je suis allé(e)**
monter	to climb	**je suis monté(e)**
partir	to leave	**je suis parti(e)**
sortir	to go out	**je suis sorti(e)**

One further minor complication with these verbs that take **être** is that the past participle 'agrees' with the subject. That is why there is an **e** in brackets on the examples above. If the **je** refers to a girl or woman, the **-e** must be added. So 'she has climbed' is **elle est montée**. Similarly with a feminine plural subject an **-es** is added; and with a masculine plural subject an **-s** is added: 'we (m.) have left' is **nous sommes partis**; 'they (f.) have arrived' is **elles sont arrivées**, and so on.

The imperfect past tense

The other sort of past tense is the so-called 'imperfect'. This is used when you are describing something, when you want to translate 'was/were doing something' or to convey the idea of 'used to'. Here are a few examples:

Je travaillais comme secrétaire.
I worked / was working / used to work as a secretary.

Ils participaient à la réunion.
They took part / were taking part / used to take part in the meeting.

Nous demandions les colis.
We asked / were asking / used to ask for the parcels.

Regardless of whether you are dealing with a verb ending in **-er**, **-ir** or **-re**, the endings are the same. To form the imperfect you take the **nous**-form of the present tense, knock off the **-ons** and then add these endings:

travailler	*perdre*	*finir*
je travaillais	**perdais**	**finissais**
tu travaillais	**perdais**	**finissais**
il/elle travaillait	**perdait**	**finissait**
nous travaillions	**perdions**	**finissions**
vous travailliez	**perdiez**	**finissiez**
ils/elles travaillaient	**perdaient**	**finissaient**

You can't be expected to master all this immediately, just be aware of the two possible forms of the past tense.

11 Try to translate the following sentences into French. Some are practising the perfect tense with **être** and others the imperfect. (Answers on p. 200.)

(a) He has gone to Paris. (**aller**)

_____

(b) We (m.) have arrived in France. (**arriver**)

_____

(c) The two women have stayed. (**rester**)

_____

(d) She has fallen. (**tomber**)

_____

(e) He was saving the company. (**sauver**)

_____

(f) They (f.) used to begin at 10 o'clock. (**commencer**)

_____

(g) He was working at the headquarters. (**travailler**)

_____

(h) Were you participating in the seminar? (**participer**)

_____

Read and understand

12 Look at Raoul Martin's CV and answer the questions below.
(Answers on p. 200.)

Raoul MARTIN
1, rue de l'Eglise
75015 Paris
Tél : 63-48-38-90

EXPERIENCES
Depuis 1990 *VACU PRODUCTS.*
– Cadre responsable du Département des Finances.

1984–90 *CHAMBOURCY*, Clamart.
– Employé de bureau qualifié dans le service financier.
– Chargé du suivi des comptes de banque et du porte-feuille.

1980–84 *BOUCLIER DE FRANCE*, Paris.
Installateurs de protection pour des particuliers.
– Chargé de la vente et de la gestion du stock.
– Etablissement des devis.

1976–80 *B.N.P.* (Succursale Paris 12ᵉ).
– Service de la caisse : guichetier-payeur, domiciliations, mécanographie, opérations diverses sur chèque.
– Habitude du contact avec un public varié.

1975–76 *SERVICE NATIONAL*, Armée de l'air.
– Officier de réserve.

1975 *LE COMPRESSEUR FROID*, Paris.
– Stage ouvrier.

FORMATION
1973   B.E.P.C.
1975   Seconde technique T1.
1981   C.A.P. de banque.

DIVERS
35 ans, célibataire.
Sport : parachutisme.

(a) Where did he do his national service?

_____

(b) What was his status when he was working for 'Le Compresseur Froid'?

_____

(c) Where did he work in the branch of a bank?

_____

(d) What sort of clients did he have contact with there?

_____

(e) Where was he in charge of sales and stock management?

_____

(f) Which area did he specialize in whilst at Chambourcy?

_____

(g) What is his job at Vacu Products?

_____

13 **ISMA**, the **Institut Supérieur du Management**, is one of France's best-known business schools. In these extracts (opposite, and on the next page) ex-students reflect on the difference the ISMA courses made to their careers. Try to understand the gist of what they are saying, then locate the French equivalents of the English phrases. (Answers on p. 200.)

Erick Monfort
(a) my training as an engineer_____

(b) in order to familiarize myself with commercial management _____

_____

(c) I acquired skills in analytical methods _____

(d) I owe it to ISMA_____

_____

Frédéric BASSI
Docteur en Pharmacie
ISMA 86

Avant mon intégration à l'Institut Supérieur du Management, je ne connaissais pas la signification des termes comme «Marketing-Mix», «CashFlow» ou «Incoterms». L'ISMA m'a permis d'acquérir ces connaissances nécessaires et indispensables pour devenir un futur cadre dirigeant de l'industrie pharmaceutique ; car avant tout, je reste un pharmacien avec tout ce que cela comporte comme spécificités particulières (déontologiques et éthiques).

Grâce au «melting-pot» et individus de sensibilités de formations différentes, grâce au contact avec des hommes de l'entreprise, j'ai pu développer :

. mes facultés d'aspiration face aux sollicitations multiples du monde de l'entreprise

. ma curiosité, mon esprit d'initiative

. mon esprit d'homme de contact et de décideur.

Cette formation d'un an est une période privilégiée qui m'a permis d'acquérir un état d'esprit général et une maîtrise de l'environnement des entreprises.

Frédéric BASSI

Frédéric Bassi

(e)   I didn't know the significance _____

(f)   in order to become a future manager _____

(g)   thanks to the contact with people (men) from commercial firms _____

_____

(h)   I have been able to develop _____

Bénédicte SAURY
Ingénieur en Agronomie
ISMA 86

Je suis rentrée à l'ISMA après une Ecole d'Agronomie, dans le but d'améliorer mes connaissances techniques dans un contexte d'Entreprise.

De plus, les industries agro-alimentaires ont actuellement un grand besoin de cadres technico-économiques, tant du point de vue Marketing qu'International. Les exportations Agro-Alimentaires ne constituent-elles pas un poids non négligeable dans notre balance des paiements ?

J'ai personnellement choisi l'option Affaires Internationales et y ai beaucoup apprécié la diversité des sujets abordés ainsi que la variété des problèmes qu'ils soulèvent : douanes, incoterms, trésorerie-devises et transports de technologie,...

Le travail en groupes pratiqué régulièrement, les études de cas, les dossiers-produits, dossiers-logistique,... permettent une application des connaissances reçues.

A l'ISMA, j'ai rencontré des gens très différents et leurs expériences ont enrichi les débats sur les thèmes abordés en cours et pendant les réflexions de groupe.

Trouver un compromis malgré ces divergences m'a permis de pratiquer une négociation de tous les jours, se rapprochant de celle que je vivrai en entreprise.

Bénédicte SAURY

Bénédicte Saury

(i)   the food and agriculture industries badly need at the moment managers with technical and economic experience

_____

(j)   our balance of payments _____

(k)   enable the application of the knowledge (information) received _____

_____

(l)   I met some very different people _____

Did you know?

Employment regulations in France

Employment relations are governed by the following main regulations:

- French Labour Law (**Droit du Travail**)

- Collective Bargaining Agreements (**Conventions Collectives**) negotiated at the national level between trade unions representing both employees and employers. These specify information such as the probation period, working conditions, and consequences of the employment contract's termination, indemnification to employees in case of absence due to illness, and the duration of paid vacations.

- Collective Company Agreements (**Accords Collectifs d'Entreprise**) are negotiated at individual company level and provide arrangements applicable to the company's sector of activity.

- Internal Regulations (**Règlements Intérieurs**). Companies with more than twenty employees have to establish the **Règlements Intérieurs**, determining rules to be followed with regard to discipline, hygiene and security.

- Employment contracts also govern personnel matters. In the case of unfair dismissal or if the formal procedure is not respected by the employer, the employee can sue the employer in court (**Conseil des Prud'hommes**). Virtually all employees in France are covered by minimum-wage legislation. Employment contracts have to specify a wage level which is at least that of the legal minimum wage (**Salaire Minimum Interprofessionnel de Croissance, SMIC**).

The Labour Code provides regulations related to working conditions such as working hours, overtime and paid vacation. The legal working week in France is 39 hours and law requires overtime payments and/or compensatory time off for any additional hours worked by non-executive employees. The statutory paid vacation time in France is five weeks per year, with eleven national bank holidays. In addition France's national system of health and unemployment insurance and retirement pensions applies to all employees in France. The system is financed by contributions from both employers and employees.

French Labour Law provides the possibility for employee representation in a company via: (i) Employee Representatives (**Délegués du Personnel**) elected for a period of one year in companies with more than ten employees. (ii) A Workers' Representation Committee (**Comité d'Entreprise**), compulsory for companies with at least fifty employees. This committee has a significant role concerning matters of collective interest and economic issues. (iii) Security, Hygiene and Working Conditions Committee (**Comité d'Hygiène, de Sécurité et des Conditions de Travail**), compulsory for companies with at least fifty employees.

The principal trade unions in France are (i) the **Confédération Générale des Travailleurs** (**CGT**), (ii) the **Confédération Française des Travailleurs** (**CFDT**), (iii) the **Forces Ouvrières** (**FO**), (iv) the trade union of executives, called the **Confédération Générale des Cadres** (**CGC**) and (v) the trade union for employers, the **Conseil National du Patronat Français** (**CNPF**).

Your turn to speak

 14 Have a go at describing your own career, starting with school and including various periods of employment. Stick to simple short sentences and use the words and phrases from dialogues 1 and 4. Speak your version out loud, but this time there is no model answer recorded.

Answers

Practise what you have learned

Exercise 1 (a) je suis rentré (*joined*) (b) je suis arrivé (c) je suis resté (d) je suis parti (e) je suis allé (f) je suis rentré (*returned*)

Exercise 2 (a) Il a d'abord travaillé au siège de Ford (vrai) (b) Il a démarré deux nouvelles usines (vrai) (c) Il est resté sept ans au Portugal (faux) (d) Il travaille depuis 1983 dans le nord de la France (faux) (e) Après ses études il est allé travailler en France (faux) (f) Après dix ans, il est rentré en Europe (vrai) (g) Il a été envoyé en Normandie (faux) (h) Il est actuellement le gestionnaire, c'est-à-dire le responsable, pour les ressources humaines (vrai)

Exercise 4 (a) Il a été débordé de travail (b) J'ai failli être renvoyé(e) (c) Nous refusons d'y aller (d) Il y a trois secrétaires bilingues qui travaillent dans la filiale (e) Rien n'est arrivé (f) Il y avait beaucoup de responsabilités (g) L'avocat a fini le nouveau contrat (h) Ils n'ont jamais travaillé en France

Exercise 6 (a) j'ai reçu (b) envoyé (c) j'ai (d) une minute (e) est-ce que vous avez (f) je pense (g) le mieux (h) ensemble (i) eventuellement

Exercise 7 (a) ii (b) vi (c) v (d) i (e) iv (f) iii

Exercise 9 (a) la Licence (b) l'école maternelle (c) le Brevet d'Enseignement Général (d) un collège d'enseignement secondaire; un lycée (e) la formation (f) le Baccalauréat (le Bac) (g) un cours d'anglais

Exercise 10 (a) école maternelle, école primaire, CES and lycée (b) after his Brevet (c) 3 years (d) management (e) road transportation firm (f) planning (g) 5 months; he didn't like the routine (h) exported foodstuffs (i) a permanent job in France

Grammar

Exercise 11 (a) Il est allé à Paris (b) Nous sommes arrivés en France (c) Les deux femmes sont restées (d) Elle est tombée (e) Il sauvait la compagnie (f) Elles commençaient à 10 heures (g) Il travaillait au siège (h) Est-ce que vous participiez au séminaire?

Read and understand

Exercise 12 (a) Air Force (b) industrial placement (**stage**) (c) Paris (d) general public (e) Bouclier de France (f) finance (g) manager of the finance department

Exercise 13 (a) ma formation d'ingénieur (b) afin de me familiariser avec la gestion commerciale (c) j'ai acquis des méthodes d'analyse (d) c'est à l'ISMA que je le dois (e) je ne connaissais pas la signification (f) pour devenir un futur cadre (dirigeant) (g) grâce au contact avec des hommes de l'entreprise (h) j'ai pu développer (i) les industries agro-alimentaires ont actuellement un grand besoin de cadres technico-économiques (j) notre balance des paiements (k) permettent une application des connaissances reçues (l) j'ai rencontré des gens très différents

THE FUTURE

You will learn

- to talk about what you think or hope will happen
- to understand arrangements made for the future
- something about the organizations which help businesses plan
  and you will be given information on the taxation system in France

Study guide

To help you keep a check on your progress, you could mark off the
various tasks as you complete them.

Dialogue 1 + **Practise what you have learned**
Dialogue 2 + **Practise what you have learned**
Dialogue 3 + **Practise what you have learned**
Dialogue 4 + **Practise what you have learned**
Ensure you know the **Key words and phrases**
Study the **Grammar** section
Do the exercises in **Read and understand**
Did you know? Taxation in France
Your turn to speak

Dialogues

1 *A new business tenant is given his programme for the day*

Tenant   Bon, je suis prêt. Quel est le programme exactement?

Director   Bon, vous allez me suivre. On va déjà aller voir Monsieur Lebrun
dans un premier temps. Ensuite, nous verrons Monsieur Breton.
Alors, Monsieur Lebrun, vous allez voir avec lui pour la question
du bail. Avec Monsieur Breton, ce sera pour votre contrat et puis
ensuite dès que vous aurez terminé cette visite on ira voir Monsieur
Chabeil pour les cours de français pour votre secrétaire.

Tenant   Et quand?

Director   Ben...tout de suite. On va commencer là, dès maintenant.

Tenant   D'accord.

Director   Si vous voulez me suivre?

le programme programme
exactement exactly
exact(e) exact
♦ **déjà** already
♦ **votre contrat** your contract
puis then
ensuite then
dès que as soon as
cette visite this/that visit
tout de suite immediately

♦ **Je suis prêt** I am ready. A woman would have said **Je suis prête**.

♦ **Vous allez me suivre** You're going to follow me. **Suivre** means 'to
follow'. One way of expressing the future is simply to use **aller** plus the
main verb in the infinitive.

dans un premier temps is another way of saying 'soon'. The more usual
word is **bientôt**.

♦ **Nous verrons Monsieur Breton** We will see M. Breton. **Nous verrons**
is the future tense of **voir** 'to see'. (The future is explained in the grammar
section in this unit.)

♦ **pour la question du bail**. Lit. 'for the question of the lease', i.e. 'to
discuss the lease'. **Le bail** means 'lease' *not* 'bail'. The French word for
'bail' is also misleading: 'on bail' is **sous caution**.

Ce sera pour votre contrat It will be for your contract. **Sera** is an
irregular future tense form of **être** 'to be'.

♦ **dès que vous aurez terminé** as soon as you (will) have finished. **Aurez**
is an irregular future form of **avoir**. Note that in French if something is
happening in the future then the future tense (here **aurez**) has to be used:
'As soon as you (will) see him' would be **Dès que vous le verrez**.

♦ **on ira voir** we will go to see. Another irregular future. **Ira** comes from
aller 'to go'. **Nous irons en France pour le weekend** 'We're going (we
will go) to France for the weekend'.

♦ **dès maintenant** straight away (lit. from now)

Si vous voulez me suivre? A polite way of asking 'Would you like to
come with me?' (lit. If you want me to follow). **Si vous voulez** is a good
way of making a polite request.

Practise what you have learned

1 Here's an exercise to familiarize you with some of the future forms of different verbs. Note down the English equivalent for the following phrases. (Answers on p. 220.)

(a) **Je serai prêt tout de suite.**

_____

(b) **Il va aller à la réunion ce soir.**

_____

(c) **Il ira au cinéma ce soir.**

_____

(d) **Elles verront la directrice à quatre heures.**

_____

(e) **Vous aurez le bail dès que vous aurez signé le contrat.**

_____

(f) **Nous irons voir l'avocat pour décider les questions légales.**

_____

2 Spot the differences! You will hear a recording of almost the same discussion, but there are seven small differences. See if you can spot them and note them down below. (Answers on p. 220.)

(a) _Je suis prête_   (e) _____

(b) _____   (f) _____

(c) _____   (g) _____

(d) _____

3 Your turn to speak. You'll be prompted to use some of the key words and phrases from the dialogue.

Dialogues

2 *A new agent asks M. Leroux, the owner of the firm, a few questions*

Agent Et bien, Monsieur Leroux, dans le cadre d'une collaboration entre nous, j'ai trois questions à vous poser, trois questions du même type. D'abord il me faudrait un stage de formation sur vos produits.

M. Leroux A ce niveau là, il n'y a aucun problème car nous sommes organisés pour cela étant donné que nous avons crée un centre...un séminaire de formation qui dure une semaine et qui vous permettra de connaître l'essentiel de ce qu'il faut pour diffuser nos produits en Angleterre.

Agent Parfait et ensuite, moi, je pense qu'il faudrait que j'approfondisse ma connaissance de la législation française.

M. Leroux Au cours de ce même séminaire il est prévu des rudiments de la législation française qui sont suffisants et qui sont prévus justement pour l'exportation.

Agent Très bien et finalement moi il me faut absolument un stage de perfectionnement en français.

M. Leroux (Alors là il y a) ... puisque vous serez de passage dans notre région quand même pendant un certain temps, je vous conseille de prolonger votre séjour et de suivre des stages de formations intensives de français diffusés par l'Institut Consulaire de Dieppe.

Agent L'Institut Consulaire de Dieppe?

M. Leroux Ah oui, l'Institut Consulaire qui donne des cours de très bonne qualité.

Agent Merci beaucoup.

- ◆ **poser** (**une question**) to ask (a question)
  d'abord first of all
  vos produits your products
  car for/because
  créer to create
- ◆ **la formation** training/education
  l'essentiel (m.) the essential
  penser to think
  les rudiments (m.) rudiments
  suffisant(e) sufficient
  justement precisely
- ◆ **l'exportation** (f.) export(ation)
  finalement finally
  absolument absolutely
  puisque since
  quand même all the same
  intensif (**intensive**) intensive
  la qualité quality

- **dans le cadre d'une collaboration entre nous** within the context of a collaboration between us. In Unit 8 you met **les cadres**, meaning 'supervisory management staff', so the meaning here – 'context' – is entirely different.

du même type of the same type. **Le même** means 'the same'.

Il me faudrait un stage de formation. Remember **il me faut**, meaning 'it is necessary for me', which is used to get over the idea of 'I need'. **Il me**
- **faudrait** is 'it would be necessary for me' or 'I would need'. **Un stage** is another common word for 'a short course'.

à ce niveau là. Lit. 'at that level', but used here idiomatically to mean 'as far as that is concerned'. **Le niveau** 'the level'.

étant donné que given that. Just learn to recognize the phrase and don't worry about the grammar involved. **Etant donné que le contrat n'est pas encore prêt** means 'given that the contract isn't yet ready'.

et qui vous permettra de connaître and which will enable you to know. **Permettre** is 'to enable/permit/allow'. Here it is in the future tense.
- **diffuser nos produits** to distribute our products. The noun from **diffuser** is **la diffusion** 'distribution'.

il faudrait que j'approfondisse ma connaissance de I would need to deepen my knowledge of. **Approfondir**, 'to deepen/extend', is linked to **profond** 'deep'. **Ma connaissance**, 'my knowledge', is linked to **connaître** 'to know'. Don't worry about the ending on **approfondir**.
- **au cours de ce même séminaire** in the course of this same seminar. **Au cours de** is a useful little phrase meaning 'during' or 'in the course of'.
- **il est prévu**. From **prévoir** 'to foresee/envisage'.

un stage de perfectionnement en français. His French is already very good but he needs an advanced course to 'perfect' his French. **Perfectionner** is the verb for 'to perfect'.

Vous serez de passage ... pendant un certain temps You will be here with us for quite some time. There is a slight ambiguity here. **Etre de passage** is normally associated with a short stay (passing through) whereas **pendant un certain temps** conveys the idea of a significant period of time. Ignore **Alors là il y a** – M. Leroux is just groping for the right way to react.

Je vous conseille de prolonger votre séjour I advise you to prolong/extend your stay. **Conseiller** is 'to advise', hence **le conseil** 'the advice' or, indeed, 'the Council'.

diffusés par offered by. **Diffuser** 'to distribute' can be used in this wider sense.

Turn over for the exercises based on this dialogue.

Practise what you have learned

4 Using the notes and vocabulary from dialogue 2, work out the French equivalent of the following sentences. (For the answers, see the next exercise.)

(a) It's in the context of the seminar in marketing that the Centre is going to organize in June.

(b) There is no problem with the lease.

(c) The week in France will enable you to get to know our products.

(d) I am going to deepen my knowledge of French legislation.

(e) Within the course of your training, you will have the opportunity of perfecting your French.

(f) Can you prolong your stay?

(g) I advise you to follow an intensive course.

5 When you have worked out the equivalents for the sentences above, switch on your recording. You'll be asked to read out your version, sentence by sentence, and you'll be able to hear the correct translation. Hopefully the two will be the same.

6 Below you will find six unfinished phrases. On the recording you will be asked to complete them using your own ideas or adapting the vocabulary of the dialogue. There is no absolutely right or wrong answer, but you will hear some suggestions from Carole and Philippe. Before you speak each phrase, pause the recording and think through what you will say.

(a) **Dans le cadre d'une eventuelle collaboration entre nous**

(b) **Il n'y a aucun problème car** _____

(c) **Nous avons créé** _____

(d) **Cela vous permettra de mieux connaître** _____

(e) **Il me faut absolument** _____

(f) **Je vous conseille de** _____

Dialogues

3 *A young businessman enquires about the first part of an MBA course*

Businessman	Quelles sont les méthodes d'enseignement?
Course organizer	L'enseignement repose essentiellement sur la méthode des cas, effectué par petits groupes.
Businessman	C'est plus pratique que théorique, alors.
Course organizer	Exactement. Un cas présente la situation réelle d'une entreprise. Les participants doivent l'analyser et proposer les éléments de mise en œuvre de la solution choisie. De cette façon les liens entre la réflexion théorique et l'application pratique sont concrètement établis.
Businessman	Ça dure combien de temps la formation?
Course organizer	Nous proposons une formation de neuf mois, de septembre à juin.
Businessman	Et qu'est-ce que ça comprend?
Course organizer	Bon, alors, ça commence avec quinze jours d'introduction aux méthodes de travail et aux techniques de vente. Ensuite, vous avez une formation de base de management pendant trois mois. Deux mois de spécialisation dans deux domaines fonctionnels de l'entreprise – c'est-à-dire marketing commercial ou affaires internationales. Puis il y a un stage de trois mois en entreprise dans le cadre de l'option choisie, en France ou à l'étranger. A la fin du stage les participants doivent avoir réalisé une étude concrète qui leur permet de faire des recommandations. Puis le cours se termine avec quinze jours de synthèse et un séminaire de politique générale d'entreprise avec des orientations stratégie et organisation, marketing commercial, finance et gestion de personnel. Il y a aussi pendant cette dernière période un jeu d'entreprise informatisé.

une méthode method
- **effectuer** to put into practice
- **pratique** practical
- **théorique** theoretical
  réel (réelle) real
  la réflexion reflection
  concrètement concretely
- **le marketing commercial** commercial marketing
  les affaires (f.pl.) business/affairs
- **(se) terminer** to conclude/finish
  la période period

Turn over for the notes to this dialogue.

l'enseignement repose essentiellement the instruction rests essentially. **Reposer** means 'to rest', both in the sense of the phrase here and in the sense of 'to relax'. **Je dois me reposer** 'I must have a rest'. Similarly, **un repos** is 'a break'.

♦ **la méthode des cas** the case-studies approach. **Un cas** can just mean 'a case', as in **dans ce cas** 'in this/that case', or in a training context it means 'a case study'.

♦ **proposer les éléments de mise en œuvre**. The key phrase here is **la mise en œuvre** 'the implementation'.

♦ **de cette façon** in this way

les liens... sont établis the links... are established

♦ **Qu'est-ce que ça comprend?** What does that comprise? **Comprendre** as well as meaning 'to understand' can also mean 'to comprise' or 'to include'. **Service compris** means 'service charge included'.

♦ **aux techniques de vente** to sales techniques. **Une vente** is 'a sale', **vendre** 'to sell'.

une formation de base basic training

dans deux domaines fonctionnels in two operational areas. **Le domaine** is a good word for 'an area' or 'a sector'.

un stage a period of training / a course / a placement

dans le cadre de l'option choisie within the framework of the chosen option. **Choisir** is 'to choose'.

♦ **à l'étranger** abroad. **Un étranger** (**une étrangère**) is not 'a stranger' but 'a foreigner'.

♦ **avoir réalisé une étude**. So the students have to complete a practical study and use this as the basis for their recommendations. **Réaliser** is 'to achieve', or 'to finish'. It is linked to the English word *realize* in the phrase 'to realize an ambition'.

gestion de personnel personnel management

♦ **un jeu d'entreprise informatisé** a computerized management game. **Un jeu d'entreprise** is 'a management game' (**un jeu** a game); **informatisé** is linked to the words we had earlier – **l'informatique** 'computing' and **l'informaticien** 'computer scientist'.

Practise what you have learned

7 Look at the dialogue and choose eight words or phrases to do with management which are the same as, or very close to, their English equivalents. Then make up a simple sentence incorporating the word. (There are some specimen answers on p. 220, though you may well have something different.)

(a) _____ _____

(b) _____ _____

(c) _____ _____

(d) _____ _____

(e) _____ _____

(f) _____ _____

(g) _____ _____

(h) _____ _____

8 Imagine you are taking down a message. Listen to the recording about a management course a couple of times to ensure you understand it and then copy the message down – use the pause control when you need more time. (Answer on p. 220.)

> MESSAGE
>
> _____
>
> _____
>
> _____
>
> _____
>
> _____
>
> _____
>
> _____
>
> _____

9 Your turn to ask questions about a management course. When you're ready, switch on.

Dialogues

4 *An employer discusses with Mme Avenel of FAF (Fonds d'Assurance Formation) how to organize his training budget*

Mme Avenel	Oui, alors pour votre formation, je vous redis que l'on peut venir en aide dans toutes les actions que vous avez à mener. C'est-à-dire rechercher les actions de formation qui sont nécessaires à votre personnel et gérer votre taxe, c'est-à-dire la somme que vous avez à consacrer à la formation du personnel de votre entreprise. C'est un des aspects de notre organisme.
Employer	Bien donc ma masse salariale sera d'environ 1 million 7 (1.700.000).
Mme Avenel	Pour un effectif de...
Employer	De 19 personnes.
Mme Avenel	De 19 personnes. Donc la taxe obligatoire étant de 0.8%, vous aurez environ 12,000 francs à consacrer à votre formation. C'est le minimum.
Employer	Bien mais alors, comment je vais pouvoir donc gérer cette formation avec ces 12,000 francs?
Mme Avenel	Alors ces sommes-là sont donc gérées par nous. Si dans une année vous n'avez pas utilisé la totalité de votre taxe, vous pouvez, on peut la rapporter sur l'année suivante.
Employer	Ça ce cumule.
Mme Avenel	Ça se cumule.

♦	**rechercher** to investigate	**nécessaire** necessary
	notre organisme our organization	♦ **un effectif** workforce
	utiliser to use	**la totalité** all (lit. totality)

je vous redis. The verb **dire** is 'to tell/say', so **redire** is 'to tell again'. It isn't quite as abrupt as in English – more like 'I'll underline what I said previously'.

l'on peut venir en aide we can help you (lit. come to your aid). Sometimes **l'** precedes **on**. It makes no difference to the meaning, it's just more polite.

toutes les actions que vous avez à mener. **Une action** is 'an initiative' or, possibly, 'a programme'. So, FAF can help in all the initiatives the employer has to take. **Mener** normally means 'to lead' but here it is linked to 'action' and used idiomatically.

gérer votre taxe to manage your (training) tax. In France the equivalent of a specific percentage of a firm's salary bill has, by law, to be spent on training.

la somme que vous avez à consacrer the sum that you have to consecrate/devote

ma masse salariale sera d'environ 1 million 7. In this context **une masse** means 'a fund'. His salary budget is, therefore, 1,700,000 francs.

la taxe obligatoire étant de... the compulsory tax being at... Mme Avenel's maths isn't very good! She should have said 13,600 francs.

on peut la rapporter sur l'année suivante you (one) can carry it forward to the following year. A nice example here of how **vous pouvez** or **on peut** are more or less interchangeable.

Ça se cumule It accumulates

Turn over for the exercises based on this dialogue.

Practise what you have learned

10 Here are some key words and phrases, together with clues as to what they mean. Match up the two lists. (Answers on p. 220.)

(a)	**une action**	(i)	**ce que l'on fait tout le temps avec de l'argent**
(b)	**gérer**	(ii)	**être responsable de**
(c)	**ma masse salariale**	(iii)	**les salariés d'une entreprise**
(d)	**l'effectif**	(iv)	**une initiative**
(e)	**obligatoire**	(v)	**être membre d'un organisme**
(f)	**l'année suivante**	(vi)	**1992 → 1993**
(g)	**dépenser**	(vii)	**ce que vous payez aux employés**
(h)	**adhérer**	(viii)	**vous pouvez payer...**
(i)	**disposer**	(ix)	**il faut le faire**

11 On the recording you'll hear another excerpt from Mme Avenel's description of the services FAF can offer. Listen through a couple of times then answer the questions below. (Answers on p. 220.)

(a) How does she say in French that it has to be paid?

_____

(b) What can FAF seek out or investigate for their clients? (3 things)

(i) _____

(ii) _____

(iii) _____

(c) Why are they able to investigate the possibilities of (ii) and (iii) above?

_____

(d) When does the tax have to be paid by?

_____

(e) What French verb does she use for 'to pay in'?

_____

12 Your turn now to ask a few questions about the services offered by FAF. Switch on when you're ready.

Key words and phrases

déjà	already
votre contrat	your contract
Je suis prêt(e)	I'm ready
suivre	to follow
Nous verrons...	We will see...
le bail	lease
dès que vous aurez terminé	as soon as you (will) have finished
on ira voir	we (one) will go to see
dès maintenant	straight away / from now
dans le cadre de	within the context of
poser une question	to ask a question
un stage	a (short) course
la formation	education/training
étant donné que	given that
diffuser des produits	to distribute products
au cours de	in the course of / during
il est prévu que	it is envisaged (foreseen) that
l'exportation (f.)	export(ation)
un cas	a case (study)
effectuer	to put into practice
pratique/théorique	practical/theoretical
la mise en œuvre	implementation
de cette façon	in this way
Qu'est-ce que ça comprend?	What does that comprise?
les techniques (f.) de vente	sales techniques
le marketing commercial	commercial marketing
(se) terminer	to conclude/finish
à l'étranger	abroad
réaliser	to achieve/realize (e.g. an ambition)
un jeu d'entreprise informatisé	computerized management game
rechercher	to investigate
un effectif	workforce
par rapport à la loi	in relation to the law
obliger	to require / oblige (someone to do something)
adhérer	to belong to (an organization)
dépenser	to spend
une dépense	expenditure
conseiller	to advise
il faudra	it will be necessary
la priorité	priority

Grammar

The future

The first thing to say is that when you want to express a future idea you can always use the easy construction which is equivalent to the *I am going to...* construction in English.

Je vais vendre ma voiture.
I am going to (I will) sell my car.

Nous allons rencontrer le directeur du personnel.
We are going to (we will) meet the personnel director.

Ils vont visiter la France en août.
They are going to (they will) visit France in August.

There have been numerous examples of the use of **aller** + infinitive in the course and you might like to flip back through the dialogues and see how the construction was used. The present tense of **aller** 'to go' is:

je vais	nous allons
tu vas	vous allez
il/elle va	ils/elles vont

In French you can also express a future idea by changing the form of the verb. Although you may not need to know the details of this for your own use, you should be able to recognize it. So, here is how it works.

With regular verbs all you do is to take the infinitive and add a set of endings. The ending depends on the subject of the verb. (With -**re** verbs such as **perdre** the final -**e** is dropped before the ending is added.)

Here is how the future tense looks for three regular verbs:

parler	*finir*	*perdre*
je parlerai	**je finirai**	**je perdrai**
tu parleras	**tu finiras**	**tu perdras**
il/elle parlera	**il/elle finira**	**il/elle perdra**
nous parlerons	**nous finirons**	**nous perdrons**
vous parlerez	**vous finirez**	**vous perdrez**
ils/elles parleront	**ils/elles finiront**	**ils/elles perdront**

So, regardless of whether the verb is an -**er**, an -**ir** or an -**re** verb, the endings for the future are the same if the subject is the same:

je	-**ai**	nous	-**ons**
tu	-**as**	vous	-**ez**
il/elle	-**a**	ils/elles	-**ont**

As ever, there are a few important exceptions, many of which you have met in the last two units. The irregularity is not in the endings – the endings set out above are valid for all verbs – but in the stem of the verb onto which the endings are added. Here in the **je** form are some of the main exceptions which you might need to be able to recognize:

je viendrai	I will come	**je verrai**	I will see
je voudrai	I will want	**je pourrai**	I will be able to
je devrai	I will have to	**je serai**	I will be
j'aurai	I will have	**j'irai**	I will go

You might also have noticed **il faudra**, 'it will be necessary to'.

13 Translate the following sentences into French. Give two versions for each – one using the **aller** + infinitive construction and one using the verb with a future ending. (Answers on p. 220.)

(a) I'll visit Dieppe tomorrow.

_____

_____

(b) He will speak to M. Lebrun.

_____

_____

(c) They will discuss the plans.

_____

_____

(d) I'll come to the trade fair.

_____

_____

(e) We will be able to decide the budget.

_____

_____

(f) He will be ready at 4 o'clock.

_____

_____

(g) Will you have the contract today?

_____

_____

Read and understand

14　**APEC**, the French national organization for the training of managers, runs short courses to enable people to reflect on where they are in their careers and where they might go in the future. In its publicity for these courses a number of questions are asked. Read through and find the French equivalents to the English phrases below.
(Answers on p. 220.)

**Si l'une de ces interrogations est la vôtre,
PERSPECTIVES
vous aidera à y répondre.**

■ Vous êtes à un carrefour de votre vie professionnelle, vous avez besoin d'éclairer votre choix :
Quelle orientation prendre ?

■ Vous venez d'accepter une nouvelle mission :
Comment la "tailler à vos mesures" ?
Comment améliorer votre efficacité et développer vos atouts ?

■ Vous êtes dans un univers professionnel en mutation.
Comment cerner votre future mission ?
Comment mesurer votre savoir-faire, déterminer vos propres objectifs ?

■ Vous voulez mieux maîtriser votre évolution professionnelle :
Comment évaluer votre potentiel ?
Quelle évolution choisir ?

■ Vous avez l'impression d'avoir "fait le tour" de votre poste. Faut-il en changer ou bien y développer de nouvelles initiatives ?

■ Vous avez plusieurs années d'expérience dans une même activité. Vos compétences sont-elles transférables dans un autre poste ? Faut-il les diversifier ou accroître votre spécialité ?

(a)　You're at a crossroads in your professional life.

___

(b)　How can you improve your efficiency and develop your strengths (trumps)?

___

(c)　a changing universe

___

(d)　How can you decide on your own objectives?

___

(e)　How can you evaluate your potential?

___

(f)　Should you (is it necessary for you to) develop new initiatives?

___

(g)　Are your skills transferable to another job?

___

15 Here are a few more ads from companies in France. Read them and see if you can answer the questions. (Answers on p. 220.)

Domiciliation de sièges sociaux

Location de bureaux équipés
Permanence téléphonique
Secrétariat service multilingue
Télex - Télécopie
Salle de réunion

Lille · Bruxelles · Paris

16 pl Général de Gaulle
59800 Lille - **20 12 33 00**

62 NCI 59 Lille   20 12 33 00

Voyagez facile, voyagez tranquille
RENAULT-VOYAGE INTERNATIONAL
LUNERAY

Agrément IATA-ATAF   Licence A14-14

• Un éventail de brochures sélectionnées parmi les
  meilleures pour vos voyages individuels ou en
  groupe.
• Billetteries AIR FRANCE - AIR INTER et toutes
  autres compagnies aériennes mondiales.
• Billetteries SNCF
• Location voiture

Réservation HOTELS et SPECTACLES
LUNERAY 76810 - Tél. 35 85 00 29

Assurances Régionales de France

« Faites confiance
à un grand groupe
régional d'assurances»

Pour contacter les **ARF** de votre Dpt,
adressez-vous à votre agence
du Crédit Mutuel

Siège social : 22 boulevard Carnot
BP 949 62033 Arras cedex

31 Crama
    62 Arras   21 71 78 78

C A C A O
BARRY

BARRY SA
BARRY INTERNATIONAL

Barry dans le monde
2500 personnes
13 usines (2 en France)
14 laboratoires
2 écoles de chocolaterie
Barry à votre service depuis 1842

Télex : 698747F
Télécopie : (1) 34 74 59 27
5 bd Michelet
78250 HARDRICOURT

102 Cacao Barry
     78 Hardricourt   (1) 34 74 72 32

EVE et EMILIE FLEURS

Situé près du Stade R. Diochon - 2, av. des Canadiens
76120 GRAND-QUEVILLY
35 73 78 47

MANUPARIS

**tous modèles
enveloppes
pochettes
sacs**
avec ou sans impression

66-72, r. Stendhal
75980 PARIS CEDEX 20

Télex : MANUMAS 220418 F
Télécopie : (1) 47 97 77 34   **(1) 47 97 03 19**

RDN
— SECURITE —
CONSTRUIT VOTRE
SECURITE DEPUIS 1940
SU.GE.MAR
22 avenue Champlain 76100 ROUEN
35 72 13 00

• Surveillance
• Prévention
• Ronde   24H/24
• Intervention
  C.R.A. agréé APSAIRD
• Télésécurité
• Surveillance à distance
• Détection électronique
• Etude et installation
• Conseil en sécurité

(a) What number would you call to order personalized plastic folders?

_____

(b) Who spends their nights delivering flowers? _____

(c) Which company has 13 factories involved with the cocoa business?

_____

(d) What's the French for 'electronic detection'? _____

(e) As well as tickets, what service does Renault-Voyage offer?

_____

(f) If you want a toehold in France or Belgium, you can ring _____
    to get fully serviced accommodation.

(g) What's the French for 'contact your Crédit Mutuel agency'?

_____

_____

Did you know?

Taxation in France

The largest source of tax revenue in France is VAT, which accounts for almost 45% of the state's total tax receips. The rest is Corporation Tax (9%), Personal Tax (20%) and other taxes (26%).

1   Value Added Tax (**Taxe à la Valeur Ajoutée – TVA**): Sales of goods are subject to French VAT when the goods are delivered in France. Services are subject to French VAT when the individual or entity has its place of business in France. The standard VAT rate is 18.6% (but it is 5.5% on most food products, books, water and other listed products, and 22% on cars, motorcycles over 240cc, and luxury items such as cameras, tape recorders and jewellery). Exports are exempt, and goods purchased in France for export may be eligible for a reimbursement of the **TVA** paid.

2   Corporation Tax: All companies, whether **Sociétés Anonymes** or **Sociétés à Responsabilité Limitée** (see the Did you know? section in Unit 10), are treated identically for tax purposes. However, to improve the competitiveness of French businesses and to promote investments in France, the standard rate of corporate income tax has been gradually reduced since 1988 (1988: 42%; 1989: 39%; 1990: 37%; 1991: 34%). The assessment of this tax is based on the principle of territoriality. Thus, corporation tax is assessed on profits deriving from business conducted in France and from profits earned abroad after they have been repatriated to France and made available for distribution to shareholders. A foreign corporation is liable to French corporation tax on its profits derived from: (i) an establishment in France, (ii) activities performed by a dependent representative in France, and (iii) a complete cycle of transactions carried out in France. Corporate tax is paid in four instalments during the relevant financial year.

3   Personal Income Tax (**Impôt sur le Revenu**) is dependent upon residence. According to French law, individuals are regarded as having their fiscal domicile in France if: (i) they have their home in France, (ii) France is the place where they perform their principal professional activities, (iii) France is the centre of their economic interests.

French residents must file by February of each year an annual income tax return stating the income earned during the previous calendar year. The tax year ends on 31 December. Married tax-payers have to file a joint tax return reporting their combined income. The year the tax-payer leaves France, he or she must file a temporary tax return reporting the income earned from 1 January to the date of departure.

4   Local taxes include:

- Real Estate Taxes (**Taxes Foncières**): These taxes are assessed on the yearly rental value of developed and undeveloped land. The tax is due annually from the property owner and is determined by the municipalities (between 15% and 30%).

- Personal Dwelling Tax (**Taxe d'Habitation**): This tax is charged on any individual who occupies a dwelling on 1 January of each year, even if he or she is not the owner. The tax is based on the dwelling rental value with deductions granted depending on the number of dependent children, and personal income tax liability.

- Business Licence Tax (**Taxe Profesionnelle**): Legal entities or individuals involved in manufacturing, trading or any professional activities in France are liable to Business Licence Tax (BLT), which is an annual tax determined by local authorities (**communes,**

départements or **régions**). BLT is assessed on: (i) the annual rental value of the tangible assets (whether owned or rented) used for carrying out the business activity, (ii) 18% of the gross salaries paid. For the purpose of promoting the creation of enterprises, temporary BLT exemptions are made available.

5 Net Wealth Tax (**Impôt de Solidarité sur la Fortune**): This tax was reintroduced in France as of January 1989. Individuals are liable for this tax only if the net value of their assets exceeds a certain limit.

France has signed double-taxation treaties with more than seventy countries, including the other members of the EC.

Your turn to speak

16 To finish the unit, and, indeed, the course, put together a few of your hopes for the future and say them out loud. Then switch on and see what other people would like to see happen.

So, **c'est fini**. It's finished. Those of us involved in producing the course all hope you have found *Breakthrough Business French* effective, and, dare we hope, enjoyable! If you've got this far and kept your head above water and kept your sanity, you've done pretty well. It's difficult to remember everything, so don't throw the recordings and book away. If you go over them every now and again, it will help you to keep your French on the boil.

Au revoir et merci

Answers

Exercise 1 (a) I'll be ready immediately (b) He's going to the meeting this evening (c) He'll go to the cinema this evening (d) They will see the director at 6 o'clock (e) You'll have the lease as soon as you've signed the contract (f) We'll go and see the lawyer to decide the legal questions

Exercise 2 (a) je suis prête (b) on ira déjà voir M. Lebrun (c) vous verrez M. Breton (d) vous le verrez pour votre contrat (e) dès qu'on aura terminé cette visite (f) nous irons voir M. Chabeil (g) nous allons commencer là

Exercise 7 (a) méthode: Je préfère la méthode audio-visuelle (b) théorique: Il vient de finir une étude théorique (c) application pratique: L'application pratique est très importante (d) management: On utilise le terme management très souvent en France (e) marketing commercial: Il s'intéresse surtout au marketing commercial (f) affaires internationales: Il faut rester en contact avec les affaires internationales (g) stratégie: Nous devons développer une nouvelle stratégie (h) finance: La finance est un élément très important dans la gestion

Exercise 8 La formation dure neuf mois. L'enseignement repose sur la méthode des cas qui présentent la situation réelle dans une entreprise. Les étudiants doivent analyser et proposer la mise en œuvre de la solution choisie.

Le cours commence le 13 septembre avec quinze jours d'introduction aux méthodes de travail et un séminaire sur les techniques de vente. Après, vous aurez trois mois de formation de base, deux mois de spécialisation, soit le marketing commercial, soit les affaires internationales, et puis un stage de trois mois en entreprise. Le cours se termine avec un séminaire sur la politique générale d'entreprise et la gestion du personnel.

Exercise 10 (a) iv (b) ii (c) vii (d) iii (e) ix (f) vi (g) i (h) v (i) viii

Exercise 11 (a) c'est obligatoire (b) (i) the most appropriate training organizations; (ii) state aid; (iii) regional aid (c) it's a new firm (d) 28 February (e) verser

Exercise 13 (a) Je vais visiter Dieppe demain / Je visiterai Dieppe demain (b) Il va parler à M. Lebrun / Il parlera à M. Lebrun (c) Ils vont discuter les plans / Ils discuteront les plans (d) Je vais venir à la foire / Je viendrai à la foire (e) Nous allons pouvoir décider le budget / Nous pourrons décider le budget (f) Il va être prêt à 4 heures / Il sera prêt à 4 heures (g) Allez-vous avoir le contrat aujourd'hui? / Aurez-vous le contrat aujourd'hui?

Exercise 14 (a) Vous êtes à un carrefour de votre vie professionnelle (b) Comment améliorer votre efficacité et développer vos atouts? (c) un univers en mutation (d) Comment déterminer vos propres objectifs? (e) Comment évaluer votre potentiel? (f) Faut-il développer de nouvelles initiatives? (g) Vos compétences sont-elles transférables dans un autre poste?

Exercise 15 (a) (1) 47 97 03 19 (b) Eve et Emilie (c) Barry (d) détection électronique (e) car hire (f) 20 12 33 00 (g) adressez-vous à votre agence du Crédit Mutuel

Vocabulary: French–English

à côté at the side
à droite on/to the right
à gauche on/to the left
à la disposition de available to
à l'appareil (m.) on the line
à l'époque (f.) at that time
à l'étranger (f.) abroad
à peine barely/hardly
à peu près approximately
à travers across/throughout
abonné (m.) subscriber
absent absent
absolument absolutely
accommodant accommodating
accompagner to accompany
accueil (m.) reception/welcome
accueillir to welcome
achat (m.) purchase
acheter to buy
action (f.) initiative
actuellement at present / now
adhérent (m.) member
administratif administrative
adresse (f.) address
aéroport (m.) airport
affaires (f.pl.) business/affairs
agenda (m.) diary (appointments)
agent de maîtrise (m.) supervisor
agent immobilier (m.) (real-)
  estate agent
agréable pleasant/nice
aider to help
aimer to like/love
ainsi thus/so
ajouter to add
aller to go
alors so
américain American
an (m.) / **année** (f.) year
Angleterre (f.) England
annonce (f.) ad
annoncer to announce
annuel (m.) / **annuelle** (f.) annual
annuler to cancel
antenne de télévision (f.) TV
  aerial
apéritif (m.) aperitif
appareil (m.) apparatus
  (telephone handset)
appareil à diapositives (m.)
  slide projector
apparemment apparently
appartenir à to belong to
appeler to call
apprendre to learn
approfondir to deepen

approprié appropriate
approvisionnement (m.) supply
appuyer to press/lean
après after(wards)
après-midi (m.) afternoon
argent (m.) money
arrivée (f.) arrival
arriver to arrive/happen
artisan (m.) craftsman
artisanal cottage-industry *adj.*
ascenseur (m.) lift/elevator
assurance (f.) insurance
atelier (m.) workshop
atelier d'intégration (m.)
  assembly unit
atteindre to reach/achieve
attendre to wait for / expect
au bout de at the end of
au choix your choice
au contraire on the contrary
au cours de in the course of
au lieu de instead of
aujourd'hui today
aussi also
aussi bien que as well as
autobus (m.) bus (within towns)
autocar (m.) coach (bus
  between towns)
automne (m.) autumn/fall
autour de around about
autre other
autre (m.) another
avance (f.) advance
avant before
avant-hier day before yesterday
avec with
avenir (m.) future
aveugle blind
avocat (m.) lawyer/solicitor
avoir to have
avoir besoin de to have need of /
  to need
avoir lieu to take place
axe (m.) axis

bail (m.) lease
bancaire banking *adjective*
bande transporteuse (f.)
  conveyor belt
banque (f.) bank
basculer to swing
basket (m.) basketball
bâtiment (m.) building
beaucoup de many / lots of
Belgique (f.) Belgium
bénéficier de to benefit from

beurre (m.) butter
bien well
bientôt soon
bienvenu welcome
bilingue bilingual
blanc (m.) / blanche (f.) white
boire to drink
boîte (f.) box
boîte de nuit (f.) night club
bon (m.) / bonne (f.) good
bon temps good time
bon voyage (m/) good journey/trip
bonjour hello / good day
bonne nuit (f.) good night
bonne route (f.) safe journey
bonsoir good evening
Bourse (f.) Stock Exchange
bourse (f.) purse/grant
bouton (m.) button
budget (m.) budget
bureau (m.) office
bus (m.) bus (within towns)
but (m.) aim/purpose

ça va? how are you?
cabine téléphonique (f.) public
   phone box/booth
cadence (f.) rate/pace
cadre (m.) manager
café au lait (m.) coffee with milk
café complet (m.) continental
   breakfast
campagne (f.) countryside
cantine (f.) canteen
capital (m.) capital (finance)
car (m.) coach (bus between
   towns)
car because/for/since
carnet de chèques (m.) cheque
   book
carrefour (m.) crossroads
carrière (f.) career
carte de crédit (f.) credit card
carte téléphonique (f.) phone
   card
cas (m.) case
catégorie (f.) category
ce (m.) / cette (f.) this/that
centre de traitment (m.) data
   processing centre
centre informatique (m.)
   computing centre
certificat (m.) certificate
c'est-à-dire that is to say
ceux (m.pl.) / celles (f.pl.) those
chacun (m.) / chacune (f.) each
   one
chaîne (f.) chain / assembly line
chambre (f.) bedroom

chaque each
château castle
chef de production (m.)
   production manager
chemin d'accès (m.) driveway
chemin de fer (m.) railway
chercher to look for
chez at (home/workplace)
chiffre d'affaires (m.) turnover
chocolat (m.) chocolate
choisir to choose
choix (m.) choice
chose (f.) thing/matter
circuit imprimé (m.) printed
   circuitboard
clavier (m.) keyboard
clef (f.) key
cœur (m.) heart
colis (m.) package/parcel
colle (f.) glue
collectivités (f.pl.)
   conglomerates / large firms
collège (m.) secondary school
   (vocational)
collègue (m./f.) colleague
combien de? how many?
comité de direction (m.)
   management committee
commande (f.) order
commander to order
comme as/like
commencement (m.) start
commencer à to begin/start
comment? how?
commentaire technique (m.)
   technical commentary
commerçant (m.) merchant/
   trader/shopkeeper
commercialiser to market
commission (f.) commission
Communauté Européenne (CE)
   (f.) European Community (EC)
commune (m.) district
compagnon (m.) colleague
complémentaire additional
complet (m.) / complète (f.)
   complete/full
composant (m.) component
comprendre to understand/
   comprise
compte bancaire (m.) bank
   account
concours (m.) competition/help
concrètement concretely
concurrence (f.) competition
concurrent (m.) competitor
confirmer to confirm
confiture (f.) jam
congé annuel (m.) annual leave

connaissance (f.) knowledge
connaître to know (a person or place)
conseil (m.) advice
conseil d'ami (m.) friendly advice
conseiller to advise
consommateur (m.) consumer
construction (f.) construction
construire to construct/build
consulaire of the council
contact (m.) contact
content happy
contrainte (f.) constraint
contrat (m.) contract
convaincre to convince
convivial convivial
coordonnées (f.pl.) whereabouts
corporel (m.) / **corporelle** (f.) of the body / physical
correctement correctly
cotation (f.) quotation
Côte d'Ivoire (f.) Ivory Coast
couleur (f.) colour
courir to run
cours (m.) course
court terme (m.) short term
coût (m.) cost
coûter to cost
crédit (m.) credit
crédits de trésorerie cash credits
créer to create
croire to believe/think
croque madame (m.) cheese, ham and egg on toast
croque monsieur (m.) cheese and ham on toast
court terme (m.) short term

d'abord first of all
d'accord OK/alright
dame (f.) lady
de bonne heure early
de la part de on behalf of
de rien don't mention it
débordé overwhelmed
décrire to describe
défilé (m.) procession/parade
défiler to parade / go past
dégustation tasting
déguster to taste/sample
déjà already
délégué (m.) delegate
demain tomorrow
demande (f.) request
demander to ask (for)
démarrer to cast off / initiate
demi (m.) half (a litre) of beer
demonstrateur (m.) demonstrator

denrées alimentaires (f.pl.) foodstuffs
département du personnel (m.) personnel department
dépendre de to depend on
dépenser to spend
dépenses (f.pl.) expenditure(s)
déposer to deposit
depuis since
dernier (m.) / **dernière** (f.) last
derrière behind
dès que as soon as
descendre to descend / get off
descendre le prix to lower the price
désirer to desire/want
désolé very sorry
desserte (f.) service (transport)
desserte ferroviaire (f.) railway network
desservir to be served by
détail (m.) detail
détenteur (m.) holder
deuxième étage (m.) second floor (US third floor)
devant in front of
devis (m.) estimate
devises (f.pl.) local currency
devoir to must / have to
Dieppois from Dieppe
difficile difficult
difficultés de trésorerie cash-flow problems
diffuser to distribute
diffusion (f.) distribution
dire to tell/say
directement directly
directeur (m.) director/head (male)
directeur général (m.) managing director
direction Tours heading for Tours
directrice (f.) director/head (female)
discuter to discuss
disparaître to disappear
disparité (f.) disparity
disponible available
disposer to have available
disposition (f.) disposition/ availability
distributeur (m.) distributor
divers diverse/various
documentation (f.) publicity material
domaine (m.) area
donc so/therefore
donner to give
douane (f.) customs

douche (f.) shower
durer to last
échangeur (m.) (traffic) interchange
échéance (f.) expiry date
école maternelle (f.) kindergarten
école primaire (f.) primary school
écouter to listen to
écran (m.) screen
écrire to write
effectif (m.) workforce
effectuer to put into practice
également equally (also)
église (f.) church
électronique electronic
emballage (m.) packaging
emmener to take (something) away
emploi (m.) job/post
employé (m.) employee
employeur (m.) employer
en assumant assuming
en dehors de outside
en effet in fact / actually
en fait in fact
en ligne on the line
en principe in principle
en urgence urgently
enchanté pleased to meet you
encore still/again
endettement (m.) debt
énergie nucléaire (f.) nuclear energy
enfant child
enfin finally
engazonnement (m.) turfing
enregistrement (m.) recording
enregistrer to record
enseignement (m.) teaching
enseigner to teach
ensemble together
ensuite then
entendre to hear
entendu agreed
entre among/between
entrée (f.) entrance
entreprise (f.) firm/business
entrer to enter
entretien (m.) meeting/interview
environ about/approximately
environs (m.pl.) surrounding area
envisageable possible/envisageable
envisager to envisage
envoyer to send
épeler to spell (out)
époque (f.) period (of time)
épouse (f.) / **époux** (m.) wife/ husband (spouse)
épuration (f.) purification

équipements de loisirs (m.pl.) leisure facilities
espérer to hope
essayer to try
essence (f.) petrol/gasoline
essentiel (m.) / **essentielle** (f.) essential
est (**l'Est**) east / the East
estimer to estimate/calculate
établir to establish
établissements de soins (m.pl.) medical and social services
état (m.) state
état d'esprit associatif community spirit
Etats-Unis (m.pl.) USA
été (m.) summer
étranger (m.) / **étrangère** (f.) foreigner
étude (f.) **de marché** market survey
étudier to study
évaluer to evaluate/consider
éventuel (m.) / **éventuelle** (f.) possible
évidemment evidently/obviously
évolution development
exact exact
exactement exactly
excellent excellent
excusez-moi I'm sorry
exemple (m.) example
exister to exist
expliquer to explain
exportation (f.) export(ation)
exporter to export
exposé (m.) presentation
exposition (f.) exhibition
extérieur (m.) outside
extrémité (f.) end/limit

fabrication (f.) production
fabriquer to produce
facile easy
faciliter to help
façon (f.) way/manner
facture (f.) bill/invoice
facturer to bill
faible weak
faiblesse (f.) weakness
faillir to fail
faire to do/make
faire du sport play sport
faire erreur to make a mistake
famille (f.) family
femme d'affaires (f.) business-woman
fer (m.) iron
fermer to close

ferré of iron
filiale (f.) branch (of a firm)
fille (f.) daughter/girl
fils (m.) son
fin (f.) end
finalement finally
finance (f.) finance
financement (m.) financing
financer to finance
finir to finish
flux (m.) flow
foire (f.) trade fair
fonction (f.) function
fonctionner to function
forêt (f.) forest
formation (f.) training/education
formation de base (f.) basic
  training
fosse (f.) pit/ditch
fosse septique (f.) septic tank
four (m.) oven
fournir to supply
fournisseur (m.) supplier
foyer (m.) household
frais (m.pl.) charges/costs
franchement frankly
fréquemment frequently
frites (f.pl.) chips / french fries
futur future

gamme (f.) product range
garder to keep
gare (f.) station
garer to park
gazon (m.) lawn/turf
gênant embarrassing/inconvenient
genre (m.) type/sort
gens (m.pl.) people
gens particuliers individuals
gentil (m.) / **gentille** (f.) nice
gérer to manage
gestion (f.) management
gestion de personnel (f.)
  personnel management
gestionnaire (m.) manager
grand big
grand ouvert wide open
gratuit free of charge
grosso modo in general / roughly

habiter to live (in)
hall (m.) hall (reception)
hébergement (m.)
  accommodation
héberger to accommodate
heureux (m.) / **heureuse** (f.)
  happy
hier yesterday
hiver winter

homme (m.) man
homme d'affaires (m.)
  businessman
hôpital (m.) hospital
horaire (m.) timetable
hors taxes before tax
hôtel de ville (m.) town hall

ici here
il y a there is / there are
immédiat immediate
imposer vos initiales to initial
imprimé printed
inciter to persuade
indicatif (m.) area code
indiquer to direct / point out
industriel (m.) industrialist
informaticien (m.) computer
  scientist
informations (f.pl.) information
informatique (f.) computing
installation électrique (f.)
  electrical installation
installer to install
instant (m.) moment
institut (m.) institute
intempéries d'hiver (f.pl.)
  winter storms
intéressant interesting
intéressé interested
intérêt (m.) interest
intermédiaire intermediary
investir to invest
investissement (m.) investment
intensif (m.) / **intensive** (f.)
  intensive

jardin (m.) garden
jardiner to do the gardening
je vous en prie don't mention it
jeu (m.) game
joli pretty/nice
jour (m.) day
journée (f.) day
jus d'orange (m.) orange juice
jusqu'à until / as far as
justement precisely

laisser to leave
lettre (f.) letter
licence (f.) degree (BA, etc.)
ligne de fabrication (f.)
  production line
ligne de production (f.)
  production line
livraison (f.) delivery
livrer to deliver
location de voitures (f.) car hire
logiciel (m.) software

loi (f.) law
loin far
long terme (m.) long term
louer to hire
lune (f.) moon
lycée (m.) secondary school (academic)

machine (f.) machine
machines-outils (f.pl.) machine tools
madame (f.) madam/Mrs
mademoiselle (f.) Miss
magnétophone (m.) tape recorder (audio)
magnétoscope (m.) video recorder
maintenant now
mais but
maison (f.) house
maison de campagne (f.) country house
maître + profession (m.) specialist
maître artisan (m.) specialist craftsman
manger to eat
manière (f.) manner
marché (m.) market
marcher to walk
marketing commercial (m.) commercial marketing
marque (f.) trademark/brand
masse (f.) amount/budget
matériel audio-visuel (m.) audio-visual material
matières fabriquées (f.pl.) finished goods
matières premières (f.pl.) raw materials
matin (m.) morning
matinée (f.) morning
médecin (m.) doctor
meilleur better
même *adverb* same
même *adjective* even
mémoire (f.) memory
mener to lead
mer (f.) sea
merci thank you
mère (f.) mother
message téléphonique (m.) telephone message
méthode (f.) method
métier (m.) profession
mettre to put
micro-composant (m.) micro-component
Midi (m.) South of France

midi (m.) noon
mieux better
minuit (m.) midnight
mise en œuvre (f.) implementation
moderniser to modernize
modifier to modify
mois (m.) month
monde (m.) world
moniteur TV (m.) TV set
monsieur (m.) sir/Mr
montant (m.) total (amount)
monter to climb
mourir to die
moyen terme (m.) medium term
multitude (f.) multitude
mutation (f.) transfer
muter to transfer

naître to be born
natif/native native
ne... aucun... no (not any)
ne... jamais... never
ne... ni... ni... neither... nor...
ne... pas... not
ne... personne... no one
ne... plus... no longer
ne... que... only
ne quittez pas hold on / hold the line
ne... rien... nothing
nécessaire necessary
nettoyer to clean
niveau (m.) level
nom (m.) surname
non no
non plus nor that
nord (le Nord) north (the North)
nord-est (le Nord Est) north-east (the North East)
nord-ouest (le Nord Ouest) north-west (the North West)
notamment in particular
noter to note
nouveau (m.) / **nouvelle** (f.) new
nu naked/bare
nuit (f.) night
numéro (m.) number
numéro de poste (m.) extension number

objectif (m.) objective
obligatoire compulsory
obliger to require / oblige (you)
occasion (f.) opportunity
oenologie (f.) oenology
œufs sur le plat (m.pl.) fried eggs
offrir to offer

ordinateur (m.) computer
organiser to organize
organisme (m.) organization
origine (f.) origin
ou or
où where
oublier to forget
ouest (l'Ouest (m.)) west (the West)
oui yes
outils (m.pl.) tools
ouvert open
ouvrier (m.) worker
ouvrier spécialisé (m.) specialist worker

paiement (m.) payment
pain (m.) bread
paperboard (m.) flip chart
papiers (m.pl) papers
par an per year
par avion by plane
par contre on the other hand
par écrit in writing
par exemple for example
par voie ferrée by rail
parallèlement in parallel
paramédical paramedical
parce que because
parfait perfect
parfaitement perfectly
Parisien (m.) / **Parisienne** (f.) from Paris (or: person from Paris)
parking (m.) carpark
parler to speak
participer (à) to take part in / participate
particulier (m.) / **particulière** (f.) specific
partir to depart/leave
pas de problème no problem
pas de quoi don't mention it
pas du tout not at all
pas encore not yet
pas grave not important
passe-temps (m.) pastime
passer to spend (time) / take (an exam)
patienter to wait / have patience
payer to pay
pays (m.) country
pays d'origine (m.) country of origin
Pays-Bas (m.pl.) Netherlands
pendant during
penser to think
perdre to lose
père (m.) father
perfectionner to perfect

période (f.) period
permettre to enable/permit
permis de conduire (m.) driving licence
Pérou (m.) Peru
personnellement personally
petit small/little
petit déjeuner (m.) breakfast
peur (f.) fear
peut-être perhaps
pile (f.) battery
piscine (f.) swimming pool
place (f.) square
planifier to plan
plaque (f.) plate
plateforme (f.) platform (freight)
plomberie (f.) plumbing
PME SME
pochette (f.) folder
polymerisé polymerized
pont (m.) bridge
porte (f.) door
poser to ask (a question)
poste (m.) post / (phone) extension
pour for / in order to
pourquoi why
poursuivre to continue/pursue
pouvoir to be able to
pratique practical
préciser to point out
premier (m.) / **première** (f.) first
premier étage (m.) first floor (US second floor)
premier temps (m.) first/initially
prendre to take
prénom (m.) first name
près de close to
présenter to introduce/present
prêt à ready to
prévoir to foresee
prévu expected (foreseen)
primaire primary
principal main
principalement principally
Principautés (f.pl.) Principalities
printemps (m.) spring
priorité (f.) priority
privé (m.) private sector
prix (m.) price
prix forfaitaire (m.) inclusive price
problème (m.) problem
prochain next
proche near
produit (m.) product
produit fini (m.) finished product
profond deep
programme (m.) programme
proposer to suggest/propose
publicité (f.) publicity/ad

puis then
puisque since/because

qualité (f.) quality
quand when
quant à as for
quantité (f.) quantity
quart (m.) quarter
quel (m.) / quelle (f.) what
quelqu'un (m.) / quelqu'une (f.)
  someone
quelque chose something
quelques some / a few
quitter to leave
quoi what

raccordement (m.) connection
raison (f.) reason
rappeler to call back
rapport (m.) report
ravi delighted
réaliser to achieve/finish
recevoir to receive
recherche (f.) research
rechercher to investigate
redire to tell again
réel (m.) / réelle (f.) real
réfléchir to reflect / think about
réflexion (f.) reflection
régler to settle (a bill)
rejoindre to join/link
remarquer to notice
remercier to thank
remettre to postpone
remise (f.) discount/reduction
remplir une fiche to fill in a form
rencontrer to meet
rendez-vous (m.) appointment
rendre visite to visit (someone)
rénovation (f.) renovation
renseignement (m.) piece of
  information
renseignements (m.pl.)
  information
renseigner to inform
rentrer to join (a firm)
rentrer to go back / go home
renvoyer to dismiss (someone)
répartition (f.) distribution
repas (m.) meal
répéter to repeat
reposer to rest/relax
représenter to represent
réseau (m.) network
réservation (f.) reservation
résider to reside/live
résoudre to resolve
responsable de responsible for
responsable (m./f.) person
  responsible

responsabilité (f.) responsibility
ressources humaines (f.pl)
  manpower / human resources
rester to stay/remain
retirer to withdraw
retour (m.) return
retraite (f.) retirement
rétroprojecteur (m.) overhead
  projector
retrouver to find
réunion (f.) meeting
revue (f.) magazine
rez de chaussée (m.) ground
  floor
rhododendrons (m.pl.)
  rhododendrons
ristourne (f.) discount
robot (m.) robot
rouge red
Royaume-Uni (m.) Great Britain
rubrique (f.) heading/listing
rudiment (m.) rudiment
rue (f.) road
rural rural

salaire (m.) salary
salarié (m.) salaried person
salle (f.) room
salle de bain (f.) bathroom
salle de conférence (f.)
  conference/seminar room
s'amuser to amuse (oneself)
sanitaire sanitary
sans without
sans doute without doubt
s'approcher to approach
s'arrêter to stop
satisfait satisfied
saucisse (f.) sausage
sauver to save/rescue
sauvetage (m.) rescue
savoir to know (something / how
  to do something)
scolarité (f.) education
se baigner to (go for a) swim
se comporter to behave (oneself)
se demander to ask oneself
se deviser to divide/split
se lever to get up
se passer to happen
se rencontrer to meet (each other)
se répartir to divide up / share
  out
se terminer to conclude/finish
se tromper to make a mistake
se trouver to be located
sécher to dry
secrétaire (f.) secretary
secteur (m.) area

selon   according to
semaine (f.)   week
séminaire (m.)   seminar
s'engager   to take a job / commit oneself
sérigraphie (f.)   silk-screen printing
service compris   service charge included
service de cars (m.)   coach service
services administratifs admin. department
servir à   to serve to
seul   alone
seulement   only
s'excuser   to apologize
si   if
siège (m.)   headquarters
s'il vous plaît   please
simplement   simply
sinon   if not
site (m.)   site
s'occuper de   to be getting on with
société (f.)   company
soir (m.)   evening
soirée (f.)   evening
sorte (f.)   sort
sortie (f.)   exit
sortir   to go out
souder   to solder
souhaiter   to want/wish
sous caution   on bail
sous-chef (m.)   deputy head
spécialiser   to specialize
stade (m.)   stage/stadium
stage (m.)   short course
sucre (m.)   sugar
sud (le Sud)   south (the South)
suffisant   sufficient/enough
suivre   to follow
sujet (m.)   subject
superbe   superb
sur   on
sûrement   for sure
sûreté (f.)   security
système d'alarme (m.)   alarm system

tailleur (m.)   tailor
tant... que...   as much... as...
tarif réduit (m.)   discount price
taux d'intérêt (m.)   interest rate
technique   technical
télécopie (f.)   fax
télécopieur (m.)   fax machine
téléphoner   to telephone
télex (m.)   telex
temps (m.)   time/weather
terminal (m.)   terminal
terrain (m.)   area/terrain
terre (f.)   earth/ground
territoire (m.)   territory

tête (f.)   head
thalassothérapie (f.)   sea-water therapy
thé (m.)   tea
théorique   theoretical
toilette (f.)   toilet
tomber   to fall
tourner   to turn
tout à fait   certainly/absolutely
tout à l'heure   soon / in a short time
tout d'abord   first of all
tout de même   all the same
tout de suite   immediately
tout droit   straight ahead
tout le monde   everybody
traiter   to handle
transférer   to transfer
transmettre   to transmit
transports routiers (m.pl.)   road transport
travailler   to work
traverser   to cross / go through
très bien   very good / very well
triste   sad
trouver   to find
TVA (Taxe à la Valeur Ajoutée)   VAT (Value Added Tax)
type (m.)   type

uniquement   solely/uniquely
unitaire   per unit
usine (f.)   factory
utilisateur (m.)   user
utiliser   to use

véhicule (m.)   vehicle
vendre   to sell
venir   to come
vente (f.)   sale
verre (m.)   glass
vers   towards
vie (f.)   life
vierge   virgin
vieux (m.) / **vieille** (f.)   old
village (m.)   village
ville (f.)   town
virement (m.)   transfer
visa (m.)   visa
visite (f.)   visit
visiter   to visit
vite   quickly
voir   to see
voiture (f.)   car
volume (m.)   volume
vouloir   to want
vouloir dire   to mean
voyageur (m.)   traveller
vraisemblablement   probably

w.c. (m.pl.)   toilet

Vocabulary: English–French

a few quelques
about environ
abroad à l'étranger (m.)
absent absent
absolutely absolument / tout à fait
accommodate *verb* héberger
accommodating accommodant
accommodation hébergement (m.)
accompany *verb* accompagner
according to selon
achieve *verb* atteindre / réaliser
across à travers
actually en effet
ad annonce (f.) / publicité (f.)
add *verb* ajouter
additional complémentaire
address addresse (f.)
admin. department services administratifs (m.pl.)
administrative administratif (m.) / administrative (f.)
advance avance (f.)
advice conseil (m.)
advise *verb* conseiller
affairs affaires (f.pl.)
after(wards) après
afternoon après-midi (m.)
again encore
agreed entendu
aim but (m.)
airport aéroport (m.)
alarm system système d'alarme (m.)
all the same tout de même
alone seul
already déjà
alright d'accord
also aussi/également
American américain
among entre
amount masse (f.)
announce *verb* annoncer
annual annuel (m.) / annuelle (f.)
another un(e) autre (m.)
any aucun
aperitif apéritif (m.)
apologise *verb* s'excuser
apparatus appareil (m.)
apparently apparemment
appointment rendez-vous (m.)
approach *verb* s'approcher
appropriate approprié
approximately à peu près / environ
area domaine (m.) / secteur (m.)

around about autour de
arrival arrivée (f.)
arrive *verb* arriver
as far as jusqu'à
as soon as dès que
as well as aussi bien que
ask (a question) *verb* poser (une question)
ask (for) *verb* demander
ask oneself *verb* se demander
assembly line chaîne (f.)
assembly unit atelier d'intégration (m.)
assuming en assumant
at (home/workplace) chez
at present actuellement
at that time à l'époque (f.)
at the end of au bout de
at the side à côté
audio-visual material matériel audio-visuel (m.)
autumn automne (m.)
availability disposition (f.)
available disponible
available to à la disposition de
axis axe (m.)

bail caution (f.)
bank banque (f.)
bank account compte bancaire (m.)
banking *adjective* bancaire
bare nu
barely à peine
basketball basket (m.)
bathroom salle de bain (f.)
battery pile (f.)
because parce que / car / puisque
bedroom chambre (f.)
before avant
before tax hors taxes
begin *verb* commencer (à)
behave (oneself) *verb* se comporter
behind derrière
Belgium Belgique (f.)
believe *verb* croire
belong to (an organization) *verb* adhérer
belong to *verb* appartenir à
benefit from *verb* bénéficier de
better meilleur/mieux
between entre
big grand
bilingual bilingue
bill *verb* facturer

bill facture (f.)
blind aveugle
box boîte (f.)
branch (of a firm) filiale (f.)
bread pain (m.)
breakfast petit déjeuner (m.)
bridge pont (m.)
budget budget (m.) / masse (f.)
build *verb* construire
building bâtiment (m.)
bus (between towns) (auto)car (m.)
bus (within towns) (auto)bus (m.)
business affaires (f.pl.) / entreprise (f.)
businessmen hommes d'affaires (m.pl.)
businesswoman femme d'affaires (f.)
but mais
butter beurre (m.)
button bouton (m.)
buy *verb* acheter
by plane par avion
by rail par train

calculate *verb* estimer
call *verb* appeler
call back *verb* rappeler
cancel *verb* annuler
canteen cantine (f.)
capital (financial) capital (m.)
car voiture (f.)
car hire location de voitures (f.)
career carrière (f.)
carpark parking (m.)
case cas (m.)
cash credits crédits de trésorerie
castle château (m.)
category catégorie (f.)
certainly tout à fait
certificate certificat (m.)
cheque book carnet de chèques (m.)
chain chaîne (f.)
charges frais (m.pl.)
child enfant (m.)
chips (French fries) frites (f.pl.)
chocolate chocolat (m.)
choice choix (m.)
choose *verb* choisir
church église (f.)
clean *verb* nettoyer
climb *verb* monter
close *verb* fermer
close to près de
coach (auto)car (m.)
coffee with milk café au lait (m.)
colleague compagnon (m.), collègue (m./f.)

colour couleur (f.)
come *verb* venir
commercial marketing marketing commercial (m.)
commission commission (f.)
company société (f.)
competition concurrence (f.) / concours (m.)
competitor concurrent (m.)
complete complet (m.) / complète (f.)
component composant (m.)
comprise *verb* comprendre
compulsory obligatoire
computer ordinateur (m.)
computer scientist informaticien (m.)
computing informatique (f.)
conclude *verb* se terminer
concretely concrètement
conference room salle de conférence (f.)
confirm *verb* confirmer
conglomerates collectivités (f.pl.)
connection raccordement (m.)
consider *verb* évaluer
constraint contrainte (f.)
construct *verb* construire
construction construction (f.)
consumer consommateur (m.)
contact contact (m.)
continental breakfast café complet (m.)
continue *verb* poursuivre
contract contrat (m.)
conveyor belt bande transporteuse (f.)
convince *verb* convaincre
convivial convivial
correctly correctement
cost coût (m.)
cost *verb* coûter
costs frais (m.pl.)
cottage-industry *adjective* artisanal
country pays (m.)
country of origin pays d'origine (m.)
countryside campagne (f.)
course cours (m.) / stage (m.)
craftsman artisan (m.)
craftsman (specialist) maître artisan (m.)
create *verb* créer
credit crédit (m.)
credit card carte de crédit (f.)
cross *verb* traverser
crossroads carrefour (m.)
customs douane (f.)

daughter fille (f.)
day jour (m.) / journée (f.)
day before yesterday avant-hier
debt endettement (m.)
deep profond
deepen *verb* approfondir
degree (**BA**, etc.) licence (f.)
delegate délégué (m.)
delighted ravi
deliver *verb* livrer
delivery livraison (f.)
demonstrator demonstrateur (m.)
depart *verb* partir
depend on *verb* dépendre de
deposit *verb* déposer
deputy head sous-chef (m.)
descend *verb* descendre
describe *verb* décrire
desire *verb* désirer
detail détail (m.)
development évolution (f.)
diary (**appointments**) agenda (m.)
die *verb* mourir
difficult difficile
direct *verb* indiquer
directly directement
director (**head**) directeur (m.) /
  directrice (f.)
disappear *verb* disparaître
discount ristourne (f.) / remise (f.)
discount price tarif réduit (m.)
discuss *verb* discuter
dismiss (**someone**) *verb* renvoyer
  (quelqu'un)
disparity disparité (f.)
disposition disposition (f.)
distribute *verb* diffuser
distribution répartition (f.) /
  diffusion (f.)
distributor distributeur (m.)
district commune (m.)
diverse divers
divide *verb* (se) deviser
do *verb* faire
doctor médecin (m.)
door porte (f.)
drink *verb* boire
driveway chemin d'accès (m.)
driving licence permis de
  conduire (m.)
dry *verb* sécher
during pendant

each chaque
each one chacun (m.) / chacune
  (f.)
early de bonne heure
earth terre (f.)
east (**the East**) est (l'Est)

easy facile
eat *verb* manger
EC (**European Community**)
  CE (Communauté Européenne)
  (f.)
education scolarité (f.) /
  formation (f.)
electronic électronique
elevator ascenseur (m.)
embarrassing gênant
employee employé (m.)
employer employeur (m.)
enable *verb* permettre
end fin (f.)
end extrémité (f.)
England Angleterre (f.)
enough suffisant
enter *verb* entrer
entrance entrée (f.)
envisage *verb* envisager
equally (**also**) également
essential essentiel (m.) /
  essentielle (f.)
establish *verb* établir
estate agent agent immobiler (m.)
estimate devis (m.)
estimate *verb* estimer
evaluate *verb* évaluer
even *adjective* même
evening soir (m.) / soirée (f.)
everybody tout le monde
evidently évidemment
exact exact
exactly exactement
example exemple (m.)
excellent excellent
exhibition exposition (f.)
exist *verb* exister
exit sortie (f.)
expect *verb* attendre
expected (**foreseen**) prévu
expenditure(s) dépenses (f.pl)
expiry date échéance (f.)
explain *verb* expliquer
export *verb* exporter
export(ation) exportation (f.)
extension number numéro de
  poste (m.)

factory usine (f.)
fail *verb* faillir
fall automne (m.)
fall *verb* tomber
family famille (f.)
far loin
father père (m.)
fax télécopie (f.)
fax machine télécopieur (m.)
fear peur (f.)

fill in a form *verb* remplir une fiche

finally enfin/finalement

finance *verb* financer

finance finance (f.)

financing financement (m.)

find *verb* trouver/retrouver

finish *verb* finir/réaliser

finish (conclude) *verb* se terminer

finished goods matières fabriquées (f.pl.)

finished product produit fini (m.)

firm entreprise (f.)

first premier (m.) / première (f.)

first floor premier étage (m.)

first name prénom (m.)

first of all d'abord / tout d'abord

flip chart paperboard (m.)

flow flux (m.)

folder pochette (f.)

follow *verb* suivre

foodstuffs denrées alimentaires (f.pl.)

for example par exemple

for (because) car

for (in order to) pour

foreigner étranger (m.) / étrangère (f.)

foresee *verb* révoir

forest forêt (f.)

forget *verb* oublier

frankly franchement

free of charge gratuit

French fries frites (f.pl.)

frequently fréquemment

fried eggs œufs sur le plat (m.pl.)

full complet (m.) / complète (f.)

function fonction (f.)

function *verb* fonctionner

future avenir (m.) / futur (m.)

game jeu (m.)

garden jardin (m.)

gasoline essence (f.)

get off *verb* descendre

get up *verb* se lever

girl fille (f.)

give *verb* donner

glass verre (m.)

glue colle (f.)

go *verb* aller

go back / go home *verb* rentrer

go out *verb* sortir

go past *verb* traverser

go through *verb* traverser

good bon (m.) / bonne (f.)

good day bonjour

good evening bonsoir

good journey/trip bon voyage (m.)

good night bonne nuit (f.)

grant bourse (f.)

Great Britain Royaume-Uni (m.)

ground terre (f.)

ground floor rez de chaussée (m.)

half (a litre) of beer demi (m.)

hall (reception) hall (m.)

handle *verb* traiter

happen *verb* se passer / arriver

happy content; heureux (m.) / heureuse (f.)

hardly à peine

have *verb* avoir

have need of *verb* avoir besoin de

have patience *verb* patienter

have to *verb* devoir

head tête (f.)

heading rubrique (f.)

headquarters siège (m.)

hear *verb* entendre

heart cœur (m.)

hello bonjour

help concours (m.)

help *verb* aider/faciliter

here ici

hire *verb* louer

hold on / hold the line ne quittez pas

holder détenteur (m.)

hope *verb* espérer

hospital hôpital (m.)

house maison (f.)

household foyer (f.)

how? comment?

how are you? ça va?

how many combien de?

human resources ressources humaines (f.pl.)

husband époux (m.) / mari (m.)

if si

if not sinon

immediate immédiat

immediately tout de suite

implementation mise en œuvre (f.)

in fact en fait / en effet

in front of devant

in general grosso modo

in order to pour

in parrallel parallèlement

in particular notamment

in principle en principe

in the course of au cours de

inclusive price prix forfaitaire (m.)

inconvenient gênant

individuals gens particuliers (m.pl.)

industrialist industriel (m.)
inform *verb* renseigner
information informations (f.pl.) /
  renseignements (m.pl.)
initial *verb* imposer vos initiales
initiative action (f.)
install *verb* installer
instead of au lieu de
institute institut (m.)
insurance assurance (f.)
intensive intensif
interest intérêt (m.)
interest rate taux d'intérêt (m.)
interested intéressé
interesting intéressant
intermediary intermédiaire
introduce *verb* présenter
invest *verb* investir
investigate *verb* rechercher
investment investissement (m.)
invoice facture (f.)
iron fer (m.)

jam confiture (f.)
job emploi (m.)
join (a firm) *verb* rentrer
join *verb* rejoindre

keep *verb* garder
key clef (f.)
keyboard clavier (m.)
know (a person or place) *verb*
  connaître
know (something or how to do
  something) *verb* savoir
knowledge connaissance (f.)

lady dame (f.)
large firms collectivités (f.pl.)
last dernier (m.) / dernière (f.)
last *verb* durer
law loi (f.)
lawn gazon (m.)
lawyer avocat (m.)
lead *verb* mener
lean *verb* appuyer
learn *verb* apprendre
lease bail (m.)
leave (holiday/vacation)
  congé (m.)
leave *verb* partir
leisure facilities équipements de
  loisirs (m.pl.)
letter lettre (f.)
level niveau (m.)
life vie (f.)
lift ascenseur (m.)
like comme
like *verb* aimer

limit extrémité (f.)
link *verb* rejoindre
listen to *verb* écouter
listing rubrique (f.)
little petit
live (in) *verb* habiter
live (reside) *verb* habiter
local currency devises (f.pl.)
long term long terme (m.)
look for *verb* chercher
lose *verb* perdre
lots of beaucoup de
love *verb* aimer
lower the price *verb* descendre
  le prix

machine machine (f.)
machine tools machines-outils
  (f.pl.)
madam madame (f.)
magazine revue (f.)
main principal
make *verb* faire
make a mistake *verb* faire
  erreur/ se tromper
man homme (m.)
manage *verb* gérer
management direction (m.) /
  gestion (f.)
management committee
  comité de direction (m.)
manager cadre (m.) /
  gestionnaire (m.)
managing director directeur
  général (m.)
manner manière (m.) / façon (f.)
manpower ressources humaines
  (f.pl.)
many beaucoup de
market marché (m.)
market *verb* commercialiser
market survey étude de
  marché (f.)
matter chose (f.)
meal repas (m.)
mean *verb* vouloir dire
medium term moyen terme (m.)
meet *verb* rencontrer
meet (each other) *verb* se
  rencontrer
meeting réunion (f.)
member adhérent (m.)
memory mémoire (f.)
merchant commerçant (m.)
method méthode (f.)
micro-component micro-
  composant (m.)
midnight minuit (m.)
Miss mademoiselle (f.)

modernize *verb* moderniser
modify *verb* modifier
moment instant (m.)
money argent (m.)
month mois (m.)
moon lune (f.)
morning matin (m.) / matinée (f.)
mother mère (f.)
Mr monsieur
Mrs madame
multitude multitude (f.)
must *verb* devoir

naked nu
native natif (m.) / native (f.)
near proche
necessary nécessaire
need *verb* avoir besoin de
neither... nor... ne... ni... ni...
Netherlands Pays-Bas (m.pl.)
network réseau (m.)
never ne... jamais...
new nouveau (m.) / nouvelle (f.)
next prochain
nice agréable; joli; gentil (m.) / gentille (f.)
night nuit (f.)
night club boîte de nuit (f.)
no non
no (not any) ne... aucun(e)...
no longer ne... plus...
no problem pas de problème
nobody ne... personne...
noon midi (m.)
north (the North) nord (le Nord)
north-east (the North East) nord-est (le Nord Est)
north-west (the North West) nord-ouest (le Nord Ouest)
not ne... pas...
not at all pas du tout
not yet pas encore
note *verb* noter
nothing ne... rien...
notice *verb* remarquer
now maintenant/actuellement
nuclear energy énergie nucléaire (f.)
number numéro (m.)

objective objectif (m.)
oblige (you) *verb* obliger
obviously évidemment
oenology oenologie (f.)
offer *verb* offrir
office bureau (m.)
OK d'accord
old vieux (m.) / vieille (f.)
on sur

on the contrary au contraire
on the line à l'appareil (m.) / en ligne (f.)
on the left à gauche
on the right à droite
only ne... que... / seulement
open ouvert
opportunity occasion (f.)
or ou
orange juice jus d'orange (m.)
order commande (f.)
order *verb* commander
organization organisme (m.)
organize *verb* organiser
origin origine (f.)
other autre
outside en dehors de / extérieur (m.)
oven four (m.)
overhead projector rétroprojecteur (m.)
overwhelmed débordé

pace cadence (f.)
package colis (m.)
packaging emballage (m.)
papers papiers (m.pl.)
parade *verb* défiler
paramedical paramédical
parcel colis (m.)
park *verb* garer
participate *verb* participer (à)
pastime passe-temps (m.)
pay *verb* payer
payment paiement (m.)
people gens (m.pl.)
per year par an
perfect parfait
perfect *verb* perfectionner
perfectly parfaitement
perhaps peut-être
period période (f.)
period (of time) époque (f.)
permit *verb* permettre
personally personnellement
personnel department département du personnel (m.)
personnel management gestion de personnel (f.)
persuade *verb* inciter
Peru Pérou (m.)
phone box/booth cabine téléphonique (f.)
phone extension poste (m.)
plan *verb* planifier
plate plaque (f.)
platform (freight) plateforme (f.)
platform (passengers) quai (m.)
pleasant agréable

please s'il vous plaît
pleased to meet you enchanté
plumbing plomberie (f.)
point out *verb* préciser/indiquer
polymerized polymerisé
possible éventuel (m.) / eventuelle (f.)
post emploi (m.)
postpone *verb* remettre
practical pratique
precisely justement/précisément
present *verb* présenter
presentation exposé (m.)
press *verb* appuyer
pretty joli
price prix (m.)
primary primaire
primary school école primaire (f.)
Principalities Principautés (f.pl.)
principally principalement
printed imprimé
priority priorité (f.)
private sector privé (m.)
probably vraisemblablement
problem problème (m.)
produce *verb* fabriquer
product produit (m.)
product range gamme (f.)
production fabrication (f.)
production line ligne de production (f.) / ligne de fabrication (f.)
production manager chef de production (m.)
profession métier (m.)
programme programme (m.)
propose *verb* proposer
publicity publicité (f.)
purchase achat (m.)
purpose but (m.)
purification épuration (f.)
purse bourse (f.)
pursue *verb* poursuivre
put *verb* mettre

quality qualité (f.)
quantity quantité (f.)
quarter quart (m.)
quickly vite
quotation cotation (f.)

railway chemin de fer (m.)
railway service desserte ferroviaire (f.)
rate cadence (f.)
raw materials matières premières (f.pl.)
ready to prêt à

real réel (m.) / réelle (f.)
real-estate agent agent immobilier (m.)
reason raison (f.)
receive *verb* recevoir
reception accueil (m.)
record *verb* enregistrer
recording enregistrement (m.)
red rouge
reduction remise (f.)
reflect *verb* refléchir
reflection réflexion (f.)
relax *verb* reposer
renovation rénovation (f.)
repeat *verb* répéter
report rapport (m.)
represent *verb* représenter
request demande (f.)
require *verb* obliger
rescue *verb* sauver
rescue sauvetage (m.)
research recherche (f.)
reservation réservation (f.)
reside *verb* résider / habiter à
resolve *verb* résoudre
responsable for responsable de
rest *verb* reposer
retirement retraite (f.)
return retour (m.)
road rue (f.)
road transport transports routiers (m.pl.)
robot robot (m.)
room salle (f.)
roughly grosso modo
rudiment rudiment (m.)
run *verb* courir
rural rural

sad triste
salaried person salarié (m.)
salary salaire (m.)
sale vente (f.)
same *adjective* même
sample *verb* déguster
sanitary sanitaire
satisfied satisfait
sausage saucisse (f.)
save *verb* sauver
say *verb* dire
screen écran (m.)
sea mer (f.)
second floor deuxième étage (m.)
secondary school (academic) lycée (m.)
secondary school (vocational) collège (m.)
secretary secrétaire (f.)
security sûreté (f.)

see *verb* voir
sell *verb* vendre
seminar séminaire (m.)
seminar room salle de
  conférence (f.)
send *verb* envoyer
service charge included service
  compris
settle (a bill) *verb* régler (une
  facture)
shopkeeper commerçant (m.)
short course stage (m.)
short term court terme (m.)
shower douche (f.)
simply simplement
since depuis/car/puisque
sir monsieur (m.)
site site (m.)
slide projector appareil à
  diapositives (m.)
small petit
SME PME
so alors/ainsi/donc
software logiciel (m.)
solder *verb* souder
solely uniquement
some quelques
someone quelqu'un (m.) /
  quelqu'une (f.)
something quelque chose
son fils (m.)
soon bientôt
sort sorte (f.) / genre (m.)
south (the South) sud (le Sud)
South of France Midi (m.)
speak *verb* parler
specialize *verb* spécialiser
specialist maître + profession
  (m.) / maître artisan (m.)
specific particulier (m.) /
  particulière (f.)
spell (out) *verb* épeler
spend *verb* dépenser
spend (time) *verb* passer
split *verb* se diviser
spouse époux (m.) / épouse (f.)
spring printemps (m.)
square place (f.)
stadium stade (m.)
start *verb* commencer (à)
start commencement (m.)
state état (m.)
station gare (f.)
stay rester
still encore
Stock Exchange Bourse (f.)
stop *verb* s'arrêter
straight ahead tout droit
study *verb* étudier

subject sujet (m.)
subscriber abonné (m.)
sufficient suffisant
sugar sucre (m.)
suggest *verb* proposer
summer été (m.)
superb superbe
supervisor agent de maîtrise (m.)
supplier fournisseur (m.)
supply *verb* fournir
supply approvisionnement (m.)
surname nom (m.)
surrounding area environs
  (m.pl.)
swim *verb* se baigner / nager
swimming pool piscine (f.)
swing *verb* basculer

tailor tailleur (m.)
take *verb* prendre
take (an exam) *verb* passer (un
  examen)
take (something) away *verb*
  emmener (quelque chose)
tape recorder (audio)
  magnétophone (m.)
taste *verb* déguster
tasting dégustation
tea thé (m.)
teach *verb* enseigner
teaching enseignement (m.)
technical technique
telephone *verb* téléphoner
telephone handset appareil (m.)
telephone message message
  téléphonique (m.)
telex télex (m.)
tell *verb* dire
terminal terminal (m.)
territory territoire (m.)
thank *verb* remercier
thank you merci
that ce (m.) / cette (f.)
that is to say c'est-à-dire
then ensuite/puis
theoretical théorique
there are il y a
there is il y a
therefore donc
thing chose (f.)
think *verb* penser/croire
this ce (m.) / cette (f.)
those ceux (m.pl.) / celles (f.pl.)
throughout à travers
thus ainsi
time temps (m.)
timetable horaire (m.)
to the left à gauche
to the right à droite

today aujourd'hui
together ensemble
toilet toilette (f.) / w.c. (m.pl.)
tomorrow demain
tools outils (m.pl.)
total (**amount**) montant (m.)
towards vers
town ville (f.)
town hall hôtel de ville (m.)
trade fair foire (f.)
trademark marque (f.)
trader commerçant (m.)
training formation (f.)
transfer *verb* muter/transférer
transfer mutation (f.) / virement (m.)
transmit *verb* transmettre
traveller voyageur (m.)
try *verb* essayer
turf gazon (m.)
turfing engazonnement (m.)
turn *verb* tourner
turnover chiffre d'affaires (m.)
TV aerial antenne de télévision (f.)
TV set moniteur TV (m.)
type type (m.) / genre (m.)

understand *verb* comprendre
uniquely uniquement
until jusqu'à
urgently en urgence
USA Etats-Unis (m.pl.)
use *verb* utiliser
user utilisateur (m.)

various divers
VAT (**Value Added Tax**) TVA (Taxe à la Valeur Ajoutée)
vehicle véhicule (m.)
video recorder magnétoscope (m.)
village village (m.)
virgin vierge
visa visa (m.)
visit *verb* visiter
visit visite (f.)
volume volume (m.)

wait *verb* patienter
wait for *verb* attendre
walk *verb* marcher
want *verb* vouloir/désirer/souhaiter
way façon (f.)
weak faible
weakness faiblesse (f.)
weather temps (m.)
week semaine (f.)
welcome *verb* accueillir
welcome accueil (m.)
well bien
west (**the West**) ouest (l'Ouest (m.))
what quel, quelle / quoi
when quand
where où
whereabouts coordonnées (f.pl.)
white blanc (m.) / blanche (f.)
why pourquoi
wide open grand ouvert
wife épouse (f.) / femme (f.)
winter hiver
winter storms intempéries d'hiver (f.pl.)
wish *verb* souhaiter
with avec
withdraw *verb* retirer
without sans
without doubt sans doute
work *verb* travailler
workforce effectif (m.)
worker ouvrier (m.) / ouvrière (f.)
workshop atelier (m.)
world monde (m.)
write *verb* écrire

year an (m.) / année (f.)
yes oui
yesterday hier

Index

Breakthrough Language Packs

Complete self-study courses

Each Breakthrough Language Pack is designed as a complete self-study course using audio cassettes and a course book. Each Pack contains:

* Three 60- or 90-minute audio cassettes or CDs
* The course book

Breakthrough Language Packs available:

Breakthrough Arabic	ISBN 0–333–56692–0
Breakthrough French	ISBN 0–333–48191–7
Breakthrough German	ISBN 0–333–56730–7
Breakthrough Greek	ISBN 0–333–48714–1
Breakthrough Italian	ISBN 0–333–48179–8
Breakthrough Russian	ISBN 0–333–55726–3
Breakthrough Spanish	ISBN 0–333–57105–3
Breakthrough Further French	ISBN 0–333–48193–3
Breakthrough Further German	ISBN 0–333–48189–5
Breakthrough Further Spanish	ISBN 0–333–48185–2
Breakthrough Business French	ISBN 0–333–54398–X
Breakthrough Business German	ISBN 0–333–54401–3
Breakthrough Business Spanish	ISBN 0–333–54404–8